Language and Identity

Previous publications by this author:

ELOQUENCE AND POWER: The Rise of Language Standards and Standard Languages (1987)

LIMITING THE ARBITRARY: Linguistic Naturalism and its Opposites in Plato's *Cratylus* and Modern Theories of Language (2000)

LANDMARKS IN LINGUISTIC THOUGHT II: The Western Tradition in the Twentieth Century (*with Nigel Love and Talbot J. Taylor*, 2001).

FROM WHITNEY TO CHOMSKY: Essays in the History of American Linguistics (2002)

Language and Identity

National, Ethnic, Religious

John E. Joseph

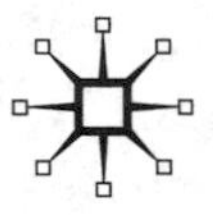

First published 2004 by
PALGRAVE MACMILLAN
Houndmills, Basingstoke, Hampshire RG21 6XS and
175 Fifth Avenue, New York, N.Y. 10010
Companies and representatives throughout the world

PALGRAVE MACMILLAN is the global academic imprint of the palgrave Macmillan division of St Martin's Press, LLC and of Palgrave Macmillan Ltd. Macmillan® is a registered trademark in the United States, United Kingdom and other countries. Palgrave is a registered trademark in the European Union and other countries.

ISBN 0–333–99752–2 hardback
ISBN 0–333–99753–0 paperback

This book is printed on paper suitable for recycling and made from fully managed and sustained forest sources.

A catalogue record for this book is available from the British Library.

Library of Congress Cataloging-in-Publication Data
Joseph, John Earl.
Language and identity : national, ethnic, religious / John E. Joseph.
p. cm.
Includes bibliographical references and index.
ISBN 0–333–99752–2 (cloth) — ISBN 0–333–99753–0 (pbk.)
1. Language and languages. 2. Identity (Psychology)
3. Sociolinguistics. 4. Nationalism. I. Title.

P107.J67 2004
400—dc22

2004043621

10 9 8 7 6 5 4 3 2 1
13 12 11 10 09 08 07 06 05 04

Printed and bound in Great Britain by
Antony Rowe Ltd, Chippenham and Eastbourne

In memory of my beloved grandparents and godparents

Tanus ibn Yusuf Abu Butrus Hubayqat / Anthony Joseph
4 Nov. 1883–20 Sept. 1963

Suraya Qamar / Sarah Amar Joseph
1 Nov. 1898–25 Apr. 1987

Contents

Preface x

1 Introduction **1**

The identity of identity 1
What language has to do with it 2
Fundamental types of identity 3
Construction and multiplicity 6
Other terms used in current research 9
Identity as a linguistic phenomenon 11

2 Linguistic Identity and the Functions and Evolution of Language **15**

Identity and the traditional functions of language 15
Identity and the phatic and performative functions 17
Does identity constitute a distinctive function of language? 20
'Over-reading': identity and the evolution of language 25
Conclusion 39

3 Approaching Identity in Traditional Linguistic Analysis **41**

Introduction 41
Classical and Romantic views of language, nation, culture and the individual 42
The nineteenth century and the beginnings of institutional linguistics 46
The social in language: Voloshinov vs Saussure 48
Jespersen and Sapir 51
Firth, Halliday and their legacy 56
Later structuralist moves toward linguistic identity: Brown & Gilman, Labov and others 58
From 'women's language' to gender identity 61
From Network Theory to communities of practice and language ideologies 63

4 Integrating Perspectives from Adjacent Disciplines **67**

Input from 1950s sociology: Goffman 67
Bernstein 68
Attitudes and accommodation 70
Foucault and Bourdieu on symbolic power 73
Social Identity Theory and 'self-categorisation' 76
Early attempts to integrate 'social identity' into sociolinguistics 77
Communication Theory of Identity 80
Essentialism and constructionism 83

5 Language in National Identities **92**

The nature of national identities 92
When did nationalism begin? 95
Constructing national identity and language: Dante's *De vulgari eloquentia* 98
Taming and centring the language: Nebrija and Valdés 102
Language imagined as a republic: Du Bellay 106
Fichte on language and nation 109
Renan and the Kedourie–Gellner debate 111
Anderson's 'imagined communities' and Billig's 'banal nationalism' 115
De-essentialising the role of language: Hobsbawm and Silverstein 119
Studies of the construction of particular national-linguistic identities 125
- Europe 126
- Asia 128
- Africa 130
- Americas 130
- Australasia and Oceania 131

6 Case Study 1: The New Quasi-Nation of Hong Kong **132**

Historical background 132
The 'myth' of declining English 134
Samples of Hong Kong English 140
The formal distinctiveness of Hong Kong English 144
The status of Hong Kong English 148
The functions of Hong Kong English 150

Chinese identities 151
Constructing colonial identity 154
The present and future roles of English 158

7 Language in Ethnic/Racial and Religious/Sectarian Identities 162

Ethnic, racial and national identities 162
From communities of practice to shared habitus 167
The particular power of ethnic/racial identity claims 168
Religious/sectarian identities 172
Personal names as texts of ethnic and religious identity 176
Language spread and identity-levelling 181

8 Case Study 2: Christian and Muslim Identities in Lebanon 194

Introduction 194
'What language is spoken in Lebanon?' 195
Historical background 196
Distribution of languages by religion 197
The co-construction of religious and ethnic identity: Maronites and Phoenicians 198
Constructing Islamic Arabic uniqueness 200
Recent shifts in Lebanese language/identity patterns 203
Still more recent developments 207
Renan and the 'heritage of memories' 208
Linking marginal ethnic identities: Celts and Phoenicians 212
Language, abstraction and the identity of Renan 215
Maalouf's utopian anti-identity 220

Afterword: Identity and the Study of Language 224

Notes 228

Bibliography 235

Index 256

Preface

This book attempts to put forward a coherent view of identity as a linguistic phenomenon in a way that will speak to people across a wide range of interests. That is, inevitably, an undertaking fraught with opportunities for failure. I am a linguist by training and profession – a broad-minded linguist, I think – but inevitably more attuned to the interests that arise from my field than to neighbouring ones, despite my best efforts. The final chapter will consider what exactly these intellectual boundaries themselves mean in terms of identity.

The Foreword to my book *Limiting the Arbitrary* (2000) explains that it attempts a historical understanding of the distinction between the natural and the arbitrary in language, upon which my earlier *Eloquence and Power* (1987) had relied too uncritically. The present book is, on one level, an effort to deal with the phenomena treated in the 1987 work, but with the natural–arbitrary dichotomy taken away, and with certain other unduly powerful concepts declawed. The most obvious of these are 'power' itself, which in those late years of the Cold War still resounded with echoes of Gramsci and Foucault, even in the writing of someone with neither Marxist nor post-structuralist theoretical commitments; and 'class', the very cornerstone of social inquiry, which before 1989 most of us were able to accept uncritically as an analytical category, but after the events of that year had to admit was a social construct of a highly ideological order, in which we as analysts, rather than the members of the 'classes' themselves, were doing most of the constructing.

The result of modifying these concepts is that the phenomena which make up language standardisation no longer appear so exceptional as they are portrayed in *Eloquence and Power*, but become difficult to distinguish from language generally. This has an effect on our understanding of language itself, making it appear no longer to be a decontextualised system of mental calculation or signification, the 'social' (or more precisely, human) consequences of which are mere side effects. Manifesting identity, and even more importantly, interpreting identity, come to be seen as central to the very existence and functioning of language.

This is not an entirely new view, but one with close precedents in some schools of eighteenth- and nineteenth-century thinking, and more distant precursors extending back to antiquity. Its current resuscitation is having an impact on a wide range of areas concerned with language, including within linguistics the study of sociolinguistics, language acquisition, discourse and pragmatics. But well beyond linguistics, the view of identity being rooted in language and vice versa has been taking on growing importance in anthropology, education, sociology, political science, literary and cultural studies, and many other areas besides.

My greatest debt of gratitude is to the Leverhulme Trust for the Research Fellowship it awarded me in 1999–2000. Other help has come in the form of grants from the Faculty Group of Arts, Divinity and Music and from the Moray Endowment Fund, the University of Edinburgh, for research on language and identity in Lebanon in the spring term of 1998, research leave from the Faculty of Arts of the University of Edinburgh in the spring term of 1998 and the summer term of 2002. The first research that led to this book was carried out on a Research Grant Award from the University of Hong Kong in 1995–96.

I am grateful as well to colleagues and students at the universities of Edinburgh and Hong Kong, the American University of Beirut and the SEAMEO Regional Language Centre in Singapore, who have contributed enormously to my understanding of language and identity. Individual debts extend to far too many people for me to be able to name every one of them, but I would be remiss if I did not cite at least the names of Rüdiger Ahrens, Chin Asher, R. E. Asher, Kingsley Bolton, Alan Davies, Theepa Dhas, John Edwards, Elizabeth Erling, Stephen Evans, Joseph Gafaranga, Mary L. Ghaleb, Christopher Heaton, Elaine Y. L. Ho, Christopher M. Hutton, D. Robert Ladd, Joyce E. James, E. F. K. Koerner, David McCrone, John MacInnes, Miriam Meyerhoff, Jim Miller, W. Keith Mitchell, Babatunde Omoniyi, Martha C. Pennington, Alastair Pennycook, Carmela Perta, Thomas M. Stephens, Talbot J. Taylor, Hugh Trappes-Lomax, Sue Wright, the two anonymous students from whom I have cited writing samples in Chapter 6, and those who took part in the name research reported in Chapter 7.

The members of my family have always played a supporting part in my work, but in this case they are feature players. I must thank especially my cousins of the Abu Butrus family in Ma'alaqa, Lebanon, as well as my father John, my wife Jeannette and our children Julian, Crispin and Maud.

It befits a book about language and identity to be more personal in nature than is the norm. One can hardly pretend to have any deep understanding of the identity issues of people among whom one has not lived and interacted for an extended period of time. It is thus that the following chapters focus on the places I have lived and worked – France, Italy, Hong Kong, Singapore, the USA and the UK – and the place in which my own identity is particularly, though only partly, rooted, namely Lebanon. I have dedicated this book to my two Lebanese grandparents because it was they who made it impossible for me not to think about identity and language every day of my life; and I have written it in part for my children, whose conceptions and births span three continents, and who are bound to confront their own issues of language and identity one day.

1
Introduction

The identity of identity

Put as simply as possible, your identity is who you are. If someone asks 'Who are you?', the answer they expect is your name. Perfectly straightforward, unless you suffer from anomia, the form of amnesia in which you forget your own identity, or unless circumstances are such that revealing your identity might be dangerous. The first of these cases is rare enough, but when does anyone actually ask you your identity except in threatening circumstances? In the worst instance, police or border guards demanding your papers at gunpoint – but even if it is just someone chatting you up in the pub, you are among strangers, which is always at least mildly unnerving.

Or maybe the person asking 'Who are you?' already knows your name. Maybe it is you looking in the mirror. Here obviously some more profound form of identity is being sought. Who are you *really*? Who are you *deep down*? Now the answers come far less easily, because who one is 'deep down' can never be fully captured and articulated in words.

Perhaps the people whose identity we feel we most fully comprehend are the great literary characters, the Lears and Emma Bovarys and, closer to earth, the Harry Potters. Their authors have captured something even more remarkable than the inner essence of an actual human being. Using language alone, they have created persons in whom readers find a resonance of their own inner being – persons in a sense more real than any actual individual. On account of being strictly linguistic in make-up, they are more knowable.

There are, then, two basic aspects to a person's identity: their name, which serves first of all to single them out from other people, and then that deeper, intangible something that constitutes who one really is, and for which we do not have a precise word. *Soul* for many people is overloaded with religious connotations that distract from its core meaning. *Ego* is similarly overloaded with Freudian baggage, and *self* and *inner self* are redolent of later pop psychology. *Identity* has the additional meaning of 'the condition of being identical', and even *personal identity* is ambiguous between one's name, which performs the 'deictic' function of indicating an individual, and that other thing we might think of as the *meaning* of one's name, which performs the 'semantic' function of telling us who that person *really* is. Other terms that have been put forward will be discussed below; but note that what we are trying to pin down here is, ironically enough, the identity of 'identity'; for when we know the word (just as with the name), then its identity becomes one with its meaning.

What language has to do with it

Imagine, if you will, a group of strangers waiting at a taxi stand. An empty taxi drives past without stopping, and the following remarks ensue:

A Out*rage*ous.
B I say.
C Fuckin hell.

Quite likely you have pictured in your mind what A, B and C look like. You can probably tell me something about how they are dressed, their background, what they do, what they are like, and whether you would like them or not. I regularly present groups of students with short dialogues like this one and have them tell me about the speakers, and it is extraordinary how much they are able to infer from what are, after all, a few squiggles on a page. That is all it takes to create a whole person in our minds, and it is most effective when the squiggles represent something the person said.

How well these inferences correspond to the 'true' identity of A, B and C is not the point. There may not be a 'true' identity – I may have made them up, and whether my understanding of their identity has any special authority is a moot question. The point is the power of our instinctive capacity to construct identities based on such minimal input. Obviously, if we *heard* the dialogue spoken by the three individuals, our interpretations of their identities would be affected by their voices, accents and other features of how they speak. And if we saw it on videotape, their appearance would affect our interpretations as well, for instance if C were wearing a Savile Row suit as opposed to old army fatigues from a charity shop. C as a woman might be interpreted differently from C as a man.

So it is not the case that language entirely determines how we conceive of a person. But how they speak, inseparably from what they say, plays a very fundamental role. In a large number of instances our contact with people is purely linguistic, taking place over the phone, by Internet, by letter, reading them as a character in a book, etc. Under these circumstances we seem to be able to size them up, to feel that we know *who they really are* – that 'deep' identity again – more satisfactorily than when we only see them and have no linguistic contact. Looks proverbially deceive.

What is more, the way we 'flesh out' our construction of other people's identities is interesting in itself. We fill the gap between the meagre linguistic and other evidence available to us, and the whole person we construct, using knowledge some of which may perhaps be 'hard-wired' into us genetically (it is impossible to know at this stage), but the bulk of which has been accumulated over a lifetime of experience of meeting people, making 'hypotheses' about what they are like, and 'testing' these hypotheses in our dealings with them. Every human being has such an accumulation of knowledge and puts it to work in every social encounter. It is as unique as our own life experience, and when we put it to work to construct the identity of someone else, we are constructing something that involves who *we* are at least as much, and often much more, than who *they* are.

I have begun with this individual aspect of language and identity because, as with having a name, it is part of everyone's everyday experience. There are many other aspects, ranging all the way up to the role of language in establishing and maintaining national identities. But they are all connected to this most fundamental level of individual experience. Indeed they proceed from it, in complex ways that much of this book will be devoted to describing.

Fundamental types of identity

Already we have seen three apparent pairs of subtypes of personal identity:

- one for real people and one for fictional characters;
- one for oneself and one for others;
- one for individuals and one for groups.

Although in each case there are clear differences involved, it is not obvious that all these differences are so fundamental as to demand that we establish six separate analytical categories. The identities of real and fictional individuals are actually not all that easy to distinguish. When it comes to the subject of a biography, it can be difficult to say whether it is a real or a fictional personage that we are dealing with. Real individuals occasionally assume 'false' identities ('identity theft' is a growing problem) and more than occasionally misrepresent their own characteristics, for example when listing their leisure-time activities on a curriculum vitae. Whether this is done intentionally or not can never be known with certainty about anyone except oneself, and even then it is not always clear, so the intent to tell the truth or create fiction is of little if any use in distinguishing types of identity. Moreover, I have suggested that fictional characters can seem more 'real' than real people, because their identities are wholly contained. It may even be that the modern desire to have a clear sense of self is the result of feeling that one completely knows a character in a novel or a film, and that by comparison oneself is messy and fuzzy, and one's self-knowledge incomplete.

Self-identity has long been given a privileged role in identity research. Further on we shall examine some of the reasons for this, and ask whether it should go on being so privileged. At this point, it will suffice to say that the identities we construct for ourselves and the identities we construct for others do not appear to be different in kind – an identity is an identity – but only in the status we accord to them, where admittedly the difference is very substantial.

The difference between individual identity and the identity of a group – a nation or town, a race or ethnicity, a gender or sexual orientation, a religion or sect, a school or club, a company or profession, or that most nebulous group identity, a social class (the list is far from exhaustive) – is most like a true difference of kind. Group (or 'communal') and individual identities function distinctly enough on the *deictic* (pointing) or name level, since group identities like 'American' or 'female' do not constitute what we normally think of as names. The 'proper' name is a word like 'Joseph' that may once have had a meaning in some language (in this case, Hebrew), but this meaning is now sublimated to the deictic function of designating particular individuals. We shall see, however, that the degree of this sublimation varies greatly from culture to culture.

'American', in contrast, is an overtly meaningful term, not just indicating certain persons but expressing something about them more significant than the mere fact that 'John' is the name their parents chose for them. On this *semantic* or meaning level, however, the difference between individual and group identity is more complex. Your 'deep' personal identity is made up in part of the various group identities to which you stake a claim, though you no doubt believe there is still a part of you that transcends the sum of these parts.

Given that the term 'name' does not always apply well to group identities, we have to find something broader. I shall suggest that we use the term *signifier*, because, although recourse should not be made to a term of art where an everyday word might do the job, in this case the model to which the term applies is supremely elegant in construction, and provides a simple framework for understanding how an identity is brought into being. It is the model of the linguistic sign as devised by Ferdinand de Saussure (1857–1913), and it consists of the conjunction of a signifier (a sound pattern, a 'word' in the usual sense) and a signified (a concept, the 'meaning' of the word in the usual sense). In Chapter 5 I shall argue that a national identity – 'Italian', for example – begins as the signifier of a signified that exists initially only as a desire. With sufficient motivation, those who hold this desire can cause it to be shared by a critical mass within the putative nation. When that happens, the signified, the 'Italian people', becomes *real* (as real as any signified can be, given that they are concepts or categories rather than actual physical objects).

Group identities would seem to be more abstract than individual ones, in the sense that 'Americanness' does not exist separately from the Americans who possess it, except as an abstract concept. Yet combinations of such abstractions are what our own individual identities are made up of. What is more, group identity frequently finds its most 'concrete' manifestation in a single, symbolic individual. The group identities we partake in nurture our individual sense of who we are, but can also smother it. Individual identity is established in part by rank relative to others with the same group identity.

This reciprocal tension between individual and group identities gives the overall concept of identity much of its power, and it has largely determined the structure of this book. What is particularly interesting about the identity of the successful literary character is that it embodies a *group* identity – the modern woman, the person trapped within social constraint, the human race generally – in the form of a plausible individual. In fact, a real-life hero or heroine or leader or star can be thought of as doing much the same thing, embodying in an especially pure form some quality that is widely shared or aspired to. The term 'sex symbol' overtly captures the symbolic nature of those it is applied to.

Ultimately this means that the distinction between individual and group identity is not so clear as it first appears; but it is robust nonetheless, and essential for understanding the overall phenomenon well enough to appreciate the ultimate dissipation of this distinction. For our purposes, then, individual and group identities shall constitute the two fundamental types, with each analysable into a deictic and a semantic aspect.

Construction and multiplicity

Certain features of the contemporary treatment of identity need to be broached in this Introduction, because, although more or less taken for granted by specialists, they can be surprising and controversial to those coming to it for the first time. The first is the assumption that our identities, whether group or individual, are not 'natural facts' about us, but are things we construct – fictions, in effect.

This is not easily accepted by someone who believes that his or her personal identity is grounded in a soul, or at least in a sense of self that is stable throughout one's life. Nor is it obvious that my identity as a man, as an American and as a Caucasian are not 'natural facts' about me, grounded as they seem to be in my bodily configuration, the fact of where I and my parents were born, and the colour of my skin. If I tried to claim that I am a black Chinese woman, *that* would be a fiction, because my true identity is as a white American man. Even if I underwent operations to change my sex and pigmentation, and became a Chinese citizen, I would still be someone who had *become* all these things. Even then they would not constitute my *true* identity.

On the other hand, whether I am a 'Caucasian' depends on what the other choices are. If one of them is 'Semitic', then perhaps that is what I am, since my paternal grandparents were Arabic-speaking natives of Lebanon, and our Semitic descent, whether it was from Phoenicians or Arabs (the politics of which will be discussed in Chapter 8), is clearly written all over my face, to judge from the number of people who over the course of my life have asked me whether I am Jewish, or made clear that they assumed I am. But my maternal descent is entirely from Europeans, 'Caucasians' so called (reflecting an outdated view of anthropological history). When required to give my race on a form I check off Caucasian, since Semitic is rarely an option, having apparently been subsumed under Caucasian for official purposes; though when there is a space for 'Other', I choose this and fill in 'hybrid'.

My Americanness too is specious. I was born in Michigan and retain a great loyalty to my state and town, but the rest of America has always felt foreign to me. I have not lived in the country for over ten years now, and Americans I meet are surprised to learn that I am American if they have heard me say so much as 'Hello', while British people immediately recognise that I am American (or possibly Canadian). Certainly as a fact of my birth I am an American, but the gamut of behavioural expectations that fall out from that fact – the *meaning* of 'American' – differs between American and British culture, and the perception of my behaviour confounds those expectations in the one case while fulfilling them in the other.

That leaves my maleness, which I do not care to call into question, though I do like to think that I am in touch with my feminine side. Yet sexual identity is probably the one that people today would be most prepared to accept can be constructed, if only because of how gender crossing and sex-change surgery have become socially accepted in recent times. Not only do trans-gender individuals receive regular exposure, with sympathetic treatment, on television talk shows, but, in Britain at least, sex change is paid for by the National Health Service if one's physician considers it necessary for one's psychological well-being. The sincerity of those who report spending their lives feeling 'trapped in a (wo)man's body' is indubitable. The question that concerns us here is this: does the fact that sexual identity *can* be distinct from physical configuration imply that *all* sexual identity is constructed? Or are these pathological cases, which implies that 'normally' sexual identity is biologically determined? Indeed, many transsexuals insist that their real inner self, their psychological sex as opposed to their physical birth-sex, was *not* something they chose or constructed, but was biologically imposed upon them.

The idea that identities are constructed is often taken to be a 'postmodern' conceit, but that is merely the result of impoverished historical knowledge. The following statement appeared in a book published more than 75 years ago: '[M]y very self, so uniquely individual in appearance, is [...] largely a social construction' (Smuts, 1927, p. 254). This was no ivory-tower philosopher speaking, let alone a postmodernist, but Jan Christiaan Smuts (1870–1950), the South African general and prime minister who played a key role in organising the League of Nations and its successor, the UN. (He wrote his book *Holism and Evolution* to pass the time while he was out of power.) Not only does Smuts consider the self to be largely a social construction, but one constructed upon *language*:

> I would never come to know myself and be conscious of my separate individual identity were it not that I become aware of others like me: consciousness of other selves is necessary for consciousness of self or self-consciousness. The individual has therefore a social origin in experience. Nay, more, it is through the use of the purely social instrument of language that I rise above the mere immediacy of experience and immersion in the current of my experience. Language gives names to the items of my experience, and thus through language they are first isolated and abstracted from the continuous body of my experience. (Ibid.)[1]

A number of things in Smuts's statement will be unpacked in the pages that follow. The first thing I wish to point out, though, is that, while it takes the view that individual identity is socially and linguistically constructed, it nevertheless assumes that 'my separate individual identity' is singular and coherent. I want to believe that this is so; for if my inner self is somehow fragmentary, all is not well. I cannot say who I 'really' am – indeed I may be in that pathological state known as schizophrenia.

Yet there are at least two senses in which each of us undeniably has multiple identities. The first is the universal fact that individuals have various roles with regard to others – child, friend, spouse, parent, teacher, colleague, boss and so on – and in these terms our identity shifts according to the context of who it is that we are with. My half-Semitic racial identity, which causes people to pick me out by sight as foreign in Western Europe, becomes irrelevant when I am in Lebanon, where people sometimes comment on my exotic Western European features.

The second sense in which identity is multiple has to do with Smuts's 'consciousness of other selves'. Obviously I cannot, in fact, be conscious of anyone else's 'self'. I cannot know what it is to be you from the inside. All I can do is to construct my own version of you, based on what I have observed of you, and of others, fashioning all this upon the template of my own unique sense of self. Everyone who knows you or simply comes into contact with you does the same. So there are as many versions of 'you' out there as there are people whose mental space you inhabit. One might argue that only your own version of you is the *real* you, and yet no one but you can know that version. Each person can only proceed as though their version of you is real for them.

There will be more to say over the course of this book about the 'repertoires' of identities that each of us possesses for ourselves and that others possess for us, and about the extent to which we can maintain belief in an underlying unity and a privileged position for our own self-representations. The working assumption will be that all these representations count, so long as it can be confirmed that they play a significant role in our interactions with others and are a part of how we think about ourselves and those around us.

Other terms used in current research

The term 'identity' itself is by no means universally accepted in the current research literature on the subject. Ivanič (1998, pp. 10–11) points out that, although identity 'is the everyday word for people's sense of who they are', the problem with it is that 'it doesn't automatically carry with it the connotations of social construction and constraint'. She gives a useful survey of 'ways of talking about "identity"' that 'foreground' these connotations, including:

- ***self*** and ***person***: a distinction made by some anthropologists and found for example in the work of Besnier (1991, 1995) and Street (1993), in which my 'self' is who I feel myself to be, emotionally and 'affectively', while 'person' is the identity I project to others in my socially defined roles.
- ***ethos***: a term used in rhetorical theory and adopted for example by Cherry (1988) to mean 'the personal characteristics which a reader might attribute to a writer on the basis of evidence in the text' (Ivanič, 1998, p. 90; see further under 'persona', below). Fairclough (1992) uses ethos as a general term for a person's identity as conceived and constructed in the context of world view and social practices.
- ***persona***: a term that originally meant a 'mask' and that has been prominent in discussions of language and identity at least since the work of Erving Goffman (1922–82; see Goffman, 1956), to refer to the self that one projects in everyday interactions. Cherry (1988) contrasts persona as an objective self (basically a social role, like 'mother', in Ivanič's interpretation) that we create in order to position ourselves within the context of those around us, as opposed to ethos, the self that consists of our own inner qualities.
- ***subject, subject position, positionings***: terms deriving from the work of the French structuralists Louis Althusser (1918–90), Michel Foucault

(1926–84), Pierre Bourdieu (1930–2002) and those they have influenced, for whom the self is a product of the 'discourse' and social 'field' in which it is located (see Chapter 4, p. 73). Since structuralism traces its origins to linguistics (see Joseph, 2001), these might seem particularly useful terms for investigating language and identity. But Ivanič notes, in line with my earlier comments on multiplicity and the quote from Smuts, that 'the singular term "subject position"' in particular is 'misleading, since it suggests one unitary position to which an individual is subject, rather than a variety of dimensions on which a person might be positioned simultaneously' (Ivanič, 1998, p. 10).

- ***subjectivity, subjectivities, positionings, possibilities for self-hood***: these are Ivanič's preferred terms, which she sees as 'carrying the connotation that identity is socially constructed and that people are not free to take on any identity they choose, but adding a sense of multiplicity, hybridity and fluidity' (ibid.).
- ***identify, identification***: it has recently become fashionable to eschew 'identity' in favour of the verb 'identify' and its nominalisation 'identification', on the grounds that these refer to a process rather than a 'fixed condition' (ibid., p. 11). In Joseph (2002a) I have drawn attention to a long tradition of reconceiving the noun 'language' in such a way as to emphasise its semantic features as a 'process' noun, which makes it verb-like in meaning and thus aprototypical of nouns. The attempts to replace 'identity' have been driven by the same dynamic.

Yet despite all these widely recognised problems with the term 'identity', Ivanič uses it not once but twice in the title of her book – and a good thing too, given that, indeed, it is 'the everyday word for people's sense of who they are'. That is the principal criterion that should be followed in the choice of all terminology. It is true that identity 'doesn't automatically carry with it the connotations of social construction and constraint', and therefore statements using this word could be taken out of context and misread as though they implied that identity is inherent and unitary. But linguists of all people should know the most basic fact about language: no attempt to unify and contain its interpretation has ever been or can ever be successful.

Each of the alternatives proposed for 'identity' is subject to its own misinterpretations, and what is more, by diverging from ordinary usage they constitute jargon, which is itself an obstacle to understanding. The use of jargon also strikes most people as pretentious – except, that is, for those whose professional identity rests upon the use of such jargon. Since that is itself one of the issues to be explored in this book, it would risk circularity if I purposely engaged in jargonising when there was a clear alternative available. So, identity it will be.

Identity as a linguistic phenomenon

Smuts believed that language gives rise to identity in the following way. First, language abstracts the world of experience into words. The encounter with language raises us above mere immediacy of experience and immersion in the current of experience. This enables us to form a conception of self rather than simply *being* ourselves. This view belongs to a tradition going back to the eighteenth-century French philosopher Étienne Bonnot, Abbot of Condillac (1714–80), who located the origins of the human mind in the transition from natural signs (as when smoke signifies fire, or screaming signifies pain) to the artificial signs of language, which forced people to *analyse* human experience rather than simply taking it in as a synthetic whole (see Chapter 3, p. 44). However, by the 1920s, when Smuts was writing, Jean Piaget (1896–1980) was already beginning to convince the psychological community that intellectual development takes place independently of language (see Chapter 4, p. 86). That may help explain why Smuts's book did not directly give rise to a social constructionist approach to identity.

Of course Piaget did not settle the issue once and for all; the question of how great a role language plays in cognition is a hardy perennial, and is likely to remain so for a long time to come. The present book is not immediately concerned with this issue. It attempts to examine the linguistic aspects of identity, and the effects of identity on language, while remaining neutral as to the 'deeper' questions of consciousness or cognitive processes. Only by doing so can the evidence adduced and the conclusions reached here hold any promise of subsequently shining objective light on those questions.

This book being concerned with how individual and group identities interact with the *directly observable* roles of language in people's lives, its justification needs to come from common, observable experience rather than from philosophical introspection. Like my predecessors of the Scottish Common Sense school, I believe that explanations of language must be grounded in common experience if they are to be credible as accounts of common experience. Hence my view that our understanding of linguistic identity must begin with what in common usage is the primary meaning of identity: the name.

That fact alone ought to make evident that identity is at root a matter of language, but it is not so evident as one might expect – especially not for linguists. The study of names has long been marginalised within linguistics, to a subarea called 'onomastics' that is rarely taught and has little institutional recognition. Yet names are the primary text of personal identity, occupying a privileged place within the language (see further Chapter 7, p. 176). They are not simply texts that proceed from the grammar of the language in the same way as other texts do; there is a particular part of grammar reserved for names, which means that they enter directly into what linguists have traditionally seen as their province. One of the long-term effects of inquiry into language and identity should be to integrate names more fully into the anthropological end of linguistics, on a par with kinship terms, deferential address and other phenomena in which culture is directly encoded into the language system.

In defining identity in terms of names or signifiers on the one hand, and their associated meanings or signifieds on the other (p. 5 above), I am asserting that the entire phenomenon of identity can be understood as a linguistic one. Beyond this, an impressive body of research in several areas of sociolinguistics, social psychology and social and linguistic anthropology points to the central importance of the language–identity nexus. Language attitudes research (see Chapter 4, p. 70) has consistently shown how quickly we form strong conceptions of each other's identities based on the way we speak. Research on linguistic accommodation, or 'Communication Accommodation Theory' as social psychologists prefer to call it (their proliferation of 'theories' being one of their own marks of professional identity) has demonstrated how the way we speak is conditioned in part by the people we are speaking to (Chapter 4, p. 72). Studies of the development of national languages have elucidated their intricate relationship with national identities (Chapter 5), and work on standard languages and language standards – ideas of correct and incorrect ways of using the language – have shown how these arise in connection with national identity, and go on to play a hugely important role in the lives of individuals by formalising hierarchies of class-based and education-based norms of usage on which each of us is judged (Chapters 4 and 5). Finally, recent years have seen much research on conceptions of 'a language' generally, and how they have been shaped by the speakers' views of who they are (Chapters 5 and 9).

Actually, in one case I shall be arguing that a prominent writer has exaggerated the foundational role of national languages in the formation of national identities. I refer to Benedict Anderson and his deservedly influential book *Imagined Communities* (1991). The problem is not, however, that the language–identity nexus itself is credited with too much importance. Rather, it is that a two-way street is treated as though it were one-way: Anderson gives all his attention to how national languages shape national identities, and none to how national identities shape national languages, which they do very profoundly.

In a 1980 article that he would adapt into a chapter of his 1982 book, the French sociologist Pierre Bourdieu looks explicitly at the nature of 'regional' and 'ethnic' identities, and makes the important point that, although they essentialise what are actually arbitrary divisions among peoples, and in this sense are not 'real', the fact that, once established, they exist as mental representations means that they are every bit as real as if they were grounded in anything 'natural':

> One can understand the particular form of struggle over classifications that is constituted by the struggle over the definition of 'regional' or 'ethnic' identity only if one transcends the opposition [...] between representation and reality, and only if one includes in reality the representation of reality, or, more precisely, the struggle over representations [...].
>
> Struggles over ethnic or regional identity – in other words, over the properties (stigmata or emblems) linked with the *origin* through the *place* of origin and its associated durable marks, such as accent – are a particular case of the different struggles over classifications, struggles over the monopoly of the power to make people see and believe, to get them to know and recognize, to impose the legitimate definition of the divisions of the social world and, thereby, to *make and unmake groups*. (Bourdieu, 1991, p. 221)

This is effectively the point of view adopted in the present book, with an added emphasis on the function of names, labels and other linguistic forms of classification-cum-text in the making and unmaking of groups along the lines Bourdieu describes.

In the end, I hope to have shown that language and identity are ultimately inseparable – again, independently from any considerations of 'consciousness'. I hope too that no one will read this book without being led to reflect about their own linguistic identity, as I myself have had to do rather intensively during the last several years of working on it. Thinking about language and identity ought to improve our understanding of who we are, in our own eyes and in other people's, and consequently it should deepen our comprehension of social interaction. Each of us, after all, is engaged with language in a lifelong project of constructing who we are, and who everyone is that we meet, or whose utterances we simply hear or read.

2
Linguistic Identity and the Functions and Evolution of Language

Identity and the traditional functions of language

Linguists and philosophers have traditionally identified the primary purposes of language as one or both of the following:

- ***communication*** with others, it being impossible for human beings to live in isolation;
- ***representation*** of the world to ourselves in our own minds – learning to categorise things using the words our language provides us with.

In Plato's *Cratylus*, Socrates says that the purpose of words is for discriminating things from one another, and for teaching each other about those things. Discriminating things from one another is what is meant by representation. Teaching each other about things is communication – where what is being communicated is, as it happens, representation. Socrates makes clear that communication is rather a poor and vulgar thing, whereas representation is a communion with the Ideal Forms of things as they exist in heaven (see Joseph, 2000a).

In the 2300 years since Plato wrote the dialogue, linguists and philosophers have maintained essentially the same view. Communication has largely been taken for granted, and the important work to be done on language has been assumed to be the understanding of its functioning as a system of representation. There have been some notable exceptions, including the figures surveyed in Chapter 3, and, in philosophy, Ludwig Wittgenstein (1889–1951), who led attempts to analyse the functioning of language as a system of representation until finally deciding that, ultimately, representation cannot be separated from communication. A language, he concluded, is nothing more nor less than the use to which it is put.

Where does linguistic identity fit into this traditional dichotomy? The fact that its operation is deeply bound up with linguistic interaction among people would seem to make it a subtype of communication. Yet group identities are certainly categories, ways of conceiving the relationship of people to one another, and the same may be said of the individual identities that represent, in part at least, repertoires of these group belongings. That would seem to qualify identity as a subtype of representation.

In fact, linguistic identity is a category that blurs the dichotomy between the two traditional functions of language. If we wished, we might break identity down into components, each of which is classifiable as communication or representation, including self-representation. But it is a type of representation so uniquely bound up with communication that one wonders how much use is served by bundling it up with representation of other sorts. As for the type of communication implied in linguistic identity, it may not be unique, but the type it is related to is a special one that will be discussed in the next section.

Another function of language that has been traditionally recognised in Western culture is that of ***expression***, where what is expressed are the feelings, emotions and passions, usually of an individual, sometimes of an entire ethnicity or gender or other grouping. Linguists and philosophers have mostly shied away from giving serious consideration to expression as a linguistic function, except in connection with the *origin* of language in its most primitive form, before its value for communication and representation were recognised. The emotions and passions are linked directly to the body, and are contrasted with the rational operation of the mind which is the basis of representation and communication.

The expression of emotion is conceived of as being on a par with animal 'language', and this gives it credibility within a modern evolutionary framework. Indeed, Charles Darwin (1809–82) himself devoted a book to *The Expression of the Emotions in Man and Animals* (1872), in the context of a heated debate involving leading linguists of the time over the basic nature of language and its connection with the mind (see below, Chapter 3, pp. 46–7). But the conception of it as pre-rational has long pushed it out of the picture within a philosophical tradition focused on rational thought. As a result, in modern times, interest in the expressive function of contemporary human language has not been part of linguistics or the philosophy of language, but of aesthetics, including aesthetically oriented literary criticism; and in a different mode, of some forms of psychology, including psychoanalysis, as well as those areas of rhetoric concerned with appealing to the emotions over reason, including propaganda and its commercial equivalent, advertising.

These aesthetic dimensions of expression are sometimes concerned with universal human emotions or particular cultural feelings, but their deepest connection is with the concept of the *individual self* – hence of identity. There is a widespread tendency to locate who one is – one's subjective self – in one's individual feelings. Even though many linguists and philosophers of language would not dispute this view, until recently they have shunned emotions as constituting an anti-rational domain that could not be subjected to rational enquiry. Throughout the humanities generally this attitude has changed drastically in the last decade and a half, but linguistics, a very conservative discipline, has been slow to embrace the change.

Identity and the phatic and performative functions

Two other, less traditional functions of language came to be widely recognised by linguists in the twentieth century, though neither was originally proposed from within linguistics. In 1923 the hugely influential book *The Meaning of Meaning* appeared. Even more influential than the main text by Ogden and Richards was one of the two 'supplements', 'The Problem of Meaning in Primitive Languages' by Bronislaw Malinowski (1884–1942), a Polish-born Lecturer in Social Anthropology at the London School of Economics. Malinowski argued that meaning is not inherent to words or to propositions, but is dependent upon what he termed the 'context of situation'. That context is often such that what we traditionally reckon to be the meaning of utterances is not their effective meaning at all. Rather, the very fact of speaking with someone, as a social act, can be the 'meaning' of the speech event, and the propositional content exchanged is irrelevant. This is the ***phatic*** function of language. Familiar examples include the 'small talk' we make with strangers and new acquaintances, the classic example being remarks about the weather.

> A mere phrase of politeness, in use as much among savage tribes as in a European drawing room, fulfils a function to which the meaning of its words is almost completely irrelevant. Enquiries about health, comments on weather, affirmations of some supremely obvious state of things – all such are exchanged, not in order to inform, not in this case to connect people in action, certainly not in order to express any thought. It would be even incorrect, I think, to say that such

> words serve the purpose of establishing a common sentiment [...]. What is the *raison d'etre* [*sic*], therefore, of such phrases as 'How do you do?' 'Ah, here you are,' 'Where do you come from?' 'Nice day to-day' – all of which serve in one society or another as formulæ of greeting or approach? (Malinowski, 1923, pp. 476–7)

He proposed the term *phatic communion* for such utterances, defining it as 'a type of speech in which ties of union are created by a mere exchange of words' (ibid., p. 478). Although he says it is as much a part of the speech of civilised people as 'savages', he believed that phatic communion constitutes the original, primitive form of human language. His claim that 'in pure sociabilities and gossip we use language exactly as savages do' (ibid., p. 479) came as a surprise to readers of the time. Even those for whom it held the modernist appeal of a return to the primitive might have been more likely to accept the notion that 'The binding tissue of words which unites the crew of a ship in bad weather, the verbal concomitants of a company of soldiers in action [...] resemble essentially the primitive uses of speech by man in action' (ibid.). At least, this would have intuitively made sense to those who had experience of such talk and could infer what Malinowski leaves unsaid – that it is dominated by profanities which make no rational sense whatever. But that is not true of the language 'we' use.

Malinowski's view aligns with the traditional one discussed above which equates expression with emotion and restricts the domain of reason to propositional content. Thus Malinowski insists:

> Are words in Phatic Communion used primarily to convey meaning, the meaning which is symbolically theirs? Certainly not! They fulfil a social function and that is their principal aim, but they are neither the result of intellectual reflection, nor do they necessarily arouse reflection in the listener. Once again we may say that language does not function here as a means of transmission of thought. (Ibid., p. 478)

But a red herring swims in each of the three sentences. Why should 'meaning' be restricted to what belongs 'symbolically' to utterances? Is phatic meaning not symbolical, quite as much as the dictionary meanings of words may be said to be? Secondly, what difference does it make whether phatic utterances are preceded or followed by 'intellectual reflection'? There is no way of determining that they are *not* followed by such reflection in anyone but oneself – and if you are the one asking the question, obviously you *are* reflecting on it. Thirdly, what is 'transmission of thought' meant to imply? It appears connected to the immediately preceding remarks on intellectual reflection, but even if there were such reflection it would not constitute transmission of thought. And if Malinowski meant that non-phatic language *does* function as a means of transmission of thought, this raises the age-old problem that we cannot determine whether 'thought transmission' actually occurs, since we do not have direct access to anyone's mind but our own. But more importantly, he fails to recognise that even language with rational, propositional content can simultaneously perform the same functions that phatic utterances do.

The huge amount of attention Malinowski's supplement received, and the impact his ideas had upon anthropologists and some particularly forward-looking linguists (notably J. R. Firth and Roman Jakobson), produced a decisive breakthrough, as well as a break. One branch of the study of language would henceforth be redirected toward *function* rather than form, where function had to be assessed *pragmatically* rather than through traditional analysis of the meaning of the component words and utterances understood in terms of their propositional content. Already in the 1930s such functional analysis was being directed not just at phatic utterances, but at all use of language, in spite of Malinowski's original attempt to separate 'primitive' from 'intellectual' types.[1]

Its effect has been to extend the recognition of what is 'meaningful' in linguistic utterances beyond their propositional content. In so doing, it has blurred the boundaries separating the propositional and the rational on the one hand from the phatic and emotional or social on the other. It has undone the exclusive priority of the wilful and conscious intent of the speaker, and has refocused attention upon the speech act as a social event in which at least two participants are equally implicated, with the unconscious aspects of their utterances potentially just as significant, sometimes more significant, than the (supposed) products of their will. Arguably, nothing has been more decisive in clearing the space for the analysis of language and identity than this, since so much of our verbal signalling of who we are takes place below the propositional level.

The ***performative*** function was first identified by the philosopher J. L. Austin (1911–60; see Austin, 1962, and Joseph et al., 2001, Chapter 7). Certain utterances, although similar in form to ones used for describing (representing) a situation or communicating information about it, in fact do neither. The verb *name* in 'I name this ship the Queen Elizabeth' (uttered while smashing a bottle of champagne against the stern) and *bet* in 'I bet you sixpence it will rain tomorrow' do not refer to something that has already happened – rather, the uttering of the sentence is itself the 'happening', the naming of the ship or the placing of the bet. As Austin put it, 'it seems clear that to utter the sentences [...] is not to describe my doing of what I should be said in so uttering to be doing or to state that I am doing it: it is to do it' (Austin, 1962, p. 6). The philosophical interest of such 'performative' utterances is that, since they are not making a statement but performing an action, there is no sense in which they can be reckoned either true or false. Truth is a judgement applied to representations of reality, not to reality itself.

Bourdieu has had a very significant impact on studies of language and identity through his assertion that claims of identity are in fact a sort of 'performative':

> Regionalist discourse is a *performative discourse* which aims to impose as legitimate a new definition of the frontiers and to get people to know and recognize the *region* that is thus delimited in opposition to the dominant definition, [...] which does not acknowledge that new region. The act of categorization, when it manages to achieve recognition or when it is exercised by a recognized authority, exercises by itself a certain power: 'ethnic' or 'regional' categories, like categories of kinship, institute a reality by using the power of *revelation* and *construction* exercised by *objectification in discourse*. (Bourdieu, 1991, p. 223)

The notion of identity as a 'performative discourse' has become a powerful one in recent years, well beyond the 'ethnic' and 'regional' categories to which Bourdieu originally applied it. By the late 1990s it had become commonplace to assert that group identities in general – be they national, sexual, generational or what have you – are claims made through performance. An identity exists by virtue of the assertions of it people make.

Does identity constitute a distinctive function of language?

There might well be cause for considering identity as a third, distinct major function of language. For now, we should be hesitant to sever links where they partially exist. One's self-representation of identity is the organising and shaping centre of one's representations of the world. Similarly, in communication, our interpretation of what is said and written to us is shaped by and organised around our reading of the identity of those with whom we are communicating.

Indeed, whether we say that identity is fundamental to the two traditional purposes of language, or constitutes a third purpose that underlies the other two, makes little difference. What matters is to understand that, if people's use of language is reduced analytically to how meaning is formed and represented in sound, or communicated from one person to another, or even the conjunction of the two, something vital has been abstracted away: the people themselves. They are always present in what they say and in the understanding they construct of what others say. Their identity inheres in their ***voice***, spoken, written or signed.

On the day of writing this page, I happened to come across this passage from Dickens's *Bleak House* (1852–53), in which an impoverished mother sits weeping and holding her baby who has just died:

> An ugly woman, very poorly clothed, hurried in while I was glancing at them, and coming straight up to the mother, said, 'Jenny! Jenny!' [. . . W]hen she condoled with the woman, and her own tears fell, she wanted no beauty. I say condoled, but her only words were 'Jenny! Jenny!' All the rest was in the tone in which she said them. (Ch. 8)

On the same day, I read in the *Sunday Times* (21 July 2002) a profile of the musician Bruce Springsteen, which says that

> The most potent political message he absorbed was in 1956, when he saw Elvis Presley on the televised Ed Sullivan Show. It was, he recalled, a liberation message.
> 'I heard it in Elvis's voice. That voice had its implications. [. . . T]hey told the story of the secret America.'

And in the same paper, the historian Simon Schama draws a direct link between ancient and modern awareness of the matter when he opens an article on modern oratory – featuring a photo of, and Schama's reflections on, the rapper Eminem – with this quotation from Cicero: 'Nothing is so akin to our natural feelings as the rhythms and sounds of voices,' wrote Cicero. 'They rouse and inflame us, calm us and soothe us and often lead us to joy and sadness.'

I do not think my coming across these statements on the same day was especially serendipitous. We are surrounded by them, and I noticed them just because my attention was fixed on the topic. The three do not imply quite the same view of 'voice'. The first and the third – Dickens via the narrator Mrs Allan Woodcourt (née Esther Summerson), and Cicero via Schama – assume that what voice connotes is *emotion*: condolence, passion, calm, joy, sadness and so on. This is actually in line with the classical view, which recognises a division of labour such that *reason* inheres in the propositional content of language, with emotion tucked neatly away into voice. The focus on propositional content is in fact part of a larger view that only reason is worth attending to, whereas emotion is a base part of our animal nature, and needs to be overcome.

But Bruce Springsteen (via the anonymous author of the profile) implies something else. What he heard in Elvis's voice was *the most potent political message* of his life, a message of liberation that was signified in *how Elvis sang*. The fact that in 1956 the cameramen working on the Ed Sullivan Show were ordered not to show his subversive swivelling hips, and that he wore a perfectly conservative suit and tie, had no body piercings and a reasonable haircut, and sang pretty innocuous fare like 'You Ain't Nothin' But a Hound Dog', means that the conditions were actually quite like those of a controlled experiment to test Springsteen's hypothesis, and its correctness would be difficult to deny.

'Liberation', as used here, is a feeling, an emotion, but *also* a message, and most significantly, a political message. It is hard to imagine a message with political content that could not be construed as 'reasonable' and put in the form of a proposition – in this case, something like 'the society in which we live, for all its claims of being devoted to "freedom" as personal liberty or as "liberation" from traditional oppressors, in fact restricts our liberty and oppresses us to a greater extent than we need to accept'. Elvis 'performs' this message by subverting the accepted values of what constitutes good performance in popular song. Actually he does not perform it alone; the screaming teenage girls are his chorus, and it is their combination that creates the convincing power of the message.

A full account of linguistic representation would have to include how the identity of the speakers is manifested by them and read by others; it would have to recognise that the speakers themselves are part of the meaning, represented within the representation. A full account of linguistic communication would have to start with, not a message, but again the speakers themselves, and their reading of each other that determines, interactively, their interpretation of what is said. All this takes us well beyond the sort of simple, logical, mathematical categorisation that 'representation' is usually taken to mean.

So too, 'communication' begins to appear as a troubling oversimplification when issues of identity come into the picture – quite apart from any scepticism we might entertain about our ability to know whether communication ever takes place in the sense we commonly understand it to do (see the remarks on 'thought transmission', p. 19 above). I have stated above as an uncontroversial rationale for the status of communication as a fundamental function of language that it is 'impossible for human beings to live in isolation', yet we are just one of many species incapable of living in isolation, and the sort of communication required for survival does not necessarily demand language.

Implicit in the current debate about the extent to which the spread of English as a world language is driving other languages, especially 'small' local and regional languages, to extinction, is a tension between the value of a world language as a means of wide communication, and the value of one's local language as a repository of cultural forms of representation (see Chapter 7, pp. 181–92). Linguists tend to assume that only the latter value has a legitimate claim to support, in part because of what it means for the authentic identity of those who speak the language. Yet those heinous instances in which people are directly forced to give up their language are the exception rather than the rule, and historically their usual result has been to strengthen the resolve to maintain the language, if only in private domains (which are the essential ones where the preservation of a language is concerned). Most of those giving up their traditional language are, on the contrary, doing so as part of constructing an identity for themselves that is bound up with a conception of modernity as communication extending beyond their village and their country to the world at large.

It is important for linguists to think about this debate in terms of the identity of the people who are abandoning their traditional languages, because our usual way of conceiving the debate – as being about one 'big' representational system wiping out the diversity of a host of 'small' ones – dwells so exclusively on the philosophical level as completely to miss the political and economic reality for the people who alone can ultimately decide to save the languages involved. If we do not take into account what it means for them, then we cannot hope to save more than a museum relic of their language – though even this is of course worth saving.

I cite this as the most important current instance of what is a general fact about the effect of reconfiguring linguistics from the point of view of identity. It displaces the whole question of the basic function of language from the philosophical sphere to the political one – or more precisely, it breaks down the division between the philosophical and the political that theoretical linguistics has so long strived to maintain, but that removes its object of study to the realm of the abstract, cutting it off from the lives of human beings.

In sum, the classical understanding of language focuses on speakers as agentive subjects and the system of linguistic knowledge that allows them to produce and understand meaningful utterances. But linguistic identity research, following upon the essential breakthrough of

Malinowski's conception of phatic communication, takes what is 'meaningful' in linguistic utterances to extend far beyond their propositional content. It is interested in all those features of utterances which hearers use to 'read' facts about the speaker – geographical and social origin, level of education, gender and sexuality, intelligence, likeability, reliability and trustworthiness, and so on. Indeed, it has been solidly and repeatedly demonstrated that interpretation of the speaker's trustworthiness from the non-propositional content of utterances bears directly upon the hearer's assessment of the 'truth value' of the proposition itself.

What this means is that, whenever we isolate language from the people who speak and interpret it and the context in which they speak and interpret it, we are not getting closer to some kind of essential *truth* about language. We are getting further from it, toward a generalisation that may well have its uses (in the case, say, of a pedagogical grammar or a computer program), but can also take the form of a pure abstraction for which the only use is to be worshipped as a kind of fetish.

But unless one locates truth solely with a supreme being or in Platonic heaven, even the 'truth' of the propositions studied by logicians is less real than the decisions which actual people make every day about whether to believe the propositions put to them by other actual people. And those decisions are made by sizing up the proposition together with the person making it – the way they speak together with any other available evidence about them.

It has been the business of sociolinguistics, as it has developed over the course of the twentieth century and particularly in the second half of the century, to examine those features within a language by which we read a person's geographical and social origins, level of education, ethnicity, age, gender and sexuality – the whole range of categorial identities into which we routinely group people (in the case of age, as age groups or generations). When I receive a phone call from a stranger, I decide within seconds, instinctively, whether it is a man or a woman, where they are from and roughly how old they are, and what sort of background they come from.

This is not information that we treat neutrally. The consistent result of research into 'language attitudes' since the 1960s (see further Chapter 4, p. 70) has been to show that we make further inferences on the basis of these initial ones. We decide whether and how much we consider the person to be intelligent, likeable, reliable, trustworthy and so on. The classical method of language attitudes research is to play tapes of people saying essentially the same thing in different accents, and in some instances with the same person speaking in more than one accent, spaced apart so that the subjects (those listening) will not realise that it is the same person. The subjects are then asked to rate the people they have heard in terms of intelligence and the other features listed above.

The results are often surprising. When asked in blind tests to rate tape-recorded voices in terms of the speaker's likeability and trustworthiness, subjects from all over Britain give the highest marks to speakers from northern England and southern Scotland, with an easterly preference in both cases. Surprisingly, this is true even for people in southern England, whom one might expect to be more trusting of people who speak as they themselves do. At the same time, there continues to be a general association of 'educated' and 'intellectual' ways of speaking with the south-east of England. The gap between the 'intellectual' and the 'trustworthy' reflects a certain cultural wariness, not always justified of course, that people who give the impression of having mastery of the language would also like to have mastery of everything and everyone else.

But the main point, in the present context, is that all of us instinctively make these decisions about the people with whom we come in contact, largely on the basis of their language – indeed, wholly on that basis if the communication is by telephone or e-mail or some other form of writing. And when we decide how *reliable* and *trustworthy* they are, we are calculating the extent to which we are prepared to believe *that the propositional content of what they are communicating to us is true or false.*

'Over-reading': identity and the evolution of language

An evolutionary account of language requires us to seek out continuities between humans and other species. Yet neither the discourses of theism or humanism have favoured this. The one portrays language as God's gift to man, the other as the uniquely human attribute that raises man to a state in which God is redundant.

The leading discourses on language have likewise been limited to considering language as a vehicle of representation or communication. In the case of representation, the notion of continuity of mental structure and function between human beings and animals goes back to Aristotle, but may be said (leaving aside numerous provisos that would need to form part of a fuller account) to have been broken with the work of René Descartes (1596–1650), who argued instead for the uniqueness of human cognition. The neo-Cartesian tradition in modern linguistics, associated particularly with Chomsky, recognises only very weak continuities between human language and the communication systems of bees, birds, dolphins, apes and so on. Stronger arguments for continuity, made in the name of Darwin (e.g. by Taylor, 1997; Lestel, 2001) are explicitly discounted by neo-Cartesians (e.g. Pinker, 1994).[2]

The structuralist approach to language as a complete and totally self-contained system, physicalised by Chomsky into a 'language organ', has further limited the possibilities of an evolutionary account of language. The distance between the 'system' of ape language and the 'system' of human language is an unbridgeable chasm. But these 'systems' are analytical projections, and genuine comparison requires us to go back to the observable behaviour from which they are projected. Chomsky's analogies from language to wings or to flying are multiply spurious. They require language to be limited to speech, not writing or signing; they take no account of bi- or multilingualism or the ability to acquire a second language; they require the erasure of all the vast construction of culture built upon language, which defies any parallel with physical organs. Above all, wings do not take entirely different shape within a species according to the environment.

But what does fit the analogy to wings somewhat is *the ability to interpret*, to 'read' features of the world of our sensory experience as signs of something not immediately available to our senses. The sort of signs I am referring to are those by which, for example, we and other creatures deduce that bad weather is coming before it has actually arrived, or infer that some other person or creature does or does not intend our harm.

If we take an evolutionary perspective on language, we will want to ask what are the analogues of linguistic behaviour in other living species, particularly the ones most closely related to us. We know of course that none of these species has developed articulated vocal speech, and on that account many linguists, including Chomsky and his school, have argued that there is no evolutionary link between man and any other species, that language is unique to humans and constitutes a 'great divide' in evolutionary terms. To be sure, the very fact that we identify distinct species implies that each species has its unique characteristics, and the tendency to focus on these uniquenesses, combined with a deep-seated reluctance to acknowledge the links between human and animal structures and behaviours, have been the great obstacles to the full acceptance of the theory of evolution and all its implications from the early nineteenth century to the present.

In the 1990s a new school of evolutionist thought on language emerged in which social considerations were put at centre stage, not as an alternative to biological explanation, but as inseparable from biology. In his 1996 book *Grooming, Gossip and the Evolution of Language,* the British psychologist Robin Dunbar located the origin of language in the needs of higher primates to form social alliances in order to deal with challenges in their environment, including from particularly powerful individuals within their own species. As the title of his book suggests, he believes that the essential functions of language for evolutionary purposes were phatic ones, with 'gossip', language of purely social content exchanged for social purposes, being the equivalent of the grooming that higher primates do to one another as an essential part of forming and maintaining their own social bonds.

> Grooming seems to be the main mechanism for bonding primate groups together. We cannot be sure exactly how it works, but we do know that its frequency increases roughly in proportion to the size of the group: bigger groups seem to require individuals to spend more time servicing their relationships. (Dunbar, 1996, p. 77)

Among baboons and chimpanzees, the average group size is 50–55 members, and this is 'pushing at the limits of the amount of time that can be devoted to grooming without digging disastrously into ecologically more important components of the time budget (such as feeding and travelling time)' (ibid.). Early humans, Dunbar believes, 'must have faced a terrible dilemma: on the one hand there was the relentless ecological pressure to increase group size, while on the other time-budgeting placed a severe upper limit on the size of groups they could maintain' (ibid.).

Language made it possible to increase group size without losing either the time needed to gather and hunt food or the social cohesion needed to counter pressures of all sorts. Because language can be directed at several people simultaneously, we can increase the rate at which we 'groom' others. But more than that, language serves a dual purpose where bonding is concerned. Dunbar notes that social bonding is 'a tricky business, because you are commiting yourself to a relationship with no guarantee that your partner will reciprocate. [...] Being able to assess the reliability of a prospective ally becomes all-important in the eternal battle of wits' (ibid., pp. 78–9). On the one hand, language serves the purposes of the individual who is seeking to make an alliance: 'It allows you to say a great about yourself, your likes and dislikes, the kind of person you are; it also allows you to convey in numerous subtle ways something about your reliability as an ally or friend' (ibid., p. 78). And, on the other hand, it serves the purposes of the person being courted as a prospective ally:

> Subtle clues provided by what you say about yourself – perhaps even how you say it – may be very important in enabling individuals to assess your desirability as a friend. We get to know the sort of people who say certain kinds of things, recognizing them as the sort of people we warm to – or run a mile from. (Ibid., p. 79)[3]

He concludes that 'Language thus seems ideally suited in various ways to being a cheap and ultra-efficient form of grooming. [...] In a nutshell, I am suggesting that language evolved to allow us to gossip' (ibid.). As Dessalles (2000) has made clear, the implication of Dunbar's proposal is that the fundamental function of human language is a *political* one.

What should be added to Dunbar's account is something he takes for granted, an ability shared broadly across mammalian species and indeed not even limited to them. We can term it *semiotic receptivity*, which is simply a way of saying that animals not only respond directly to things in their environment, as plants do, but 'read' things in their environment, and respond to their interpretation. For example, forest-dwelling animals have highly developed abilities to interpret sounds in their environment as indicating approaching predators or prey. Household pets can develop an exquisite ability to read the actions and attitudes of the humans around them (and vice versa). Signs of sexual receptivity and readiness have to be read, and here there is much misinterpretation, including among human beings with our highly developed communicational systems.

Where exactly to draw the line between direct response to environmental stimuli and response mediated by 'reading' is a difficult problem, and a crucial one. It is made harder by the fact that we human observers are unlikely to become aware of such responses in other species, or convinced that they really are responses rather than just coincidental movements, unless they are so regularly repeated as to have become a matter of habit in the animal concerned. When we describe an action, human or animal, as habitual, we are saying that its occurrence is not willed by the being who performs it, but takes place at least partly independently of their will. The notion of reading, on the other hand, implies the role of a mind in processing sensory data and determining how to respond to it.

Pavlov's famous experiments training dogs to develop predictable responses to bells and other arbitrary noises showed how powerful is the ability to create responsive habits so automatic as to seem to obviate the mind altogether. The bell rings, the dog salivates. Is anything intermediary transpiring in the dog's brain, between the electric impulse of the bell sound being transmitted from the eardrum and the impulse to the glands to salivate? It is clear that the dog went through a stage (the 'training') where something intermediary clearly did transpire, namely that the dog was given food. When food in the mouth triggers salivation, we are not inclined to think of this as involving any kind of interpretation, but simply as a mechanical response of the glands. We know that every day we ourselves unconsciously salivate while eating, and it is not easy for us to imagine other species having a higher level of consciousness than ourselves. As the dog gradually learned to associate the bell with food, however, and began salivating even without food being presented, it looked like a relatively complex cerebral operation was taking place, and the fact that an arbitrary stimulus, the bell, was involved, seems justification enough for thinking about it in terms of the dog's 'mind'. But even then we have to say that once the response is fully conditioned, the dog performs it 'mindlessly'.

The same is likely to be said when the response appears not to have been learned by the individual animal but *genetically* conditioned, inherited from ancestors whose natural inclination to perform the response gave them an evolutionary advantage. Running under cover in response to the sound of an approaching predator is an obvious example. The more automatic the response, the less we are apt to imagine a mind through which it is mediated. Of course many would reject any notion of an animal 'mind' as a scientifically inadmissible notion, and some of these reject the whole notion of mind, even in humans, as an unnecessary metaphysical accretion whose existence is incapable of objective verification. This was the basis of behaviourism, though many people who do not consider themselves behaviourists share this view. This is not the place to consider the problem of mind generally, only to consider how, if there is a human mind involved in language, it relates to the analogous workings in other species.

Again, the answer is that in every case it is difficult to say with any certainty what level or kind of mental operation is involved, but there are cases in which, if we say that human beings are reading and interpreting things in their environment, we are obliged to say that other animals are doing so as well. And to return to the central point, those are the aspects of human interpretative behaviour which are evolutionarily deepest. They have to do not with what we say, the signs we produce, but with what we receive through our senses and interpret.

What makes man *not* unique is his status as a 'reading', interpreting animal.

At the individual level, too, every human being's initiation into language begins with the passive experience of learning to read the sights and sounds and other sensual data around one, including the reading of how one's own 'mindless' cries and grimaces provoke reactions in one's caretakers. This is passive up to the stage where the infant begins manipulating those signs, presumably at a point when he or she might or might not give a signal and chooses to do so. That point is hardly less nebulous than with animals, since we cannot query infants about their intentions. (We do have somewhat more reliable intuitions about our own species than others, but the fallacy of projecting adult intentions onto infant minds is not really different in kind from anthropomorphism.) Research on language acquisition has always focused on production rather than understanding, in part because production can be observed directly, understanding only indirectly, and with very young children, not altogether reliably; but no doubt also in part because of the general assumption that the most specifically human kind of semiotic behaviour, the production of articulated speech, is the real beginning of language, rather than any aspect that is evolutionarily deeper.

If we turn this around, and think about language as starting from this very general kind of semiotic receptivity and reading, other changes of perspective follow. We can begin to think of human language as having a primary purpose other than one of the two traditionally ascribed to it, communication (from the point of view of a speaker having an intention and wishing to transmit it to listeners) and representation (of the universe, as analysed into the logical categories which languages are thought by some philosophers, at least, to contain). Before either of these, and in many regards enveloping them both, language exists, in this reversed perspective, for the purpose of *reading the speaker*.

Sociolinguistics is concerned with how people read each other, in two senses. First, how the meanings of utterances are interpreted, not just following idealised word senses and rules of syntax as recorded in dictionaries and grammars, but in the context of who is addressing whom in what situation. Secondly, how speakers themselves are read, in the sense of the social and personal identities their listeners construct for them based on what they say and how they say it (a complex process, since most speakers' output is already shaped in part by how they have 'read' their listeners). For example, consider the brief conversation on p. 2 among those left standing in the queue after the taxi drove past without stopping. Reading the conversation, one conjures up the scene in one's mind, and if asked, one can give quite detailed descriptions of the speakers. Without exception, B and C will be described as polar opposites in terms of social status, education and age, and possibly sex, and A will be described as more like B than C. Readers can usually even express, if asked, their feelings about these three people, who are entirely fictional, and whom they have imagined based upon a few squiggles on a page. This is admittedly a somewhat extreme example, since C has been given a taboo word in a non-standard spelling. But in fact every day each of us repeatedly undertakes this process of constructing our reading of people we encounter, in person, on the telephone, on the radio or the screen, or in writing, including on the Internet, based upon their language – what they say and how they say it.

One thing which understanding-based research on language acquisition has taught us is that the first thing infants learn to respond to in the language spoken to and around them is intonation. They learn to read the emotions of the speaker based upon patterns of melody, volume, pitch, rhythm, eventually the repetition of phonological patterns (alliteration, assonance, rhyme), all before understanding the meanings of words and sentences. Thus a baby will respond joyfully to the sentence *Drop dead ya little bugger* uttered in a soft, lilting tone, and will burst into tears upon hearing the sentence *How's daddy's little darling then* uttered in a loud, raucous one. Speakers, knowing this intuitively, tend to 'baby talk' to infants. What is true here of infants remains true when they grow into adulthood. They continue to read and react to patterns of various sorts below the surface of the words and sentences being spoken to them, and the people who speak to them continue to adjust their utterances, again in a patterned way, according to how they perceive their audience. Uncovering these patterns is a large part of the work of sociolinguistics.

Speakers are always able to read a much wider spectrum of language patterns than they themselves would ever produce. That is obviously the case with languages one knows well; but one can even listen to a language one does not know at all and still read things about the speaker, the context and perhaps even the meaning. The fact that interpretative ability outstrips performance ability means that our knowledge of language is really far broader than an analysis of our output could ever hope to show. This is related to the key insight behind generative grammar, that our knowledge of language (our 'competence' in early versions of the theory) is more powerful than our performance ever reveals, a fact which generativists then interpret to mean that our knowledge of language could never be built up solely from hearing the 'degenerate' performance of those around us, but must instead be based essentially on a 'universal grammar' that is built into the structure of the human brain, and that operates autonomously from any other cerebral structures of perception, intelligence and so on. For example, how do English speakers know that, to the sentence *John asked Ralph what Sue gave Mary*, there can correspond the question *Whom did John ask what Sue gave Mary*? but not the questions **Who did John ask Ralph what gave Mary*? (answer: *Sue*) or **Whom did John ask Ralph what Sue gave*? (answer: *Mary*). No one is ever taught that questions like the latter cannot be formed, yet at least in clear-cut cases like these speakers invariably know it. The generativist answer is that they must be born knowing it; whatever cannot be learned must be specified in universal grammar. Again, this 'universal' grammar is universal only to humans, and therefore represents a great divide in evolutionary terms, a giant mutation in genetic ones.

But the evolutionary perspective suggested here, which focuses instead on what is shared across species, takes its point of departure in an inclination to read and interpret, a semiotic receptivity, which is much more truly universal. It admits what generative grammar must ignore, that there is no direct evidence for the existence of a universal grammar hard-wired into the brain, or even for a linguistic system in the brain that is organised at such a high level that it makes sense to characterise the things people say as 'degenerate' in comparison with it. As for the considerable knowledge of language which speakers can be shown to possess yet cannot have learned directly, this approach accepts the plentiful and growing evidence which has accumulated over the last two decades from computer-based approaches to language showing that computer programs, which have an infinitely simplified structure compared to that of the human or even animal brain, possess an exceedingly powerful capacity to project inferences from small amounts of data. In other words, it is entirely plausible that knowledge of language which speakers have not been directly taught has nevertheless been systematically projected from the linguistic forms to which they have been exposed. The plausibility is all the greater if, like a growing majority of cognitive psychologists, we follow Piaget rather than Chomsky and assume that whatever cerebral structures are involved in language production are not strictly autonomous, but overlap and interact with structures of general perception and intelligence, all of which together constitute the faculty of interpretation.

Sociolinguistics provides overwhelming evidence that this is the case. Everywhere we look, we find people understanding and producing language *not* in an autonomous way, but completely mixed up with their reading of the people they are speaking or listening to and the situational context they are in. Now the question arises: what is *real* language? Is it what ordinary people do out in the world? Or is it the abstractions which linguists deduce must be in their brains, but cannot directly observe? The generativist says that the only kind of language worth knowing about scientifically is that universal grammar hard-wired into the brain, which cannot be observed directly in the speech or writing of any human being (degenerate performance), even under laboratory conditions, but must be deduced based upon its ability to account systematically for the things that can and cannot be said in any human language. The sociolinguist says that, on the contrary, real language is what we hear and see. All our analyses and deductions are abstractions from this, and being abstract, are less real. This of course is part of an ancient and much broader dispute concerning the real, which divides the religious believer from the materialist, and even among religious believers has given rise to various sectarian and scholastic divisions. Our positions on 'real language' are likely to reflect our more general opinions in this regard, though it is a complex matter, since, for example, Chomsky is apt to characterise universal grammar as a physical, material reality despite the total lack of physical or material evidence for it. In other words, the generativist looks to the sociolinguist like an anti-materialist trapped in a metaphysical labyrinth of his own devising; but the generativist sees himself as uncovering the physical architecture of the human mind, while the sociolinguist is collecting butterflies.

The evolutionary sociolinguistic perspective I am describing here – which is by no means the one taken by all sociolinguists – can help us see where the problems lie. It does not start from an unobservable abstraction rhetorically transformed into a physical part of the brain, but from what we can see and hear around us. It suggests that language is part of a broader, non-species-specific capacity for organising, reading and interpreting sensory data in our environment, reacting to these interpretations, and affecting the environment with one's own grist for the interpretative mills of other beings. It is not at all clear, objectively speaking, where 'language' begins and ends within this broader capacity, though various cultural traditions (including the one we call 'linguistics') have given their own definitions to language which are worth attending to. Take again our interpretation of the brief conversation about the taxi. Some of it requires knowledge of the English language – the meaning of *outrageous*, for instance. Or perhaps not in this case: one can imagine playing a tape of the conversation to people who know no English, and their being able to read, strictly from the way in which the utterances are made on the level of sound, what the speakers are expressing, with their readings matching those made by people who know English. Other elements, including those which guide our reading of the speakers as people, involve extraordinarily complex bits of interwoven contextual knowledge that are not clearly part of knowing 'English' as such. Some of them are more akin to what the dog or horse senses in the voice, than with 'the English language' imagined as a set of correspondences between words and meanings plus rules for combining them. And yet, the interpretations a speaker of English is able to make of these utterances, by bringing 'the English language' into what now becomes an infinitely complex interplay with these evolutionarily deeper interpretational systems, reach levels of detail which it is impossible for us to imagine in the mind of another species.

But just what is 'the English language' in this perspective? Not the whole of the ability of English speakers to interpret the speech or writing of other English speakers, nor even their capacity for producing interpretable signs. For as noted above, these capacities inevitably exceed the boundaries of any given language, and even of human language. If the first task of sociolinguistics is to understand this broader interpretative capacity, its second task is to account for how specific interpretative traditions come to be conventionalised, institutionalised and passed from generation to generation, within social groups of various sorts, including the grouping we call the classroom. There has in the past been a strong tendency, which has been breaking down in recent years, of considering classroom teaching as something 'unnatural' and apart from normal social life. Nowadays sociolinguists are more apt to recognise that the classroom is a social grouping like any other, and teaching and learning are social and linguistic activities like any other. One still encounters references to 'natural' language data that are meant to exclude anything produced in a classroom, at least if it involves the teacher; one can even imagine contexts in which such a distinction is useful, although the use of the term 'natural', with the connotation that the other kind of discourse is somehow 'unnatural', is meaningless. In any case, classroom discourse is a crucial element in that second task of sociolinguistics, accounting for how the specific interpretative traditions we call 'languages' are formed and maintained.

We thus take 'languages' to be cultural traditions which have been formed out of a universal attribute, which is not some specific and autonomous grammatical unit of the brain that is merely imaginary at this point, but a universally observable capacity to interpret signs. For any given language, there is not just a single cultural tradition it represents, but several, in some cases many, including perhaps religious ones, legal ones, ones formed for purposes of teaching and learning, logical or philosophical ones, and ones formed by modern linguists of various theoretical leanings. Different traditions may form for the 'same language' in different places. In historical terms, the single most powerful element in the creation and maintenance of these traditions has been *memory*, at every level from the individual to the cultural. Prior to the invention of writing, it was not obvious that individual and cultural memory could be distinguished; at least, cultural memory had to be invested in certain individuals and their ability to memorise and pass on oral tradition. Writing has allowed the storage of cultural memory separately from living individuals, something which has in one sense made cultural historical memory more powerful, but in another sense much weaker, since writing captures such a small part of language. If writing captured anything like the whole of language, we would expect different actors' interpretations of Hamlet, for example, to be identical. The actor's art finds its space in what the written word does not say, just as the pianist's or conductor's art has its space not in getting the printed musical notes right, but in interpreting all that they fail to capture.

But if languages are cultural traditions, how can we account for the facts of child language acquisition? Children pass through relatively regular stages of babbling, one-word, two-word and telegraphic utterances, with individual children progressing at somewhat different paces but still through relatively clear stages across languages. This is no more difficult to explain without universal grammar than with it, so long as we dispense with the incredible Chomskyan notion that language functions have nothing to do with anything else that goes on in the brain. Like all young animals, children are not born with fully fledged abilities of cognition or even perception. These general cerebral capacities develop over the first few years of life; learning language plays an important part in this development, as it is through the words they are taught that children learn a particular tradition of how to see, hear, smell, taste, feel, categorise and interpret things. If perception were purely physical and universal, we should expect all the languages of the world to recognise more or less the same colours, for example, when in reality languages vary vastly in the colours they differentiate and name.

Languages, then, are cultural traditions built upon foundations common to many animal species, namely cerebral structures and physical dispositions for perception, cognition, reading and interpretation, all of which interact with each other. The learning of a specific cultural tradition begins while the young individual's perceptual, cognitive and interpretative capacities are still being formed, and it shapes those capacities. The interactions are so complex as never to produce exactly the same outcome in any two individuals. And yet, patterns emerge among people who interact and share the experience of learning the cultural tradition. These patterns include the regional, social class, generational, sexual and other identifiable features within a language that sociolinguists attend to. They include patterns which are acquired not only in the home and at the playground, but in formal education – for in another instance of difference from generative grammar, we need not take it as axiomatic that the child's acquisition of its mother tongue is complete by the age of four, and that any changes which occur thereafter are trivial. This again is an idealisation which reflects a certain political bias against the effects of education, and which moreover flies in the face of common experience.

It should be clear that we are not going to take sociolinguistics as dealing with the trivial, unsystematic leftovers of 'real' linguistics, which alone tackles the essence of language, the speaker's mental grammar which has been produced by the triggering of parameters already hard-wired in at birth – indeed, well before birth, presumably at some stage when the human embryo has become distinct from that of a chicken. Quite the contrary. Our position is that if any kind of linguistics has a claim to greater reality it is sociolinguistics, the study of the audible and visible, rather than the deductive and imaginary; the study of the evolutionarily continuous and viable, rather than one that desperately hopes Darwin is mistaken. It is through a series of historical accidents that the approach we are taking here is not simply called linguistics *tout court*; in a logical world, this approach would be called linguistics, and all the rest theoretical or speculative linguistics. Of course I am not opposed to the latter approaches; I even teach them, and work within them at times. What I reject is any view of language that takes such a reductive approach that vowels or consonants or rules of syntax become more 'real' than people who speak. *People speaking* is the subject of this book.

'Reading' in the sense of interpreting identity fulfils the criteria for an evolutionary basis to language. It also underpins both representation and communication. This harks back to something like the behaviourist position (consider Pavlov's dogs, Skinner's pigeons), but without making any a priori decision about the relationship of 'instinctive' animal behaviour to human behaviour. However, if two animals of the same species react differently to the same stimulus, then 'reading' might be an apt characterisation of the mental process involved.

There is no reason to think that the interpretative needs of early humans were different from those of modern ones or of animal species or of the traditional accounts: food, sex and protection from danger. Food and, in a more complicated way, sex, required accumulation of territory and capital. That gave rise to danger, which in turn required more capital to finance weaponry. The recent evidence that early human groups who migrated off to form colonies wore shell jewellery to make themselves recognisable to those from the homeland, if it is a correct interpretation, implies the projection of an identity. This would have been important for reasons having to do with sex and danger, and perhaps also food, if trade was going on between homeland and colony. This is semiotic behaviour, somewhat comparable to sexual or combat display, but denoting something fundamental about who one is. The appropriation of jewellery by Neanderthals shows however that 'the signifier is independent of the signified' in a way that perhaps has no parallel in physical display – or perhaps does. The important point is that the expression of something like ethnic identity is at least contemporaneous with the beginning of language. Language would itself provide a marker of identity less easy to copy than shell jewellery – though still copyable.

What seems like the paradox of identity can also be understood in this evolutionarily connected way. On the one hand, identity is about 'sameness' (its etymological root) – being Chinese or Muslim connects one with other Chinese or Muslims to form a category of Chineseness or Muslimness, of which a particular individual may be a prototypical or marginal member. On the other hand, identity is about who one is uniquely – first of all a name, then a self that consists of the various identities (in the first sense) of which one partakes, and finally, for some people, a completely individual essence that escapes all categorisation beyond association with this particular person. Note that these oppositions actually intertwine: identity-as-sameness is principally recognised through contact with what is different, while identity-as-uniqueness is established largely through the intersection of identity-as-sameness categories. The twin impulses to sameness and uniqueness can plausibly be linked to the observable behaviour of mammalian species that prefer exogamy (outgroup breeding), which favours the production of viable offspring by improving the gene pool, yet which depends upon close family–tribal–species ties to ensure the nurture of the offspring and the protection of the group as a whole – and, crucially, to ensure the recognisability of close relatives with whom breeding must be avoided. The 'in-law' relationship is a key example of this drive to extend and recreate families ('samenesses') by incorporating suitable outsiders ('differences') in order to keep inimical outsiders at bay.

In psychological terms, individual identity starts with the ego, which, already at the time of its emergence is encountering the social forces that will cause the superego to develop. Group identities contribute to the establishment of both the ego and the superego. Yet in the ego there is always the need for unique possession. Is it possible to imagine, say, a group of Buddhist nuns who have so entirely given over their selves to divinity and groupness that no petty envy or resentment ever enters their hearts? Perhaps, but we would be obliged to say that they have risen above being human. At the other extreme, a person who valued only his individuality and no group belonging would be marked as a sociopath and a danger to the community. Linguistically these facts have their counterparts in the fact that no two people, however close, are linguistically identical – this would be hard to prove in the case of two nuns who have taken a vow of silence, so we had better specify that it is impossible to demonstrate that any two people are identical in their production and comprehension of language. It is a falsifiable proposition – it would suffice to show that two people *were* so identical. Caveat: identity will depend on the categories and criteria of linguistic analysis used. At the same time, group identities tend strongly to correlate with shared linguistic features – the major finding of sociolinguistics – to which it may be added that (1) group identities are sometimes manifested *primarily* through shared linguistic features, and (2) these features are not necessarily fixed in a given individual, whose knowledge of his language always includes a wide range of features (so that he can understand speakers from outside his group), which in some cases he can deploy actively, for example in the case of linguistic accommodation.

The notion that our knowledge of language consists fundamentally of abstract representations of sound–meaning correspondences depends heavily upon the observable fact that we are able to interpret very different utterances of the same words as having the same meaning. But this ignores the fact that we interpret much else from the precise way in which the word is said – mainly, information about the speaker, including his or her background, intentions, credibility. In other words, we read an identity onto the people whose words we hear and read. We can call this more precisely ***over-reading***, since the data on which it is based is (nearly) always inadequate to support the inferences made. There is no logical reason why linguistic patterns must reflect other attributes of the person who displays them. But this is how linguistic identity functions in general: we read the identity of people with whom we come into contact based on very subtle features of behaviour, among which those of language are particularly central. From the observable behaviour of other species we can plausibly call this an evolutionary inheritance, without running the risk that we are anthropomorphising by attributing 'interpretation' to other species.

This is not to suggest that such over-reading is inherently misguided or problematic, except when it engenders prejudice. The process is so ubiquitous and powerful, taking place in every encounter between people, that without it the entire range of processes which we call meaning and communication would be, if not impossible, at least of a vastly different form. Indeed, it is possible to argue that this process of over-reading is shared with other species, and that it therefore predates language in human evolutionary development. Certainly a tremendous amount of survival value inheres in the ability to size up the truth or falsity of what people tell us. Identity, and the reading of identity, form, in other words, the fundamental basis of human communication and interaction upon which 'language' in the usual sense is grafted.

Conclusion

The traditional recognition of representation and communication as the essential functions of language is based on a privileging of the active agency of the subject that is itself a historical product and an obstacle to a theory of language reconcilable with evolutionism. If we assume instead a primordial language subject-cum-object reacting interpretatively to the world around it, then interpretation becomes the primordial linguistic function. Abolishing the privileged status of the subject allows us to reincorporate the traditional role of the emotions into the analysis of language, adding a further evolutionary dimension, ending the monopoly of the cognitive. Forgoing the fiction of the complete self-contained language system gives us the further evolutionary dimension needed – we recognise it as an analytical artefact rather than a physical organ.

At this point it is no longer clear that there is any 'essential function' of language, because even this assumption implies the subject-agency of the inventor of a tool. We can, however, distinguish those things in the world that act in response to other things, and that, when they react in ways that are not wholly predictable, or involve a symbolic dimension, may be said to react interpretatively. When the reaction consists of trying to place an individual person or thing in a category with others, it is the ascription of an identity. Thus we might say that identity is a subcategory of representation – except that it extends beyond the bounds of representation as traditionally conceived, i.e. as the cognitive act of a subjective, agentive mind. We may want to widen the definition of representation, or else keep it in this restricted sense while recognising its limitations. As for identity, we can define it as the category (or set of categories) into which a person (or less often, animal or object or abstraction) is read as belonging, expressible as or (in the case of a proper name) consisting of a noun phrase or adjective phrase. I say 'is read as belonging' rather than 'belongs' in order to make clear that our experience does not include knowledge of any absolute identity, which can exist only in a Platonic heaven or, what amounts to the same thing, and equally unknowable, the mind of God.

Both in recent models and in the wider history, there is a key underlying paradox: although the goal of the social sciences is to determine what is behind the illusion that individuals act as wilful subjects, there is a strong methodological reluctance to move away from putting the individual as wilful subject at the centre of the social science universe of discourse. This chapter has included an attempt to motivate such a move, by arguing for an approach grounded in *reading* and *interpretation* that, among other things, has evolutionary plausibility. Inquiry into language and identity poses fundamental challenges to linguistics as traditionally conceived, reaching as far as the definition of language itself and its place within human life and evolution. I have tried to show that an understanding of language without consideration of identity can never hope to be complete, to indicate how such a consideration can enrich our understanding of language, and to draw attention to some of the methodological issues that cannot be skirted if it is to do so in any sort of serious way. The next chapter will examine the methodologies that have actually developed for understanding of the topic, together with their theoretical underpinnings.

3
Approaching Identity in Traditional Linguistic Analysis

Introduction

This chapter examines theories and methods developed within the study of language that form the background to the contemporary study of language and identity, assessing their achievements and their limitations. Along with the next chapter, which looks at the contributions from fields not concentrating on the study of language as such, it does not pretend to be a complete survey of the models developed, but limits itself to particular lines of research that paved the way toward current approaches.

Certain overarching trends have characterised the developments that will be surveyed here. These include:

- a move from seeing those aspects of language that are connected with identity as being mere by-products of another activity (such as communication of information) to being an important, directly functional activity in their own right;
- a move from seeing language itself as a determinate structure that directly determines important aspects of the lives of its speakers, to seeing it as something the speakers themselves control and use to their own ends;
- a move from focusing uniquely on the self-identity of an individual or group, to a granting of equal importance to the interpretations others make of a person's or group's identity;
- a move from identifying the 'groups' relevant to identity solely in terms of institutionally recognised categories and toward 'micro' groups;

- a move from *essentialism* to *constructionism*, in other words from analysing linguistic identity as a given and fixed aspect of who an individual or group is, to something changeable and variable as it is constructed and performed.

The first three of these shifts are closely interconnected; they will be taken up as much in the next chapter as in the present one. The last shift will be discussed in detail in the next chapter, where questions will be raised about whether, in fact, identity itself does not represent a phenomenon of essentialising within everyday human behaviour, and if so, whether our analysis of it should really eschew 'essences' altogether.

Classical and Romantic views of language, nation, culture and the individual

The growth of interest in language and identity toward the end of the twentieth century represented no historical novelty, but the working out of themes, ideas and tensions that had characterised European and American thinking since the eighteenth century. The Romantic period saw a decisive pendulum swing in the ancient debate over whether the form of a language is directly connected to the people who speak it. On one side of this debate was Aristotle (384–322 BC), who maintained that 'What is in the voice symbolises the passions of the mind/soul, [which] are the same for all people' (*On Interpretation*, 16a3–8, my translation; see further Joseph, forthcoming a). The word translated here as 'passions', *pathemata*, means everything the mind undergoes, for example in response to sensory input. Aristotle believed that such 'passive' mental experience was the basis for everything the mind does actively in thinking, and his position, as stated here, is that such experience is universal, the same for all human beings regardless of where they are from or what language they speak.

What many found unsatisfying in the Aristotelian position was that it gave no clue toward answering one of the most basic linguistic questions – why, if mental experience is the same for all, do different languages exist? The answer suggested by Aristotle's view is: mere accident. But neither this, nor Aristotle's belief that the signs of language signify their meanings purely by convention, was widely satisfactory in a culture that for centuries had interpreted deep significance into every aspect of its world, weaving complex myths of linkage and causation. So it is no surprise that a generation later, Epicurus of Samos (341–270 BC) would argue on the contrary that

> And so names too were not at first deliberately given to things, but men's natures according to their different nationalities [*ethnē*] had their own peculiar feelings and received their peculiar impressions, and so each in their own way emitted air formed into shape by each of these feelings and impressions, according to the differences made in the different nations by the places of their abode as well. (Epicurus, *Letter to Herodotus*, 75–6, translation by Bailey, 1926)

Epicurus is widely remembered as the philosopher who put the body at the centre of his moral considerations, and here he is maintaining that from the bodies of the members of an *ethnos* there arise nationally or racially distinct feelings and impressions, and that these directly shape the language of that *ethnos*. What Epicurus put forward in this letter was the first surviving theory of language and identity, and a strong theory it was, holding that members of different nationalities and ethnicities differ in their feelings and even their sensory perception of the world around them, and that these feelings and impressions are what produced their particular languages.

This would explain why there are different languages, and why, on the whole, language boundaries appear to coincide with boundaries between peoples; and it means that our language is not just an accidental part of who we are as a people, but has been directly moulded by the most fundamental part of who we are, our bodies. It offers too something that most people have always wanted to believe – that *we* are different from *them*, deeply different, in language (which is obvious), in mind (less obvious, but indirectly observable in differences of custom and culture) and body (the least obvious, except that we are sensitive to microscopic, trivial similarities and differences, such as of skin colour).

The Epicurean view appealed to those in ancient world, such as Lucretius, author of *De rerum natura* (first century BC) for whom the differences among peoples appeared to be such an obvious fact as to constitute a first principle from which other, more mysterious phenomena should be explained. Yet Epicurus had produced nothing like the massive, encyclopaedic body of work of Aristotle, who, by the late Middle Ages had such a unique stature that he was known simply as 'the philosopher'. This status began to be challenged in the late fifteenth century with the rediscovery of Plato. When an even more direct challenge to the academic authority of Aristotle was mounted in the sixteenth and seventeenth centuries, it was done in the name of 'neo-Epicureanism'.

By this time, too, imperial and colonial expansion were bringing European peoples into much more direct and sustained contact with non-European peoples than at any time since Imperial Rome, and of course even Rome had had no contact with the Americas. The sheer scale of human ethnic and cultural differences was imposing itself on the European mind, exciting anthropological curiosity and demanding plausible historical explanation within a culture that accepted the biblical account of creation – accepting too that the account could be metaphorical, though just how metaphorical was a matter of significant sectarian dispute.

For a churchman-cum-scientist like Condillac (see p. 11), it went without saying that explanations must be reconcilable both with observable facts and with the Bible, and in his *Essai sur l'origine des connoissances humaines* (1746) he used the Fall of Man through the disobedience of Adam and Eve to define a breach in human history that would allow something like both the Aristotelian and Epicurean view of mind and language to stand. For Condillac, the prelapsarian mind, the state of Adam and Eve before original sin, and to which we shall return when we die, has the universal characteristics described by Aristotle, being structured by what Descartes in the previous century had called 'innate ideas'. The post-lapsarian mind, however, has lost contact with these God-given innate ideas, and must therefore be restructured based on the experience of the senses, i.e. the body. It is the tabula rasa that John Locke (1632–1704) had argued for in the neo-Epicurean tradition, contra Descartes.

Seven years after Condillac's *Essai*, Jean-Jacques Rousseau (1712–78) reacted to it in his *Discours sur l'origine et les fondemens de l'inégalité parmi les hommes* (1753), which imagines how the very different forms of language and thought observable among various peoples could have arisen historically. The same sort of enquiry would be pursued further a generation later in Germany by the Romantics, such as Johann Georg Hamann (1730–88) and Johann Gottfried Herder (1744–1803). By now there has re-emerged an ancient belief that climate, landscape, race, national character and language are all intimately and inseparably bound together, so that, as with Condillac, whatever conventional character languages exhibit is ultimately superficial. The choice of conventions is never in any sense free to individuals, and even in its origin it was not arbitrary, being determined by that conjunction of causes which together define what will eventually be called the *Volksgeist*, the national spirit, the 'genius' of a people that is reflected in their language and other 'folk' creations.

The fullest development of this Romantic outlook would come in the posthumously published *Über die Verschiedenheit des menschlichen Sprachbaues und ihren Einfluss auf die geistige Entwickelung des Menschengeschlechts* (1836) by Baron Wilhelm von Humboldt (1767–1835). Based upon his broad and deep study of reports of languages from all corners of the world, Humboldt proposed that languages can be categorised into a handful of types based upon how they structure information into words. The isolating type, of which Chinese is the prototypical example, has one word corresponding to each idea, regardless of whether it is a 'root' idea or simply a modification. The agglutinating type, which includes the American Indian languages as well as the Turkish–Mongolian family, goes to the opposite extreme, constructing enormously long words that correspond to whole sentences in other language types. In the middle is the inflecting type, which includes Sanskrit and the entire Indo-European family, which start with 'root' words and add prefixes, suffixes, infixes, etc. to them to indicate various smaller differences that specify or colour the root meaning without however fundamentally changing it.

As the title of his work indicates, Humboldt believed that a people's intellectual development is influenced by the structural typology of its language. Chinese, he maintained, is a superior language for the expression of ideas, and the works of classical Chinese literature are unparalleled manifestations of ideas in their pure, detached form. Sanskrit, on the other hand, is a superior language for the expression of human thought processes, which operate like the structure of the inflecting languages themselves, starting off with a root idea and then modifying it in a secondary way. So it is no accident, Humboldt believed, that, just as Chinese has produced the greatest expression of pure ideas, the Indo-European languages have produced the greatest works in the realm of human thought.

Two further aspects of Humboldt's theory need to be explained. Over time, language change can move the structure of a language away from the typology of its historical source. Thus Modern English retains relatively few traces of its inflectional origins; in many respects it is more like Chinese than like Sanskrit in the way it 'packages information' into words. For a Romantic thinker like Humboldt, however, this present-day reality counts for naught. Whatever a language is at its origin, it will remain that for ever, despite the superficial historical vicissitudes that may hide this. The 'genius' of the language is unaffected – and we should remember that the word *genius* itself is etymologically connected to *genesis* and *genetic*, all having to do with origin. Secondly, there are within any given people certain rare individuals whom we identify as 'geniuses', the original sense of this having been that such individuals somehow embody that originary essence of their people and culture. For the Romantic, those geniuses alone are *true* individuals, in that they alone do not simply act in ways determined by their national–cultural inheritance, but add to that inheritance, carrying it further forward.

By the mid-nineteenth century it would be a received idea that a cardinal difference between 'civilised' and 'primitive' peoples was that, among the latter, there are no individuals in the proper sense. Everyone in a primitive race is intellectually equal, the view went, whereas in a civilised race one finds enormous differences of intelligence between the sexes (considered as a whole) and between the privileged and the working classes. The peasantry of a civilised country thus had much in common with the natives of a primitive country, although only the former were thought capable of producing the occasional genius. Of course, upon being recognised as a genius, the individual in question would, by definition, leave the class from which they had sprung.

This is a fitting point to recall that group identities, particularly national and ethnic identities, are double-edged swords. On the one hand, they fulfil the positive function of giving people a sense of who they are, of belonging to a community, in the absence of which one can feel a sense of alienation that can have disastrous consequences. On the other hand, such belonging is always constructed through difference from 'others' – a categorial distancing that can all too easily turn into a desire for segregation, and to hatred. It is at least as crucial for us to understand these destructive aspects of identity as its positive ones, since only through understanding them can we contribute to the important work of battling ethnic and national hatred, prejudice and oppression, without at the same time sacrificing those beneficial elements of identity that are essential to the healthy life of individuals and societies.

The nineteenth century and the beginnings of institutional linguistics

As linguistics became institutionalised in the nineteenth century, a breach opened up where the Humboldtian connection with thought and culture was concerned. Its most public expression was in the widely followed debates between the Oxford professor of comparative philology, Friedrich Max Müller (1823–1900), and the American Sanskritist and linguist William Dwight Whitney (1827–1894). Müller, following in the spirit of Humboldt, maintained that '*There is no thought without words, as little as there are words without thought*' (Müller, 1873, p. 419, italics in original). Thought and language come into being simultaneously. Language is a physical endowment, a living thing, which shapes the culture and thought of a people, for better and for worse. Mythology, Müller maintained, was 'a disease of language' (Müller, 1861, p. 11). Whitney argued that language was nothing of the sort – languages are institutions, historical products created by people to encode already existing thought. Admittedly, once created they take on a metaphorical 'life of their own' that causes them to elude the control of individuals. They are 'democratic' institutions maintained by and subject to the 'will of the people', which is something of quite a different order from individual will.

Whitney's views would have a profound impact upon a young Swiss aristocrat named Ferdinand de Saussure (1857–1913), who encountered Whitney's work (and once met the man himself) while studying Indo-European historical linguistics in Germany. Saussure embraced the Whitneyan conception of language as an institution, consisting of arbitrary signs. But where the relationship of language to thought was concerned, Saussure fundamentally agreed with Max Müller. As Whitney conceives of the institutional nature of language, it must be the case that thought exists first, and languages follow as arbitrary systems for encoding thought. If thought and language come into being simultaneously, as Max Müller insists, then the link between the two, and thus between words and their meanings, is not arbitrary but natural.

Although Saussure believed Whitney had got this wrong, he also thought the American had provided the solution:

> To make it evident that languages are pure institutions, Whitney very rightly insisted on the arbitrariness of signs; and he thereby placed linguistics on its true axis. But he did not follow it all the way through, and did not see that this arbitrariness separates languages from all other institutions. (Saussure, 1922 [1916], p. 110)

If we take arbitrariness seriously, and make it the first principle of the linguistic sign, then the word and its meaning can come into existence simultaneously without this implying any deterministic connection between them. Saussure believed, like Max Müller, that the meanings of words are brought into existence when the word is created and not before; but the creation of the word is nothing more than the establishment of an arbitrary institutional link between a sound pattern (or as he would eventually call it, a signifier – see p. 5) and a meaning (signified). The second fact, Whitney's insight, trumps the first without the first being wrong.

Saussure, who will be discussed further in the next section, would succeed posthumously in setting twentieth-century linguistics on the track of investigating language as an arbitrary system in which, not only are signifiers arbitrarily linked to signifieds, but signifieds are not bound in any way to 'real-world' items which they conceptualise. Such a model of language allows only a 'weak' conception of the language–identity link, in which identities are not deeply grounded in anything like the ethnic body but are really conventional labels for culturally conventionalised categories.

Throughout this long history a fundamental paradox has endured. My language is a fundamental part of who I am, culturally and mentally (at least in the sense that it is the vehicle of my thinking), and yet other people can learn my language or I theirs. Language boundaries tend to coalign with ethnic boundaries, yet, especially as a speaker of a 'world language' like English, I am surrounded by evidence that the two are readily crossed, and that indeed both linguistic and ethnic 'boundaries' are metaphorical and incapable of being pinned down scientifically. And while cultural differences are real and powerful, I nevertheless have much in common with members of other linguistic cultures, more perhaps than I have with various subcultures within my own language. The development of linguistics in the twentieth and twenty-first centuries would continue to trace a shuttle path between the poles of this paradox.

The social in language: Voloshinov vs Saussure

Posthumously assembled and published in 1916, Saussure's *Course in General Linguistics* would within a decade and a half assume the status of foundational text for structuralist linguistics. Saussure declared that *langue*, a language, is a 'social fact', and that social force holds the system together so powerfully that no individual can change the language. Changes occur in *parole*, 'speech', and if eventually the social community accepts the change, the system moves to a new state, a new *langue*.

An example of such change can be found in the word *social* itself. For Saussure, it signifies (following its Latin etymology) binding together, whatever it is that makes a collectivity of individuals act in the same way. His calling language a social fact is connected to his assertion that every member of the speech community possesses the language in identical form. But already by the 1920s *social* was being used in many people's *parole* with a different implication, indeed virtually the opposite of Saussure's. It was associated with what, within a collectivity, distinguished certain subgroups from others. By the second half of the century, this meaning had become dominant.

A crucial force behind the change was Marxism, which turned into a political reality with the Russian Revolution of 1917, a year after Saussure's *Course* was published. In the newly constituted USSR, the *Course* was initially received as consistent in spirit with the 'formalism' then in vogue, and its remarks about the social nature of language were interpreted as harmonious with the Marxist view that every central facet of human experience is social in its origin and operation. For the Marxist, however, the 'social' immediately implies the political: socially differentiated subgroups vying with one another to further their interests at the expense of the others.

But over the course of the 1920s serious questions were raised about how commensurable formalism was with this basic Marxist view. Mikhail Bakhtin (1895–1975) and members of the intellectual circle he led came to the realisation that the social space which language occupies for Saussure is not political: there is no scope for one speaker to manifest power over another, because *langue* has no individual dimension – that belongs entirely to *parole*. The member of Bakhtin's circle who took on Saussure most directly was Valentin Voloshinov (1895–1936), in *Marxism and the Philosophy of Language* (1929). Here, as in certain other works by those close to Bakhtin, his ideas are so closely interwoven with theirs that it remains unclear to what extent Bakhtin should be considered the co-author or indeed the author (see Todorov, 1981).

For Voloshinov, Saussure's *Course* represents the most striking and thoroughly developed form of what he disparagingly terms 'abstract objectivism' (Voloshinov, 1973 [1929], p. 58). It defines the boundaries of language to include 'not the relationship of the sign to the actual reality it reflects nor to the individual who is its originator, but the *relationship of sign to sign within a closed system* already accepted and authorized' (ibid., italics in original). Rather than deal with actual utterances, it considers only the language system abstracted away from them. Saussure does at least move beyond the Romantic view of language as a facet of individual consciousness. Yet his refusal to engage with 'history', in the Marxist sense of the actions of actual people (the 'base', as opposed to 'superstructure'), denies his approach any claim to genuine social substance in the Marxist sense. For Voloshinov,

> Every sign, as we know, is a construct between socially organized persons in the process of their interaction. Therefore, the forms of signs are conditioned above all by the social organization of the participants involved and also by the immediate conditions of their interaction. (Ibid., p. 21)

Signs are ideological in their very nature, and social existence is not merely reflected in them but 'refracted' by them. For the sign is not like a smooth mirror, but one with a cracked and irregular surface, created by the 'differently oriented social interests within one and the same sign community, i.e., by the class struggle' (ibid., p. 23). When Voloshinov declares that 'Sign becomes an arena of the class struggle' (ibid., p. 23), he makes language central to the 'base', a Marxist declaration that language and politics are inseparable, maybe even indistinguishable. 'Linguistic creativity [...] cannot be understood apart from the ideological meanings and values that fill it' (ibid., p. 98).

No speech act is individual; they are always social, even if the addressee exists only in the speaker's imagination. And indeed, every word we utter is generated in interaction with an imagined audience in our mind, before any real audience ever hears or reads it. Thus, according to Voloshinov and Bakhtin, language is inherently 'dialogic', and it is a fundamental error and illusion of 'bourgeois' linguistics to conceive of it as monologic, generated simply by the individual psychology of a speaker. The discrete systems that linguists normally study coexist with a multiplicity of different ways of speaking that are constantly intermingling with each other, a condition for which Bakhtin (1975, written in 1934–35) introduces the term 'heteroglossia':

> A unitary language is not something given but is always in essence posited – and at every moment of its linguistic life it is opposed to the realities of heteroglossia. But at the same time it makes its real presence felt as a force for overcoming this heteroglossia, imposing specific limits to it [...]. (Bahktin, 1981 [1975], p. 270)

This tension constitutes the arena of the class struggle where voices and signs are concerned.

Voloshinov died in the 1930s, and his and Bakhtin's writings fell into obscurity until their rediscovery in the 1960s. By this time, many of their ground-breaking ideas had been arrived at independently by later Marxists, post-Marxists and even non-Marxists, and when their work began to be translated into French and English, they seemed perfectly contemporary despite a remove of 40 years. Saussure and Voloshinov offer two clearly differentiated modes for approaching the social and political in language. Saussure's is based on an understanding of the social as what binds people together, Voloshinov's as what keeps them apart. The latter accords better with what 'social' has now come to signify in sociolinguistics and the social sciences generally. Yet so relentlessly does Voloshinov pursue the argument that language is ideological from top to bottom that he makes the terms 'language' and 'politics' appear tautological – it ceases to be clear what one can say about the relationship between them that would be meaningful.

Nevertheless, some 40 years after his death, Voloshinov would succeed better than anyone previously in winning people over to the view that the 'politics of language' is not simply a matter of what people do with language, but that language itself is political from the bottom up. The linguistic sign embodies the social relationships of its users. In this sense, their social identity is present in the language itself. Thus a significant space was opened up for the academic study of language and identity.[1]

Jespersen and Sapir

In Western Europe and America, meanwhile, attention to either the personal or the social dimension of language was deeply unfashionable. The historical–comparative inquiry that had come to define the field in the nineteenth century, with Germany as its centre, abstracted language users out of the picture. Saussure's *Cours* at least made clear where the place of the individual language user lies – in speech (*parole*) rather than in language proper (*langue*). Saussure said that a linguistics of *parole* should eventually develop, but made clear that, for the time being at least, the sole legitimate object of linguistic inquiry was *langue* in itself and for itself.

Two linguists of the period are noteworthy for their readiness to confront the dominant ideology of the day. Among European linguists outside the USSR, the one most closely attuned to the political and individual aspects of language was the Danish Anglicist Otto Jespersen (1860–1943). In a remarkable book entitled *Mankind, Nation and Individual from a Linguistic Point of View* (1925), Jespersen, following in the footsteps of the slightly older Danish linguist Adolf Noreen (1854–1925), analysed the role of the standard language in the life of individuals who, particularly in cities, were increasingly using it alongside, or indeed in place of, the local dialect of their birthplace. Other linguists tended to treat the standard language as less 'real' – merely a lingua franca, unlike the local dialects in which individuals were believed to be psychologically rooted. Jespersen maintained that, as urban living shifted from being restricted to a small fraction of the population toward being characteristic of the majority,[2] the linguistic reality was such that the standard language could no longer be treated as a mere symbol in the life of the nation.

> The greatest and most important phenomenon of the evolution of language in historic times has been the springing up of the great national common-languages – Greek, French, English, German, etc. – the 'standard' languages which have driven out, or are on the way to drive out, the local dialects purely conditioned by geographical factors. (Jespersen, 1925, pp. 39–40)
>
> [...] Standard languages are *socially* determined. [...] One may mention great political unifications, and be it observed, unifications on the lines of nationality; [...] finally the enormous growth of many great cities which attract a population from outside. (Ibid., pp. 64–5, italics in original)
>
> [I]n great towns the immigrants from different parts of the country get their dialect rubbed down in intercourse with one another with the result that the population of a great town comes to talk in a manner which one would not expect from its geographical situation. (Ibid., p. 57)

Nor could use of the standard language be discounted as a mere ornament in the linguistic life of an individual. Although it might be true in geographical terms that, with standard-language forms, 'the person using them does not betray by his speech where he comes from' (ibid., p. 40), use of the forms does place the person socially. The standard language was now a part of the individual's linguistic identity quite as much as the mother dialect – even those who did not know the standard language were now marked by this fact.

With the exception of work by members of the Prague Linguistic Circle such as Bohuslav Havránek (1893–1978) and Jan Mukařovský (1891–1973) in the 1930s (see Havránek, 1932, 1938; Mukařovský, 1932), however, the sort of serious inquiry Jespersen envisioned and initiated into standard languages and their role in the lives of speakers would not be taken up again until the 1960s. An account of their development from that point forward can be found in Joseph (1987), published at a time when considerations of standard language had begun to merge with broader inquiry into the 'ideologies' of language (the subject of a later section) by which the cultural beliefs underpinning linguistic identity are maintained.

Across the Atlantic, the anthropologist and linguist Edward Sapir (1884–1939), one of the founding figures of 'American structuralism' (cf. Joseph, 2002a, Ch. 7), stands out for his enduring interest in case studies of individual language users and in his ultimate desire – never fully achieved – to frame the study of language within the fuller context of the human 'personality'. In his field research on American Indian languages, Sapir paid attention to people who were considered unusual users of their language, and wrote several studies on such individuals. One of the most remarkable of his early works, *Abnormal Types of Speech in Nootka* (1915), focused on how speakers of this American Indian language of Vancouver Island vary the language to indicate characteristics of the person being spoken about. The variations involve the use of the diminutive suffix -'is or the augmentative -aq', plus, what is more unusual, changes to the consonant system. In many cases the characteristics in question are physical or moral deformities, and the linguistic changes are also used when speaking of animals which the Nootka culture associates with these characteristics. So, for example, in speaking of or to dwarfs, the diminutive suffix is used, as when speaking of or to children, but in addition, all sibilants (*s, z, sh*, etc.) are palatalised, i.e. pronounced with the tongue drawn back toward the hard palate, altering the sound. These palatalised sibilants are also used when speaking about little birds such as sparrows or wrens. Some other examples are shown in Table 3.1. Sapir noted that the interpersonal effect of using these special forms when speaking *to* the person possessing the characteristic, or in his or her presence, is complex and subtle, and depends in part on the personalities of the individuals concerned. Some of the forms are likely to cause offence, are these are only used to poke fun or tease. Other forms can be used in a kind-hearted way to let the person know that the speaker attaches no great importance to the defect.

Sapir made clear that the Nootka phenomenon is by no means unique, but an especially salient example of something that occurs in *all* languages, namely, 'the use in speech of various devices implying something in regard to the status, sex, age, or other characteristics of the speaker, person addressed, or person spoken of, without any direct statement as to such characteristics' (Sapir, 1949 [1915], p. 179). A 1933

Table 3.1 'Abnormal' language in Nootka (from data in Sapir, 1915)

Characteristic	*Suffix*	*Consonant change*	*Also used in speaking of*
Child	-'is		Those one wishes to belittle
Fat, abnormally large	-aq'		
Abnormally small	-'is	Sibilants palatalised	
Eye defects	-'is	Sibilants → laterals	Deer, mink
Hunchbacked	-'is	Sibilants → thickish, with lower jaw protruding	
Lame	-'is	Meaningless element *Lc* or *Lci* inserted somewhere before suffix	
Left-handed		*tcH*[a] inserted after 1st syllable	Bears (believed to be left-handed)
Circumcised male		Meaningless element *ct'* inserted after 1st syllable	
Greedy		*tcx* inserted after 1st syllable	Ravens

encyclopaedia article Sapir wrote made the following statement projecting much of what research on language and identity would be about more than half a century later:

> Language is a great force of socialization, probably the greatest that exists. By this is meant not merely the obvious fact that significant social intercourse is hardly possible without language but that the mere fact of a common speech serves as a peculiarly potent symbol of the social solidarity of those who speak the language. The psychological significance of this goes far beyond the association of particular languages with nationalities, political entities, or smaller local groups [...].
>
> In spite of the fact that language acts as a socializing and uniformizing force, it is at the same time the most potent single known factor for the growth of individuality. The fundamental quality of one's voice, the phonetic patterns of speech, the speed and relative smoothness of articulation, the length and build of the sentences, the character and range of the vocabulary, the scholastic consistency of the words used, the readiness with which words respond to the requirements of the social environment, in particular the suitability of one's language to the language habits of the persons addressed – all these are so many complex indicators of the personality. [...] All in all, it

> is not too much to say that one of the really important functions of language is to be constantly declaring to society the psychological place held by all of its members. (Sapir, 1949 [1933], pp. 15–18)

In the section on 'Essentialism and Constructionism' below, I shall revisit this statement to point out how it deviates from present-day assumptions. But this does not diminish its historical significance. Here is the leading anthropological linguist of his day (and his century) calling for the functional analysis of language to take account of its 'constantly declaring to society the psychological place held by all of its members'. The call would be almost totally ignored for decades to come.[3]

If you ask an ordinary educated person what three things they know about from twentieth-century linguistics, the most common answers will be Saussurean sign theory, Chomskyan innateness (or maybe 'deep structure') and the 'Sapir–Whorf Hypothesis', not necessarily in that order.[4] Ask them to say what the Sapir–Whorf Hypothesis is, and they will probably reply with the 'strong' version, that 'one's perception of the world is determined by the structure of one's native language' (*New Shorter Oxford English Dictionary*, 1993, under 'Whorfianism'), or perhaps the 'weak' version, that 'the structure of a language partly determines a native speaker's categorization of experience' (ibid., under 'Sapir–Whorf Hypothesis'). These ideas have apparent links with the German Romantic views discussed on pp. 44–6 above, although I have shown elsewhere that they were more directly stimulated by later sources including Ogden & Richards (1923), in which Malinowski (1923) was contained.

Sapir came to believe that the sorts of idiosyncratic conceptualisations one finds in every human language, such as those in Table 3.1 from Nootka, are evidence that the members of that linguistic culture think differently from people in other cultures. Consider the example of Nootka speech used to refer to left-handed people, being marked by the same feature used in speaking of bears, which the culture believes to be left-handed. A Nootka speaker categorises things in the world in such a way that left-handed people and bears belong to the same category. No similar categorisation exists for speakers of English or other European languages. Whorf famously analysed expressions of time in another American Indian language, Hopi, and concluded not only that the Hopi conceived of time in a completely different way from speakers of what he termed SAE ('Standard Average European'), but that the Hopi conceptions were actually closer to the conceptions developed by modern physicists.[5]

Whorf's writings do not relate directly to the question of language and identity, but they have served an important indirect purpose as the touchstone for modern linguists arguing that languages have a deep connection to the thought and culture of the people who speak them. Chomsky and other linguists of 'universalist' bent have never had any time for the Sapir–Whorf Hypothesis. Cognitivists who have tried to test the hypothesis have turned up results that admit of various interpretations. Yet linguists arguing for the importance of protecting and preserving 'endangered languages', or simply explaining why language matters in the understanding of identity, have been highly prone to falling back upon Whorfian statements that every language divides the world up differently, and that language is essential, not accidental, to cultural formation, cohesion and transmission. In Chapter 5 we shall encounter a recent attempt to analyse national linguistic identity within the Whorfian framework.

Firth, Halliday and their legacy

Back in Britain, J. R. Firth (1890–1960), the country's first professor of linguistics and a self-proclaimed non-Saussurean,[6] laid the ground for a politicised analysis of language within the basic framework of structural analysis, by locating a space for political meaning within a systemic analysis of language (see further Joseph, 2003). Structuralist approaches proceeded by analysing everything down to its constituent parts, and assumed that the whole utterance could be understood as nothing more than the sum of these parts. Firth argued that the putting-together itself, the *collocation* of parts, created meaning at least as much as what the individual parts contributed. In the course of a discussion of Edward Lear's limericks, Firth proposed 'to bring forward as a technical term, meaning by "collocation", and to apply the tests of "collocability"' (Firth, 1957 [1951], p. 194). 'One of the meanings of *ass*,' he famously writes there (ibid., p. 195), 'is its habitual collocation with an immediately preceding *you silly* [...].' Firth insisted that 'meaning' must be broadly construed to embrace not just words, but actions, and *the people who speak the words and do the actions*.

> The commonest sentences in which the words *horse, cow, pig, swine, dog* are used with adjectives in nominal phrases, and also with verbs in the simple present, indicate characteristic distributions in collocability which may be regarded as a level of meaning in describing the English of any particular social group or indeed of one person. (Ibid.)

The very idea of 'describing the English of any particular social group or indeed of one person' was already novel for its time; the notion that, for purposes of such description, collocability might constitute a level of meaning of comparable importance with word meaning was nothing short of radical. Firth strove to make this clear:

> The statement of meaning by collocation and various collocabilities does not involve the definition of word-meaning by means of further sentences in shifted terms. Meaning by collocation is an abstraction at the syntagmatic level and is not directly concerned with the conceptual or idea approach to the meaning of words. One of the meanings of *night* is its collocability with *dark*, and of *dark*, of course, collocation with *night*. (Ibid., p. 196)

Another statement in the same article goes further still. In discussing how meaning operates at the level of phonology, Firth writes: 'Surely it is part of the meaning of an American to sound like one' (ibid., p. 192).

This is one of those elliptical and gnomic statements which already in Firth's lifetime earned him a reputation for being better understood in the 'translations' of his best students, such as R. H. Robins (1921–2000) and M. A. K. Halliday (b. 1925), than in the original. However one interprets this particular statement – and it does require interpretation, since it is far from obvious in what sense 'an American' has 'a meaning' – it is clearly about language and national identity. I understand it as follows: labelling or identifying someone as 'an American' (whether it is oneself or another person) implies certain expectations about the form of English they speak. When told that someone is an American who does not have an American accent, we experience cognitive dissonance. Something is deeply amiss.

It would be Firth's students, notably Halliday, who would pave the way toward a form of text analysis based upon uncovering the hidden ideologies that structure the use of language. Halliday is both a Marxist and a structuralist – the perception of the two as opposed ideologies faded in the 1960s, when the prominent Marxist theorist Althusser (mentioned in Chapter 1) came to be labelled as a structuralist by everyone but himself.[7] By developing a 'systemic–functional grammar' aimed at comprehending both the social and semiotic dimensions of texts, Halliday (see e.g. Halliday, 1978) provided the tools for the 'critical linguistics' developed by Roger Fowler (1938–99) in collaboration with a group of younger scholars (see Fowler, 1987; Fowler et al., 1979). This in turn led to the 'critical discourse analysis' (CDA) of Fairclough

(1989, 1992), which marries critical linguistics with the perspectives of Foucault and Bourdieu (the subjects of a later section), and sees itself as capturing the 'dynamic' nature of both power relations and text production by uncovering the hegemonic structures within texts. This is in contrast with earlier analyses, including those of critical linguistics, which concerned themselves with static relations and how they are encoded.

Another set of significant present-day approaches to language and identity traces its roots to this tradition. 'Critical applied linguistics' (CAL) is a cover term for a diffuse range of inquiries into language, texts, pedagogy and cultural politics, united by an interest in modern critical theory and politicial commitments that, as Pennycook (2001) points out, are both post-liberal and post-Marxist, but beyond that are difficult to specify. CAL has been influential in convincing foreign-language teachers that the work they do has a direct impact on the identities and the lives of those they teach, and moreover that their students are active agents in the shaping and reshaping of their own identities through linguistic and other means. Pennycook's (2001) survey of CAL actually contains just one reference to Halliday, and none at all to Firth, instead positioning CAL as the continuation of continental traditions including those of Jürgen Habermas as well as the French structuralists Foucault and Bourdieu. I believe its history can be more accurately characterised as a grafting of these continental branches onto what is essentially a Firthian–Hallidayan tree. Some versions of CAL will be examined in more detail in Chapter 7 (pp. 181–92), in the context of the spread of English.

Later structuralist moves toward linguistic identity: Brown & Gilman, Labov and others

From the death of Sapir in 1939 onwards, the mainstream of linguistic inquiry was occupied by structuralist analysis of the system of particular languages, with particular attention to phonemic analysis of the sound system. Actually, the beginnings of modern sociolinguistics were taking place in this period (see Joseph, 2002b, Ch. 5), but the trend was strongly toward the study either of a whole language system or the universal features shared by all such systems, rather than the variation within them.

In 1958 a symposium on 'Language and Style' was held in Cambridge, Massachusetts, bringing together a range of people from linguistics, psychology and literary studies to explore a range of topics related to 'style', a concept given wide definitional berth for purposes of the meeting. Several of the papers published in the proceedings volume in 1960 would become classics, but probably the single most influential one was co-authored by the psychologist Roger Brown (1925–97) and a linguist with interests in the analysis of literary texts, Albert Gilman (1923–89). Their paper, 'The Pronouns of Power and Solidarity', presented the distinction between familiar and deferential pronouns of address (Spanish *tu/Usted*, French *tu/vous*, German *du/Sie*, etc.) as a system for establishing and maintaining interpersonal relations that is directly embedded into grammar.

The paper is an implicit critique of the structuralist view of the language system as autonomous and aloof from the mundane politics of *parole.* It is reminiscent of the then forgotten Voloshinov's conception of language as the arena of the class struggle, except that Brown & Gilman consider only interpersonal relations and not the broader political picture. They show how the *tu*-type forms are used to keep social inferiors in their place, but also to manifest tender intimacy to a child or a lover, political solidarity with one's peers, or a personal bond to God. It can, in other words, function to break down the social boundaries between individuals as much as to maintain them, the meaning of each utterance being dependent upon the surrounding political context.

Brown & Gilman paved the way for much research into such phenomena across a wide range of languages, and led ultimately to the 'politeness theory' of another Brown (Penelope) & Levinson (1987). Their approach was built upon the concept of *face* as developed by the Canadian sociologist Erving Goffman, who was mentioned in Chapter 1 (p. 91) in connection with the related term *persona*, and will be discussed further in Chapter 4 (pp. 67–8). Since any linguistic exchange between speakers is inherently face-threatening, language must include means for expressing politeness in order for face to be maintained. Brown & Levinson propose that linguistic politeness can be analysed universally on the basis of three independent variables:

- social distance between speaker and hearer
- their relative power
- degree of imposition associated with the required expenditure of goods or services.

Kasper (1994) surveys a range of subsequent studies that have tested Brown & Levinson's model empirically and found it wanting in one or more aspects, and raises various bases on which its claimed universality is dubious.

Although sociolinguistic research has quite a long history and was well along in its development by the 1950s, William Labov's work of the early 1960s was primarily responsible for getting it institutional recognition as an academic discipline worthy of significant research funding. Labov's first significant published article, 'The Social Motivation of a Sound Change' (1963), dealt with the English dialect of Martha's Vineyard, an island off the coast of Massachusetts, which shows what is sometimes called 'Canadian raising', in which the diphthongs in words like *right* and *house* are pronounced as /əy/ and /əw/ rather than /ay/ and /aw/. This feature is not found in the dialects of the US mainland spoken by the large numbers of people who 'summer' on Martha's Vineyard, and with whom the Vineyarders (year-round residents) have a complex relationship of dependency and resentment. Following Jespersen's statement about how 'the immigrants from different parts of the country get their dialect rubbed down in intercourse with one another', one might have expected this feature to have been levelled out of the Martha's Vineyard dialect through the extensive, regular contact with large numbers of speakers from the mainland. But in Labov's view, this is precisely what has strengthened the feature and caused it to be maintained:

> It is apparent that the immediate meaning of this phonetic feature is 'Vineyarder'. When a man says [rəyt] or [həws], he is unconsciously establishing the fact that he belongs to the island: that he is one of the natives to whom the island really belongs. (Labov, 1963, p. 307)

Apart from the word 'unconsciously', which is a red herring – for whether the effect is 'conscious' or not makes no difference (and is impossible to determine) – this is very much the sort of analysis of the effect of linguistic identity on language form that would be characteristic of work in the 1990s and since.

However, it was not yet the kind of interpretation that the linguistics establishment was prepared to accept as scientifically valid, and it was from that establishment that Labov was determined to gain recognition for sociolinguistic research. The work through which he succeeded in gaining that recognition, such as Labov (1966), downplays such interpretation grounded in identity in favour of a more 'objective' presentation of the distribution of linguistic variables by social class, with heavy reliance on statistics to establish their significance. Arguably, if Labov had not done this, sociolinguistics would not have become a standard part of the linguistics curriculum in most countries, and would never have developed the cadres of researchers who, a couple of decades on, would pick up the thread of his initial focus on identity, interweaving it with what had been achieved in the meanwhile by social psychologists and others.

From 'women's language' to gender identity

Many non-European languages have separate grammatical systems for use by men and women, and at least since the 1940s American linguists had suggested that, although the sex-based differences in European languages are subtler in form, they too might be analysed as distinct systems (Furfey, 1944; Haas, 1944). The linguist who would finally do this in a way that would establish gender distinction in language as an important and enduring topic was Robin Lakoff. In a 1973 article that was expanded into a book two years later, she argued that languages, in both their structure and their use, mark out an inferior social role for women and bind them to it. As with deferential address and interpersonal relationships, gender politics is incorporated directly into the pronoun systems of English and many other languages, through the use of the masculine as the 'unmarked' gender (as in 'Everyone take his seat'). Lakoff's book fed into a movement to change such usage, so that now it is more common to say 'his or her' or use 'their' as a singular pronoun, a usage formerly considered solipsistic but now on its way to acceptability. Lakoff points to features that occur more frequently in women's than in men's English, such as tag questions, hedges, intensifiers and pause markers, which as marks of insecurity and of the role women are expected to occupy are fundamental to maintaining the status quo in gender politics. Her interpretations received independent support from conversation analysis data (Sacks, 1992; Sacks et al., 1974), showing that in discussions involving both men and women, the occurrence of interruptions is very unequal, with women many times less likely to interrupt men than the other way round.

O'Barr (1982) would argue that in fact the features Lakoff identified should not be considered part of 'women's language', but of 'powerless language', since their occurrence is in fact greater among men *or* women who occupy low-prestige jobs and are less well educated, than among persons of the same sex with a higher level of education and more prestigious employment. O'Barr's particular concern was with the effects which 'powerless' and 'powerful' language produces in the courtroom situation; his data show that juries generally give more weight to testimony that does not include the features Lakoff pointed out, although this depends somewhat on their preconceptions of where the witness testifying ought to be on the sociolinguistic scale. O'Barr's findings have been taken as suggesting that the fairness of trial by jury is compromised by the inherent politics of language, though it is not at all clear that any attempt at remedying this would be either equitable or indeed possible.

Lakoff's work was soon followed up by Thorne and Henley (1975) and Spender (1980), and led both to the discourse analyses of women's language practised by Tannen (1994), and to the more politically oriented work of Cameron (1992, 1995). Tannen (1990), an international bestseller, would give rise to a very considerable industry of personal and marital therapy based upon the notion that men's and women's different modes of conversing box them into separate cultures, the walls of which need to be broken through in order for genuine communication to occur and the politics of marriage to be kept peaceful and productive. This is wholly inimical to the Marxist view that gender differences are trivial, class distinctions being the only ones that matter. But even many non-Marxists question whether it is ultimately in the interests of women or other 'powerless' groups to insist on their cultural difference, rather than working for integration.

Historically, the discourse on language and gender was able to break into 'mainstream' linguistics without exciting anything like the scepticism aroused by the Sapir–Whorf Hypothesis, even though the conclusions it was pointing toward were the same, namely, that distinctive forms of language equate with distinctive modes of thought. This was worrisome in the case of the Sapir–Whorf Hypothesis, probably because in the wake of the Second World War and the exposure of Nazi genocide, few were terribly inclined to explore ethnic differences in a way that might potentially be turned to such ends. The discourse of gender difference in language arose two decades later in a very different atmosphere, the context being a movement for the liberation of women. When Lakoff identified features of women's language that appeared to hold women back in society, this served to strengthen people's realisations of how society was indeed biased against women and to bolster the case for positive social change. Once the notion of men's and women's language was accepted, the more general idea of the language–identity link had been admitted through the back door, as it were. The way was opened for the study not only of sexual orientation identity, but for group identities of all sorts beyond those national and ethnic ones traditionally associated with language difference.

Some people lack a clear national identity, and probably more still lack a religious identity, for the reasons just described. The relatively few people who feel they lack an ethnic identity – white English people, for example – generally do so because they are at the peak of a socio-ethnic triangle, where their ethnicity carries little symbolic value except the negative one of distinguishing them from all the 'ethnics' around them. No one, however, lacks a gender identity. They may have a confused gender identity, or a double (but not confused) gender identity, or any other permutation. But to be human and to lack *any* gender identity is unimaginable – particularly since, even if one were to *feel* no gender identity, others would still impose one or more on them.

For sheer ubiquity, as well as for its central importance in our daily life, gender identity tops the list of the various entries in a person's identity repertoire. It is not an identity for which people have, as of yet, gone to war, at least not in the literal sense. But from a Darwinian perspective, the construction of gender identity is blatantly crucial when it comes to reproductive success, and this is already true in the feather displays of dominant male birds and the genital displays of receptive females – whence it is a short step to fashionable haircuts, lipstick (which functions differently in the construction of male and female gender identities), and the symbolic wearing of earrings and, of course, the linguistic performance of gender and sexual orientation identities.

From Network Theory to communities of practice and language ideologies

In her 1980 book *Language and Social Networks*, Lesley Milroy reported data from sociolinguistic studies she conducted in Belfast which she interpreted as requiring modification of certain notions taken as given in earlier work, particularly in the Labovian line. The 'social class' of an individual did not appear to be the key variable allowing one to make predictions about which forms of particular linguistic variables the person would use. Rather, the key variable was the nature of the person's 'social network', a concept Milroy traced back to Barnes (1954), a sociological study of a Norwegian island parish. The concept had more recently figured prominently in work by such sociologists as Boissevain and Mitchell (Mitchell, 1969; Boissevain, 1974; Boissevain & Mitchell, 1973). Milroy defined social network as

> the informal social relationships contracted by an individual. Since all speakers everywhere contract informal social relationships, the

> network concept is in principle capable of universal application and so is less ethnocentric than, for example, notions of *class* or *caste*. (Milroy, 1980, p. 174)

Individuals' personal networks are analysed as relatively 'dense' or 'multiplex'. Milroy found that, where close-knit localised network structures existed, there was a strong tendency to maintain non-standard vernacular forms of speech. The maintenance of vernacular forms had been difficult to explain in a model such as Labov's, based on a scale of 'class' belonging, where accordance with norms of standard usage marked one as higher on the social hierarchy and thus entitled to the benefits that accrue to higher status. Since most people desire such benefits, why do they not simply do the rational thing and start to speak like their social 'superiors'? Labov's early work on Martha's Vineyard had suggested that the answer lay in identity, specifically in the value of belonging to a group who, although not highly placed in socio-economic terms, could nevertheless claim something valuable for themselves (in the Martha's Vineyard case, authenticity). Milroy's book provided the first statistical backing for such an explanation.

What it did not attempt to do was to explore the nature of the identity that emerged from the network, or even to ask whether it *did* emerge from it, or whether on the contrary the identity created the network. It simply established the significance of linguistic identity for the benefit of those sociolinguists who believed only in the value of rigorous statistics and eschewed interpretation as unscientific, and did so on their own terms. Moreover, by cutting the legs out from under the criterion that had been the very basis of sociolinguistic research – social class – it opened the way for investigation of *any* criterion on which a social network might be based. Investigations could no longer be looked down upon as trivial if the differences they examined were not based on class, except, of course, by confirmed Marxists, for whom by definition class will always be the be-all and end-all.

One thing Milroy had made clear about the inner workings of the social network was that, although it depended somewhat on amount of personal contact, what was really essential to it was the fact that the members of a social network share *norms*, behavioural tendencies but also systems of belief that encompass language but extend beyond it as well. As attention turned to understanding the nature of these norms, two widely publicised views, one having to do with how textual meaning operates, the other with the nature of nationalism, plausibly had an impact. Stanley Fish (1980) had devised the concept of the 'interpretative community' to explain how it is that, on the one hand, people read different meanings into the same text, while on the other hand, we do not evaluate all such readings equally, but consider some as valid and dismiss others as absurd. Fish argued that various norms of reading exist and are propagated and manifested culturally, within groups of varying size, including even (rarely) groups of one. An interpretative community is a group sharing such a set of norms. Its members may never come into direct physical contact with one another; their shared norms may be spread by a source such as the educational system, or books or the media. Around the same time, Benedict Anderson proposed a new understanding of the 'nation' as an 'imagined community', whose members, like that of the interpretative community, will never all meet one another let alone have the sort of regular intercourse that creates a 'network'. What binds them together is the shared belief in the membership in the community.

Notably with the work of Penelope Eckert, sociolinguistic investigation of groups ideologically bound to one another shifted from statistically based examination of social networks to more interpretative examination of *communities of practice*. The community of practice is 'an aggregate of people who come together around mutual engagement in an endeavor' (Eckert & McConnell-Ginet, 1992, p. 464), in the course of which emerge shared beliefs, norms and ideologies (see further Wenger, 1998; Meyerhoff, 2002). These of course are not limited to linguistic and communicative behaviour. The advantage of the community of practice is its openness – any aggregate of people can be held to constitute one, so long as the analyst can point convincingly to behaviour that implies shared norms, or, better still, can elicit expression of the underlying ideologies from members of the community. This line of research is thus continuous with another one that has focused more directly on the normative beliefs or ideologies by which national and other group identities are maintained. Some early work along these lines was published in Wodak (1989) and Joseph & Taylor (1990), and subsequently a great deal more has appeared, e.g. in Schieffelin et al. (1998), Verschueren (1999), Blommaert (1999b) and Kroskrity (2000).

The next chapter will examine the input that has come into the study of linguistic identity from areas of study other than linguistics. The dividing lines are blurry, to be sure, since some such input has informed each of the approaches described in the present chapter – indeed, up through Humboldt, any attempt to separate linguistic from anthropological, psychological or social inquiry is quite anachronistic. Similarly, the figures discussed in the next chapter have not failed to learn from the work linguists have done.

4
Integrating Perspectives from Adjacent Disciplines

Input from 1950s sociology: Goffman

Goffman's work was introduced in the preceding chapter (p. 59), and its impact on the study of language is explored in more detail in Joseph et al. (2001, Ch. 11). When conducting his doctoral research in the Shetland Islands in the late 1940s, Goffman arrived at the view that

> The human tendency to use signs and symbols means that evidence of social worth and of mutual evaluations will be conveyed by very minor things, and these things will be witnessed, as will the fact that they have been witnessed. An unguarded glance, a momentary change in tone of voice, an ecological position taken or not taken, can drench a talk with judgmental significance. Therefore, just as there is no occasion of talk in which improper impressions could not intentionally or unintentionally arise, so there is no occasion of talk so trivial as not to require each participant to show serious concern with the way he handles himself and the others present. [...]
>
> In any society, whenever the physical possibility of spoken interaction arises, it seems that a system of practices, conventions, and procedural rules comes into play which functions as a means of guiding and organizing the flow of messages. [...]
>
> The conventions regarding the structure of occasions of talk represent an effective solution to the problem of organizing a flow of spoken messages. In attempting to discover how it is that these conventions are maintained in force as guides to action, one finds evidence to suggest a functional relationship between the structure of the self and the structure of spoken interaction. (Goffman, 1956, pp. 225–7)

This 'structure of the self' as presented in speech, the persona, was what Goffman was developing the analytical tools to describe in a way that would be acceptable within the scientific rhetoric of sociologists. He found that the concept of 'face', which Western cultures generally associated with those of East Asia, was actually necessary for understanding human interaction in any culture.

> [W]hen a person volunteers a statement or message, however trivial or commonplace, he commits himself and those he addresses, and in a sense places everyone present in jeopardy. By saying something, the speaker opens himself up to the possibility that the intended recipients will affront him by not listening or will think him forward, foolish, or offensive in what he has said. And should he meet with such a reception, he will find himself committed to the necessity of taking face-saving action against them. [...]
>
> Thus when one person volunteers a message, thereby contributing what might easily be a threat to the ritual equilibrium, someone else present is obliged to show that the message has been received and that its content is acceptable to all concerned. (Goffman, 1956, pp. 227–8)

Goffman introduced a distinction between *negative face*, the desire not to be imposed or intruded on, and *positive face*, the desire for approval. Members of any social group possess both kinds of face.

It would be well into the 1960s before linguistics opened its gates to the sort of interpretive inquiry that Goffman had been pioneering, in part because a critical mass of linguists did not see 'discourse' – texts extending beyond the length of the phrase or sentence – as falling within their bailiwick. The gradual shift in this view was as important as any other single development in eventually getting the detailed study of linguistic identity off the ground.

Bernstein

One particularly strong and controversial set of views on language and social identity brought the issue to the top of the educational as well as the sociolinguistic agenda for two decades. In late 1950s London, Basil Bernstein (1924–2000), trained in both sociology and linguistics, attempted to apply the Sapir–Whorf Hypothesis to the analysis of class difference in language. The undertaking would prove influential and controversial in equal measure.[1]

In the early 1960s Bernstein became the colleague of Halliday and his wife Ruqaiya Hasan, and by his own account the encounter was decisive for his subsequent work (see Bernstein, 1996, pp. 148–9). He introduced a distinction between two types of language, 'public' and 'formal', which he later renamed as *restricted code* and *elaborated code*, and under this terminology his views attracted notoriety throughout the English-speaking world. Bernstein was clearly saying – despite his later vehement but disingenuous denials – that only middle-class people have true personal identities and full cognition of their world. Working-class people have strong social identity, shared with others who speak only the restricted code:

> In the case of a restricted code the speech is played out against a back-cloth of assumptions common to the speakers, against a set of shared interests and identifications, in short against a cultural identity which reduces the need for the speakers to elaborate verbally their intent and make it explicit. (Bernstein, 1964, p. 58)

But restricted code lacks the resources that allow verbal signalling of one's identity as an individual. It

> functions to permit the signalling of social rather than personal identity. The latter tends to be signalled through non-verbal and expressive means rather than through elaborate varying of verbal selections. [...] The code strengthens solidarity with the group by restricting the verbal signalling of personal difference. [...] A strong sense of social identity is induced probably at the cost of a sense of personal identity. (Ibid., p. 63)

When these statements were interpreted in the only reasonable way they could be – as meaning that the language of the working classes renders their speakers cognitively deficient and indistinct as individuals – and when objections were raised to this, Bernstein reacted with shock, and over subsequent decades altered his statements to make them sound less like negative judgements on the working classes. He responded robustly to anyone who criticised statements such as the ones above, and while he deserves credit for shifting his stance (see especially Bernstein, 1996), he never came to grips with the inescapable implications of the early work that made his name. Efforts to rehabilitate him in the 1990s have not resulted in his reformulated views on social difference, language and identity having wide influence. They are still seen as being based on a form of linguistic determinism that has gone out of fashion, replaced by a view of individual agency that few accept as being tied in any way to social class.

Attitudes and accommodation

Contemporaneously with Labov's early work, the Canadian social psychologist Wallace Lambert began exploring people's attitudes toward the 'other' language in a bilingual situation like that in Montreal. His findings were not in accord with the predictions he made. Especially in a politically charged situation like that of 1960s Quebec, one might have expected French speakers to have uniformly negative attitudes toward English and vice versa. What Lambert found was considerably subtler than that.

When he asked people to rate speakers on specific traits such as intelligence, industry, likeability, trustworthiness and so on, it turned out that certain traits were associated with French speakers or English speakers, regardless of whether those whose opinions were being sought were themselves speakers predominantly of English or of French. For example, when a tape of someone speaking in French was played, followed by a tape of someone saying essentially the same thing in English, those listening to the two tended to say that the English speaker was more intelligent and industrious. Even people who were themselves French speakers tended to rate the English speech samples higher on these traits. However, when it came to features such as likeability, French speakers tended to say that the French speaker on the tape was more likeable, and English speakers that the English speaker on the tape was more likeable.

A much-vaunted methodological feature of Lambert's research was the use of 'matched-guise' testing, in which some of the taped samples played were of the same individual speaking, first in one language and then in the other. Those hearing the tapes, not knowing that it was the same individual they were listening to (the samples would be interspersed with bits by other speakers to make this less evident), consistently gave different ratings for the personal traits when it was French the individual was speaking and when it was English. This appeared to prove that their evaluation of the speaker as a person was dependent solely upon the language chosen, and not on any other factor such as voice quality or speech style.

Later researchers into language attitudes would be severely critical of Lambert's early work and the matched-guise technique, which, as one critique puts it,

> means, essentially, that a single speaker records all versions of a message appearing in a given experimental design, for example, dialects A, B, and C. An important assumption, which to our knowledge has not been tested, is that respondents perceive the speaker to be equally skilled in presenting each version. If this assumption is unknowingly violated, differences in respondents' evaluative reactions to dialect versions, for example, may be falsely attributed to the dialects themselves when in fact they are a product of idiosyncratic differences in speaker fluency. (Bradac et al., 2001, p. 139)

Furthermore, Lambert's early studies 'used attitude questionnaires which relied heavily on bipolar scales; they were experiments, hence decontextualized' (ibid., p. 140).[2] This criticism reflects a serious shift that has taken place in social science methodology over the last two decades. In the 1960s the focus of concern was on obtaining statistically significant data under conditions that could be replicated by other researchers. The ideal setting for this was the laboratory, in which conditions could be controlled to the fullest extent possible. By the 1980s the view became widespread that data obtained in this way, in a setting so unlike the contexts of ordinary language use, were not in fact able to shed significant light on real language. Data should instead be obtained by 'ethnographic' means, with the researcher entering directly into the contexts of use. It is not the case that the newer mode has completely ousted the older one; they currently constitute the grounds for something of a civil war among social scientists inclined in the one or the other direction. But the rise of interest in language and identity has come predominantly from the ethnographic end of the spectrum, for reasons that will become clearer in the section on 'Essentialism and constructionism'.

Whatever the shortcomings, Lambert's findings and those of the whole tradition of work he established, pursued and has guided many others in pursuing, were important in helping to establish the significance of sociolinguistics in the 1960s. They were taken to show that our relationships with other human beings are established fundamentally on instinctive judgements we make about them, in which the language they use figures prominently and can, in some cases at least, determine our judgement independently of any other factor.

In the 1970s another social psychologist, Howard Giles, a Briton transplanted to California, undertook a detailed and wide-ranging programme of research into a related phenomenon. The fact is that when we encounter someone and make judgements about them based on how they speak, our own way of speaking typically changes in response to those judgements. 'Speech Accommodation Theory' was the term originally used for the study of how our use of language is affected by our perception of the people we are speaking with; this has subsequently been broadened to 'Communication Accommodation Theory' so as not to cut the linguistic features of accommodation off from its other manifestations (in gesture, for example).

Here the old fascination with the speaker as wilful subject is mitigated by a realisation, comparable to that of Voloshinov, that the 'speaker' is neither a given nor a constant, but is constructed in interaction with interlocutors and ultimately inseparable from them. More generally, this perspective on individual subjects had come into sociology with the 'exchange theory' of Homans (1958), which supplied Giles and his collaborators with certain key insights. Its import has become clearer over recent years as accommodation research has moved away from an initial tendency to portray the phenomena as automatic and rather simplistic in nature (speech convergence occurring when there is sympathy between interlocutors, divergence when there is social distance). Thakerar et al. (1982) introduced the notion of 'perceptual/subjective accommodation', in which, 'Although a speaker's intent, or even actual behavior, may signal one meaning, the listener's interpretation of the speaker's act may not be consistent with the speaker's intent. The listener may not detect the behavior or may misinterpret the speaker's meaning' (Shepard et al., 2001, p. 38). Boves et al. (1990) found that 'perceived status of the interacting partner affected speech behaviors such that subjects' ratings of their partner were based more on stereotypes held about the relations between status and speech than the actual speech itself' (ibid., p. 47).

Bell (1984) made a strong critique of Labovian sociolinguistics for its failure to recognise the central importance of accommodation in language behaviour. Speech 'style' had always figured as a key variable in Labov's research, and had been treated by him as relatively straightforward and unproblematic, varying according to the amount of attention speakers pay to what they are saying. Bell rejects this attention-based view of style as a 'nonstarter', and argues that style is instead a matter of 'audience design': '[A]t all levels of language variability, people are responding primarily to other people. Speakers are designing their style for their audience' (Bell, 1984, p. 197).

Nowadays we might take the notion of 'audience design' still further, and hold that, in accommodating, speakers actually *design their audience*, rather than simply react to an audience that exists as a given. What linguistic accommodation means for language and identity is that it is not simply the case that I have *one* linguistic identity and that it is somehow essentially bound up with who I 'really am'. When I accommodate, I become 'someone else' linguistically, based on my perception of the person I am accommodating to. The latter point is particularly important: what I accommodate to is not another person, but *the identity I have constructed for that person.* Furthermore, my very act of accommodation and the degree to which it extends (for there are individual differences in how much we accommodate), becomes a feature of my own linguistic identity. If I fail to accommodate at all, that too is a feature.

Foucault and Bourdieu on symbolic power

In France in the mid-1950s, the ethnologist Claude Lévi-Strauss was primarily responsible for generalising a 'structuralist' movement that tried to analyse all of culture based upon methods and categories imported from linguistics. One of the most important figures to emerge from this movement in the 1960s would be Michel Foucault (1926–84), a cultural historian who stands at the cusp of the 'post-structuralism' that from about 1968 onward would call these categories into question.

What essentially distinguishes Foucault from his Marxist counterparts was his belief that the objects of knowledge, including language as well as the concepts that constitute its signifieds, are *not* produced by subjects thinking, speaking and acting intersubjectively (i.e. not as independent agents, but in interaction with one another).[3] Rather, Foucault believed, the objects of knowledge are produced by 'power' itself, with which they have a mutually constitutive relationship.

> We should admit that power produces knowledge ([...]); that power and knowledge directly imply one another; that there is no power relation without the correlative constitution of a field of knowledge, nor any knowledge that does not presuppose and constitute at the same time power relations [...]. In short, it is not the activity of the subject of knowledge that produces a corpus of knowledge, useful or resistant to power, but power-knowledge, the processes and struggles that traverse it and of which it is made up, that determines the forms and possible domains of knowledge. (Foucault, 1977 [1975], pp. 27–8)

Foucault is sometimes misrepresented by his opponents – a category that runs the gamut from Marxists to conservative 'anti-relativists' – as holding that neither power nor knowledge nor any other reality is anything but a mere linguistic construct. His critique of Western thought is actually much more subtle and powerful than this. Power, operating through language, determines the parameters of what is knowable (the *episteme*), which change from epoch to epoch. What has however led to dissatisfaction among many people who were initially inspired by Foucault to focus on language and power is that, beyond a certain point, thinking in terms of 'power' thus abstracted becomes an obstacle to understanding who exactly is doing what to whom, and how. It plays too into a widely held but false dichotomy according to which only those 'in power' actually have and make choices, while the vast majority of people only think they are making choices when in fact they are simply living out inevitabilities forced upon them by the power structure. Since this is essentially the Marxist view,[4] it is ironic that Foucault has become the focus of so much Marxist scorn in recent years.

Pierre Bourdieu (1930–2002) attempted to reconnect the Marxist and structuralist lines by renouncing the structuralist dismissal of the human 'subject'. He conceives of every area of human activity as a socially charged 'field', in which the players are neither signs as in earlier structuralism, nor manifestations of power as in Foucault, nor the more traditional conceptions of the Romantic individual or the Marxist social subject, but instead instances of what he terms *habitus*, definable as 'a set of dispositions which incline agents to act and react in certain ways' (Thompson, Intro. to Bourdieu, 1991, p. 12).[5] These dispositions are inculcated into us from early childhood, and they generate practices that are regular without being governed by any 'rule'. The habitus is inhabited by an active human agent who is defined by the system but, crucially, not merely its passive object. The agent engages in exchanges of symbolic power with other agents, each of whose habitus is linked to the rest in the shared field.

Bourdieu (1982) applies this form of analysis specifically to language, and has been much cited in the subsequent sociolinguistic literature. He describes the standard language as a 'normalised' product that creates possibilities for symbolic domination.

> The distinctiveness of symbolic domination lies precisely in the fact that it assumes, of those who submit to it, an attitude which challenges the usual dichotomy of freedom and constraint. The 'choices' of the habitus (for example, using the 'received' uvular 'r' instead of the rolled 'r' in the presence of legitimate speakers) are dispositions

> which, although they are unquestionably the product of social determinisms, are also constituted outside the spheres of consciousness and constraint. The propensity to reduce the search for causes to a search for responsibilities makes it impossible to see that *intimidation*, a symbolic violence which is not aware of what it is (to the extent that it implies no *act of intimidation*) can only be exerted on a person predisposed (in his habitus) to feel it, whereas others will ignore it. It is already partly true to say that the cause of the timidity lies in the relation between the situation or the intimidating person (who may deny any intimidating intention) and the person intimidated, or rather, between the social conditions of production of each of them. And little by little, one has to take account thereby of the whole social structure. (Bourdieu, 1991, p. 51)

Bourdieu's impact has been considerable both inside and outside France, especially in those branches of the social sciences that are reluctant to take things any further in the direction of individual agency than Bourdieu does in his rather conservative balancing act that seeks to find a middle ground between freedom and constraint. To the less conservative, his outlook appears to be a 'deterministic process of reproduction: We can trade forms of capital, but as Jenkins (1992) observes, Bourdieu fails to show how actors can actually intervene to change how things happen' (Pennycook, 2001, p. 126).

Yet, in shifting the perspective from identity-production alone to identity-reception, we undo much of the rightful opposition to structuralist analysis and create a space in which Bourdieu's habitus is explanatorily useful. Even the individual who in a wilful, active way undoes the identity they were born and socialised into and takes on a new identity (thus undercutting the very basis on which the habitus stands) is still going to be perceived, interpreted and measured by those around them in terms of their relative place within a network of social hierarchies based on the distribution of cultural capital. The identities others interpret onto us, in other words, will be shaped by their own habitus, at least to the extent that they are not doing it explicitly. Pennycook is right to identify deliberate intervention as the side of human social behaviour that Bourdieu fails to explain, but that was not what he set out to explain. Such deliberate individual action does not really pose any kind of social problem, from Bourdieu's perspective. The problem, rather, is how to explain the actions agents undertake that are not deliberate, and the cases where they undertake a deliberate course of action but find themselves unable to achieve it because of their own strong 'dispositions'.

Social Identity Theory and 'self-categorisation'

In the early 1970s, Henri Tajfel (1919–82), a social psychologist and colleague of Howard Giles at Bristol, developed Social Identity Theory, which in the years following his death came to be the single most influential model for analysing linguistic identity. Tajfel (1978) defined social identity as 'that part of an individual's self-concept which derives from his knowledge of his membership of a social group (or groups) together with the value and emotional significance attached to that membership'. Within this simple definition are embedded at least five positions which in their time were quite revolutionary:

- that social identity pertains to an individual rather than to a social group;
- that it is a matter of *self-concept*, rather than of social categories into which one simply falls;
- that the fact of *membership* is the essential thing, rather than anything having to do with the nature of the group itself;
- that an individual's own knowledge of the membership, and the particular value they attach to it – completely 'subjective' factors – are what count;
- that emotional significance is not some trivial side effect of the identity belonging but an integral part of it.

Beyond this, Social Identity Theory marked a break with other approaches in the fact that it was not concerned with analyses grounded in a notion of 'power', but simply in the relative hierarchisations that we seem instinctively to impose on ourselves, most particularly in our status as members of 'in-groups' and 'out-groups', which would come into even greater prominence in the 'Self-Categorisation Theory' that developed as an extension of the original model, notably in the work of Tajfel's collaborator Turner (see Tajfel & Turner, 1979; Turner et al., 1987; Turner, 1991; McGarty et al., 1994). Moreover, Social Identity Theory took the social 'myths' or 'ideologies' which groups engender for themselves – including the stereotypes they apply to out-group members (see Tajfel, 1981) – as serious constitutive elements of identities, rather than dismissing them as attempts at 'objective' analysis were wont to do.

Numerous offshoots of Social Identity Theory will appear in the remainder of this chapter as well as in the chapters that follow, for example the important analysis of national identity by Tajfel's sometime collaborator Michael Billig, discussed in Chapter 5. With accelerating effect during the first two decades after his death, Tajfel's work, either directly or indirectly, reoriented thinking about identity away from its earlier focus on the analyst's objective view to the subjective experience of the individual concerned, and away from a sense of identity as imposed categorisation to one of performed self-categorisation. The stress on the simple dichotomy of in-group and out-group helped to provide methodological comparability across the wide range of identities to which people applied the theory. In due course, inevitably, many would come to feel that it is too limiting, particularly because of the focus on *self*-categorisation. Although this was a crucial step in moving the analysis of linguistic identity away from the 'objective' authority of the social scientist and toward understanding how ordinary people establish and manifest identity in their language and discourse, it still made it seem as though identity was essentially something each subject produces for himself or herself. It did not allow sufficient space for the *reception* or *interpretation* of one's identity by others to be seen as no less constitutive of identity.

Early attempts to integrate 'social identity' into sociolinguistics

In the 1960s two figures, one in America and one in Britain, were pursuing their own individual paths toward an identity-based analysis of utterances in multilingual or multidialectal communities. The first was John J. Gumperz, a specialist in the languages of northern India who collaborated closely with Dell Hymes in establishing an approach called the 'ethnography of communication'. The book *Language and Social Identity* which Gumperz edited in 1982 marked a watershed in the history of the topic, starting with its very title. The papers in the volume are focused on the analysis of conversations in which the participants are from different 'cultures', the cultural divides being ethnic in most cases but based on gender in one paper and on gender and ethnicity together (by Tannen) in another. Surprisingly, in view of the volume's title, there are no references to Social Identity Theory, and very few to any psychological work at all – despite the fact that the collection was funded by a US National Institute of Mental Health grant (see the book's introduction, p. x). Gumperz presents his approach as a form of social anthropology, yet the tradition represented in the citations is that of linguistics and sociolinguistics, including many of the figures named above; and although this book does in certain respects push the research into language and identity significantly forward, it nevertheless sticks quite firmly to basic Saussurean assumptions about the primacy of the linguistic system as something imposed on speakers, who are its relatively passive users. The book begins by claiming that

> [W]e seek to develop interpretive sociolinguistic approaches to human interaction which account for the role that communicative phenomena play in the exercise of power and control and in the production and reproduction of social identity. Our basic premise is that social processes are symbolic processes but that symbols have meaning only in relation to the forces which control the utilization and allocation of environmental resources. (Gumperz & Cook-Gumperz, 1982, p. 1)

The shadow of Foucault and Bourdieu (who is cited here) looms over the references to 'power and control' and 'production and reproduction'. 'Communicative phenomena' play a role in the *exercise* of a power and control that are already given; no possibility is suggested of their actually helping to *constitute* power and control. The insistence that 'symbols have meaning only in relation to' forces of power, which could have come straight out of Voloshinov (who is not cited in the book), leaves no space for individuals to interpret, project and 'perform' symbolic meaning.

Echoing what no doubt was the rationale for the mental health funding, the authors claim that 'modern bureaucratic industrial society [...] increases the importance of communication processes', while at the same time modern society is characterised by 'unprecedented cultural and ethnic diversity', and 'When backgrounds differ, meetings can be plagued by misunderstandings' (ibid., p. 2). In sum, there is a crisis in social identity caused by the fact that bureaucracy is making us more reliant upon communication, while population mobility makes communication less reliable. Implicitly, then, the conversation analyses pursued in *Language and Social Identity* are aimed at solving a broad social problem by identifying obstacles to communication that occur between people whose social identities differ. What would be the more enduring legacy of this research is presented as one of its (perhaps unexpected) findings rather than as one of its methodological premises:

> We customarily take gender, ethnicity, and class as given parameters and boundaries within which we create our own social identities. The study of language as interactional discourse demonstrates that these parameters are not constants that can be taken for granted but are communicatively produced. (Ibid., p. 1)

The full implications of this statement are not pursued in the studies that make up the book, but would have to await a fuller engagement by linguists with developments in social psychology.

The other individual referred to in the opening paragraph of this section was Robert Le Page of York University, who in the late 1960s produced a series of papers expressing dissatisfaction with existing sociolinguistic methods that had arisen in his attempts to apply those methods to the analysis of Caribbean Creole English. Labov's work had shown how speakers use linguistic variation to signal some particular identity, whether ethnic, social, occupational or gender based, but did not provide, in Le Page's view, scope for understanding how multiple identities are signalled simultaneously. Le Page attempted to do this by analysing each utterance a speaker makes as an 'act of identity' that can be interpreted multidimensionally as manifesting very complex sets of belongings. Le Page stressed the fluidity of linguistic identity and the breadth of the choices available to signal them, and it was perhaps the stressing of this that distinguished him from Labov more than his actual descriptive apparatus, despite Le Page's sometimes strong criticisms of sociolinguists for being not only doctrinaire but ethnocentric (see Le Page, 1977, p. 173; Milroy, 1980, p. 203). He also stressed the role of acts of identity in holding a language together, 'focusing' it in the face of forces contributing to its diffuseness.

The 1985 book *Acts of Identity* which Le Page co-authored with Andrée Tabouret-Keller was the first book-length treatment of linguistic identity. Subtitled *Creole-based approaches to language and ethnicity*, it put forward, particularly in its closing chapters, a model for seeing how ethnicity is constructed in discourse that has by now become quite normal in the analysis of any linguistic identity, not just Creole ones. Further marking 1985 as the *annus mirabilis* for the study of the topic, *Language, Society and Identity* by the Canadian social psychologist John Edwards would offer the first general synthesis of approaches to language and identity developed within both linguistics and social psychology, applying them directly to issues of language conflict and shift from across the globe. Edwards's aim was, to be sure, very different from that of Gumperz and Le Page, since he was not looking 'into' conversations or other texts for direct linguistic evidence of the language–identity link. Rather, he was considering broader social and policy issues and their implications (including educational ones) for the populations who speak minority languages. He devoted considerable attention to the attempt to revive Irish Gaelic by making it a required school subject in the Republic of Ireland – a move that, far from improving the language's vitality, may have had the opposite effect, since requiring a language as a school subject seems to be the most effective way to guarantee that the younger generation will resent it and reject it. Nonetheless, Edwards pointed out, Irish national identity remains strong and vibrant, and the symbolic role played by the common maintenance of a small number of Irish words (to designate governmental and other national institutions, for example) appears to be sufficient to satisfy the need for a linguistic component to national identity. Edwards suggested that it is irrational to expect people to make the huge cultural investment needed for full-scale maintenance of a 'heritage' language if it is the case that a much smaller form of maintenance will serve the functional purpose.

Communication Theory of Identity

The list of alternative terms for identity in Chapter 1 shows how strongly the whole tradition of thinking and talking about it has been biased in the direction of *self*-identity, as if this was the only form of identity that mattered. This bias probably results from the historical fact that this tradition began with attempts to analyse what Smuts calls 'consciousness of self', which itself descends from still earlier introspective inquiry into the nature of the soul. Yet it is surprising that even those who talk about 'social identity' nevertheless focus on how the social roles which an individual plays construct and constrain their self-conception, with at best secondary consideration of the identity they possess for the other people who constitute their social world.

In social psychology, Michael Hecht has been active over the last decade in moving the analysis of identity away from self-conception and toward an understanding of how our various 'layers' of identity are constructed in interaction with others. Hecht's 'Communication Theory of Identity' is articulated in Hecht (1993), with the 'layered perspective' added in Baldwin & Hecht (1995). The theory recognises four layers or levels of identity:

- *personal identity* or an individual's conception of self. Often called self-concept, this level captures who a person thinks that he/she is;
- *enacted identity* or how an identity is expressed in language and communication;
- *relational identity* or identities in reference to each other;
- *communal identity* or identities as defined by collectivities (Hecht et al., 2001, p. 430, italic added).

The differentiation of personal and enacted identity – a who-I-am for myself and a who-I-am for others – represents clear progress toward the goal of pushing research on language and identity in the other-oriented direction. Where it can be taken further, I believe, is in the recognition that 'enacted identity' has an entirely different status from personal identity, because, unlike the latter, it lacks what we might call a *privileged interpreter*. With personal identity as Hecht defines it, the self is the sole authority capable of determining what it is. With enacted identity, there is no such authority – everyone who encounters the individual constructs their own interpretation. The notion of a unified 'enacted identity' is an abstraction that imposes a false veneer of unity upon what is bound to be a diversity of interpretations, each of which has as much to do with the individual doing the interpreting as with the one being interpreted.

Why should a social psychologist want to deal in such abstractions as 'enacted identity'? For one very obvious and well-motivated reason, and, I think, for two further, subtler reasons. The first is that social sciences have always been averse to the whole notion of wilful individual interpretation, seeing that as the domain of the humanities. Social 'science' conceives itself as existing in order to determine what is *really* happening when we are under the *delusion* that we are making wilful choices. This is not meant as a criticism of Hecht, but a recognition that an abstraction like 'enacted identity' is structurally capable of finding acceptance within a social science community that would shun the alternative of a plethora of individual interpretations. It is, in other words, a deception necessary for strategic reasons that have to do with the sociology of academic disciplines, until such time as the social sciences are prepared to come to grips with the reality the abstraction masks.

The second motive I referred to is that enacted identity, as a unified concept, provides a counterweight to personal identity, useful for dislodging the latter from its uniquely privileged place. I have noted that enacted identity, the who-I-am for others, lacks a privileged interpreter.

It has however one uniquely *un*privileged interpreter, namely, the self. I am the last person likely to know who I am for others, because who I *want* to be for them – which may or may not be the same as who I am for myself – blocks my view. Again, the strategic importance of establishing that identity is not limited to personal identity is undeniable. But, in a sense, we surreptitiously reaffirm the unique importance of personal identity by skewing our analysis in this way. Indeed, enacted identity as Hecht conceives it is still something the self authors and 'expresses', keeping the self firmly on centre stage. Ultimately, we need to account for the self as both producer and consumer of its own enacted identities. It is a matter of common experience that people can and spontaneously do articulate how they think others have seen them, how they think they have come off in a particular social situation. This moreover is an important part of their 'self-concept', blurring the distinction between the personal and the enacted.

The third motive for the abstraction of enacted identity is that it does not simply fail to recognise the absence of a privileged interpreter, it implies that there is such an interpreter, and that it is the social psychologist undertaking the analysis. Again there are academic–sociological factors at work, in the form of norms, enforced by journal referees and editors, which may require one to adopt a stance of pretended omniscience. A construct like enacted identity, which empowers an analyst to turn whatever he or she sees into what is seeable, bolsters omniscience for as long as one can get away with it.

That brings us to Hecht's 'relational identity', which is of quite a different order from the others in the list because it is a part of each of them, not an alternative to any of them. Every identity is at least partly relational, constructed in reference to other identities. Even when an identity is purely relational – when a person or group is identified just by virtue of difference from some other person or group – that identity is still going to fall into the personal/enacted or communal category.

In defining 'communal identity' as 'identities as defined by collectivities', Hecht introduces an ambiguity: would the identity of a particular individual, as a collectivity defines it, be a communal identity? For example, would the popular conception of the singer Michael Jackson's identity be a communal identity? Or an enacted identity? The way Hecht and his collaborators use the term communal identity suggests that its definition should be 'identities as defined *for* collectivities'. In any case, their definition begs the question of how anything gets defined *by* a collectivity. To understand group identities, it is to how individuals assert those identities that we must first look.

The self or selves that the individual wants to project is of great interest, but our understanding of it is severely limited if we try to cut it off from how that person's identity is received and interpreted – 'read', to use the term introduced in the previous chapter – by others. The distinction is parallel to that between 'authorial intent' and 'reader response' approaches to textual meaning, which rest upon opposing views of where 'real meaning' lies. Is it in what an author (or speaker) means to say, or in what he or she is heard to say? Either way we answer, there are enormous problems (for a good treatment, see Lecercle, 1999). With authorial intent, they start with the impossibility of determining what anyone but ourselves 'really meant', given that they might be lying, or have been purposely ambiguous, or might even not know themselves what they really meant, for instance if it was driven by unconscious motives. With reader response, the problem is how to prevent any statement from meaning whatever anyone is determined to read into it – but separating plausible readings from implausible ones rests fundamentally on our interpretations of whether a reading does or does not fall within the range of those meanings the author could conceivably have meant or have agreed to, an inherently speculative enterprise. The essential thing is to recognise that *both* authorial intent and reader response have a role to play in the determination of meaning. Ditto for identity: both self-identity and the identities others construct for us go into making up our 'real' identity.

It is probably fair to say that for the last 40 years sociolinguists and social psychologists have both been disappointed in the others' failure to provide an adequate model for their own purposes. Yet, given the rather extraordinary intellectual distance each side has traversed over those decades, it is doubtful that any model could have been adequate, at least for very long. The next section looks at one of the more dramatic changes that has taken place, and considers whether it is perhaps in the nature of a pendulum swing, for which restoration of a certain equilibrium might be in order.

Essentialism and constructionism

On the methodological plane, there have been two fairly polarised approaches to language and identity in work over recent decades. The first is an 'essentialist' approach in which categories such as nationality, class, race, gender, etc. are taken as givens, in terms of which people's linguistic behaviour can be analysed. Although dominant until into the 1990s, this approach has always coexisted with another, 'constructionist' one, which is more interested in identity as a 'process' in which individuals construct categorial belonging, both for themselves and for others with whom they come in contact.

In Chapter 1 it was noted that as early as 1926 Smuts was arguing for a view of the self as a social construction grounded in language. In so doing he was placing himself within a venerable tradition. Already in the Middle Ages, disputes arose between 'realists', who believed that abstract concepts, including the names of classes of things like tables and chairs, were God-given and therefore natural in kind, and 'nominalists', who believed that such concepts were human creations and therefore arbitrary. These two views harked back to ancient arguments about the nature of language, and ensured that the debate about whether language was essentially a natural endowment or a human construction would by no means disappear in the second millennium.

Any approach to language that looks beyond 'people talking' to find a system that structures what they say, can be described as a form of essentialism, the modern equivalent of medieval realism and ancient naturalism. More precisely, we could call realism and naturalism both forms of essentialism, and note some modern essentialists, though not all, maintain precisely the positions held by medieval realists and ancient naturalists. But what unites all linguistic essentialists is the belief that deep and true functioning of language is to be located outside the human will, usually in some version of an unconscious mind; or in 'society', still understood as some sort of quasi-metaphysical force emanating from groups of people and above the individual will; or in the workings of semiotic systems themselves, again some kind of nebulous, metaphysical realm.

Linguistic essentialism, which includes virtually the whole of modern linguistics, is a fascinating discourse which proceeds from an intriguing rhetorical move, when grammar, which originated historically as a device for language teaching, was reconceived as actually existing in the human mind. When exactly this move originated is unclear – possibly in the seventeenth century, when medieval grammars were unwittingly reinterpreted in the wake of Descartes as analysing, not a mirror of the mind, but the mind itself. In any case, the move has been repeated by subsequent generations of linguists in the eighteenth, nineteenth and twentieth centuries, with intriguing results, though not ones that can reasonably be taken as having a monopoly on a 'scientific' approach to language.

The linguists discussed above who, in the first half of the twentieth century, were trying to shift attention away from grammar and onto speakers, were all doing battle against this core essentialism, though usually only in order to install some other essentialism in its place. Sapir, for example, tried in many of his writings to frame the study of language within the fuller context of the human 'personality'. In the passage quoted on pp. 54–5 above, Sapir is struggling to break free of an essentialist view of language, and partly succeeds, but cannot rid himself completely of certain essentialising assumptions:

> Language is a ***great force*** of socialization [...].
> [T]he mere fact of a common speech serves as a peculiarly potent ***symbol*** of the social solidarity of those who speak the language.
> The fundamental quality of one's voice, the phonetic patterns of speech [...] – all these are so many complex ***indicators*** of the personality.
> [O]ne of the really important functions of language is to be constantly ***declaring*** to society the psychological place held by all of its members.

From today's point of view, where this passage remains essentialist is, first, in taking language to be a force acting upon people, on its own as it were; and secondly, in treating linguistic facts as *symbols* and *indicators* of some social and psychological reality that appears to exist independently of them. Constructionists would not say that 'the mere fact of a common speech serves as a peculiarly potent symbol of the social solidarity of those who speak the language'; they would not consider it a 'mere' fact, to start with, and they would take it to be much too deeply a part of any conceivable measure of 'social solidarity' to be seen merely as 'symbolising' it. The eight types of linguistic features listed in the second paragraph are not accurately described as 'so many complex indicators of the personality', when 'personality' is an abstract category we use to express a holistic sense of how we interpret a person's identity and emotional constitution, and the features in question are part of what we interpret. Nor is it enough to say that language is 'constantly declaring to society the psychological place held by all of its members', when in fact – in so far as 'psychological place' really means anything and is not mere 'psychobabble' – language is central to *establishing* an individual's psyche and place in the social order.

Still, Sapir saw how much was being missed by abstracting language away from such concerns altogether, and had he lived longer, Yale in the early 1940s might have become the cradle of a constructionist approach to language. But the Sapirian tradition has remained alive in anthropological linguistics, largely through the work of Dell Hymes, who in the 1950s was teaching at Harvard, as were a few other key figures who will be discussed below. Serious interest in the linguistic study of the individual has recently been revived by Johnstone (1996).

Studies of how children construct their language and indeed their whole 'world' in interaction with parents, caretakers and peers go back at least to the nineteenth century, and reached a high point in terms of both theoretical formulation and empirical observation in the 1920s, 1930s and after with the work of Piaget (see Chapter 1, p. 11). Both Piaget and the Russian psychologist Lev S. Vygotsky (1896–1934) made significant strides toward constructionism, and in fact Vygotsky's direct criticisms of Piaget (1929) would help Piaget considerably in this regard. Vygotsky criticised Piaget for characterising children's thought and speech as predominantly egocentric, with social aspects being secondary developments. In contrast to this, Vygotsky states his own view as follows:

> The primary function of speech, in both children and adults, is communication, social contact. The earliest speech of the child is therefore essentially social [...]. At a certain age the social speech of the child is quite sharply divided into egocentric and communicative speech. ([...]) Egocentric speech emerges when the child transfers social, collaborative forms of behavior to the sphere of inner-personal psychic functions [...]. Egocentric speech, splintered off from general social speech, in time leads to inner speech, which serves both autistic and logical thinking. (Vygotsky, 1962, p. 19)

The neo-Vygotskyans, led by James Lantolf (see e.g. Frawley & Lantolf, 1985; Lantolf, 2000), use statements like this as the basis for a theory of language learning which is non-essentialist, depending not on any kind of mental endowment in the individual but attending instead to social exchange and negotiation, putting it very much within the constructionist spirit – more actually than Vygotsky himself, whom they read with excessive charity in their desire to canonise him as their intellectual forebear. Vygotsky is not really talking about social construction of speech or language. He remains focused on the individual emitting speech, and is only arguing about whether the *purpose* of that speech is egocentric or social. This is really about the *intention* of the speaking child to direct his speech to himself or someone else. Note that Vygotsky talks about *the child*, which gives not an individualist perspective but its opposite. He implies that all children are the same with respect to the intentions of their early speech, when of course children cannot be asked to confirm what their intentions are, so that everything depends upon the interpretation of the observer. Might it not be that some children's early speech is primarily egocentric, while others' is primarily communicative? The failure to leave open this possibility is indicative of a form of essentialism. One might well ask whether it even makes sense to try to characterise speech in terms of this dichotomy. Might it not be that speech is, or can be, *simultaneously* egocentric and communicative? Might not the sharp division which Vygotsky says emerges between the two types be imposed by the perspective of the analyst?

But the even bigger question that constructionists might wish to put to Vygotsky is: Why focus so single-mindedly on the person speaking? For whatever the 'primary function of speech' may be, the primary function of language is certainly the *interpretation* of what others say to us. No one disputes that interpretation and learning are inseparable. The strongest argument for focusing on speech alone is the methodological one that speech is directly perceptible and recordable and therefore verifiable, whereas interpretation is a matter of private mental experience. In dealing with adult language we can find evidence for interpretation in the discourse itself and the actions that accompany it, and can even ask the subjects what they meant or understood by a particular utterance, though we cannot necessarily take their answers at face value. With child language we are pretty well limited to actions as our source of evidence for interpretation. But note that none of these methodological worries are shared by Vygotsky, who unabashedly reads motives into the early speech of children he observes and then declares what is the inner mental state of 'the child'.

In the late 1950s an effort began to confront and combine the work of Piaget, Vygotsky and other developmental psychologists with the findings of structural linguistics. It might have happened earlier except for certain accidents of history. The linguist most deeply interested in child language from the 1930s through to the 1950s, Roman Jakobson (1896–1982), was Piaget's exact contemporary and followed his work. Once he became established at Harvard in the late 1950s, his talents as an intellectual magnet who recognised no academic boundaries put him at the centre of a coming together of researchers in psychology exploring child language and intelligence from a post-Piagetian direction, and linguists abandoning the Bloomfieldian behaviourist strictures against scientific inquiry into unobservables, including the human mind.

One of those at Harvard at this time was Jerome Bruner, who like Jakobson developed links across academic disciplines and emerged as the key figure in the constructionist approach to language and mind, of which he remains today the *éminence grise*. Bruner welcomed Noam Chomsky's approach because of the liberation it provided from the stimulus–response behaviourism then dominant under the aegis of B. F. Skinner, Bruner's boss in the Harvard psychology laboratory. But Bruner believed that Chomsky's view of an innate, language-specific faculty in the human mind provides nothing more than a rough point of departure for the understanding of language acquisition. Further knowledge requires abandoning Chomsky's view for that of Piaget, which Chomsky explicitly denies, that we are indeed born with something in our minds, but that these are schemata for general learning, not specific to language. As Bruner put it in a 1983 monograph:

> Whatever original *language* endowment may consist of and however much or little of it there may be need not concern us. For whether human beings are lightly or heavily armored with innate capacities for lexico-grammatical language, they still have to learn how to *use* language. *That* cannot be learned *in vitro*. The only way language use can be learned is by *using* it communicatively. The 'rules' of language use are only lightly specified by the rules of grammar .... Not that such rules are not of deep interest: they may tell much about the shape of mind. It is only that infants learning language are *not* academic grammarians inferring rules abstractly and independently of use.
>
> Whatever else language is, it is a systematic way of communicating to others, of affecting their and our own behavior, of sharing attention, and of constituting realities to which we then adhere just as we adhere to the 'facts' of nature. (Bruner, 1983, pp. 119–20, italics in original)

To be a constructionist of the Brunerian sort, one must believe that it is important to study individual cases of language learning – and not to approach them as instances of the inevitable unwinding of a genetically predetermined language acquisition device, in which the important thing is to filter out accidental particularities so as to arrive at an idealisation of language acquisition. Rather, the constructionist takes the 'accidental particularities' as what is really real and interesting, and capable of opening up insights about how people in general learn to speak, without however having to put them through a formal process of idealisation that risks distorting them to fit some essentialising Procrustean bed of linguistic theory.

In most scientific enterprises having to do with human activity, such a procedure is commonplace. In medicine and psychiatry, singular cases get written up, and conclusions are deduced from an interpretation of the singularity. One wants to know about the person's history, environment and habits as well as any relevant genetic information. The conclusions might not have any direct relevance to any other individual, yet are enlightening for the physician or psychiatrist whose work is after all largely an interpretative one. Constructionists see their work in much the same way: general understanding is of course an ultimate goal, but the study of particular cases can be an important path toward it.

What is perhaps most important in the quote from Bruner is his point that language is a systematic way of constituting realities. This is the direction his work would continue to take in the 1980s and since (see e.g. Bruner, 1990), investigating how we as children and indeed adults construct realities for ourselves through language, so that the acquisition of language is actually inseparable from how we come to constitute our perception and understanding of the world around us. In the 1990s, this view was taken a step further: namely, to understand *language itself* as something the individual constructs, rather than something given in advance that is systematic and that the individual 'acquires'. In this sense, a language is a text, a story about talking that is at the same time a story about ourselves, indeed that *creates* our selves.

But at the same time Bruner backed away from his own strong constructionist position toward one that allows a role for Chomskyan innatism as well. Although some of his followers would break with him over what they saw as a retrograde move (see Joseph et al., 2001, Ch. 12 for details), Bruner, in the wisdom of his advanced age, deserves credit for stepping back to observe the question *sub specie aeternitatis*. If there were nothing to either the 'nature' or the 'nurture' position, the debate between them would not have endured for virtually as long as human history. Neither position appearing likely to go away, a synthesis of the two seems likelier to approach the truth than a one-sided adherence to the one or the other.

In a similar way, it is easy to fall into a well-entrenched rut of describing the recent history of ideas about language and identity as a movement from essentialism to constructionism. Such accounts are unintentionally deceptive, in that, while many today proclaim themselves constructionists, no one claims to be an essentialist. Essentialism, a pejorative term, consists of whatever constructionists do not like. When constructionists talk about essentialism they are, ironically enough, 'essentialising' history. This is not to say that what they are opposing should not be opposed or at least questioned. When 'class' and 'power' continue, as a heritage of the Romantic era and its aftermath, to be treated as though they were not constructs at all, but given in nature, the fallacy must be declared. But there is a price to pay. When one has lost faith in such categories, analytical rigour becomes much harder to attain, and the discourse of language and identity risks passing beyond mere fuzziness and into a realm of pure rhetorically driven tautology. The methodological ideal is therefore to strive for the intellectual rigour of essentialist analysis without falling into the trap of believing in the absoluteness of its categories, and to maintain the dynamic and individualistic focus of constructionism while avoiding the trap of empty relativism.

There is a further reason for not eschewing essentialism entirely in the study of language and identity. It is that constructing an identity is in fact constructing an essence – this was Bourdieu's point in the statement quoted in Chapter 1 (p. 13) about 'struggles over classifications, struggles over the monopoly of the power to make people see and believe, to get them to know and recognize, to impose the legitimate definition of the divisions of the social world and, thereby, to *make and unmake groups*' (Bourdieu, 1991, p. 221). This process depends for its operation on a widespread belief in the essentialism of identities. That is what motivates and shapes its creation, and the analyst who refuses any truck with essentialism risks missing a factor of the highest importance in the identity's construction. In other words, essentialism versus constructionism is not as mutually exclusive a distinction as it is normally taken to be, when what is being constructed is, in effect, an essentialising myth. To reject essentialism in methodology is to say quite rightly that our analysis must not buy into the myth, but must stand aloof from it to try to see how it functions and why it might have come into being in the belief system or ideology of those who subscribe to it. Yet there must remain space for essentialism in our epistemology, or we can never comprehend the whole point for which identities are constructed.

The second half of this book, starting with the next chapter, will inquire into the social construction of three particularly powerful types of 'essentialised' identities, alongside consideration of how individuals construct, deconstruct, reconstruct, manifest, perform, read and interpret those identities as part of their own identity repertoire. The social and individual dimensions cannot be neatly separated from one another for analytical purposes, because, if anything is clear from the first half of the book, it is that those dimensions are in fact inseparable. They represent different ways of conceiving and observing the same phenomena, rather than distinct phenomena.

5
Language in National Identities

The nature of national identities

'Nation' is an inherently ambiguous word, used sometimes in its etymological sense of people linked by nativity, birth, as when one speaks of the Hebrew nation or the Cherokee nation. More often it is used in its extended sense of an expanse of territory, its inhabitants and the government that rules them from a single, unified centre – the British nation, for instance. When the etymological and extended senses of nation coalesce, the term 'nation-state' is sometimes used. Thus Ireland (Eire) would count as a nation and a nation-state, whereas the United Kingdom is only a nation in the extended sense, comprising as it does at least four nations in the etymological sense, the English, Northern Irish, Scots and Welsh. Scotland, Wales and others of their type are sometimes called 'nations without states'.

There is a problem in that the two basic senses of 'nation' can never *really* coalesce. For them to do so, no one but members of the nation-by-birth would inhabit the national territory, and no member of the nation-by-birth would live outside the territory. Such a perfect mapping constitutes the 'ideal' of the nation-state – a dystopian rather than a utopian ideal for anyone but the most rabidly puristic nationalist.[1] In the modern world, affirmation of belief in the nation-by-birth has been strongest whenever a political nation has perceived itself to be under threat from 'outsiders', either because immigration has made the population visibly diverse, or because of imperial or colonial dominance. In France over the last two decades, support for the National Front party, or FN (motto: 'La France pour les Français') has consistently been strongest in those regions with the highest concentration of recent immigrants – initially, North African immigrants, and now, increasingly, East Europeans. In 2002 the founder and leader of the FN, Jean-Marie Le Pen, advanced to the final stage of the French presidential election. In Scotland, the Scottish National Party (SNP) flourished in the Thatcher years, when painful economic restructuring measures imposed on the whole of the UK were felt by many Scots as imperial oppression by the old enemy, England. Since the partial devolution of political authority to a re-established Scottish Parliament by the Blair government in 1999, the SNP has found itself struggling for a role that will rekindle its support.

In the USA, the instant proliferation of flags after the attacks on the World Trade Center and the Pentagon on 11 September 2001 was a stark visual example of how we instinctively look to symbols of national identity in reaction to a national attack, which is what the destruction of these buildings was blatantly designed to be perceived as. Until the attack and its aftermath, one might have thought the symbolic value of the World Trade Center, given its name, had to do with international capitalism. But its dominant position on the New York skyline seems to have been interpreted by those who perpetrated the attack as a proposition, that the USA and 'international' capitalism are inseparable. What was a still greater surprise was how much the towers apparently counted as a national symbol even for Americans living thousands of miles from New York, who have never visited the city and normally think of it as embodying values quite the opposite of their own. Possibly its 'national' value was created by the attack itself. In any case, within weeks the USA led an international coalition to invade Afghanistan and overthrow the Taliban government, which was hosting Osama Bin Laden, the mastermind of the 11 September attacks, and 18 months later it would lead a smaller coalition to invade Iraq and oust Saddam Hussein, who had had nothing directly to do with the attacks but was perceived as the great national enemy alongside Bin Laden.

The constructionist turn described in the preceding chapter has affected the analysis of national identity at least as much as any other form of identity. Indeed, the repeated reconfigurations of national boundaries in the wake of the two world wars, the reorganisation of the USSR and Eastern bloc countries in 1989–91, and the recognition of sub-national entities in Western Europe in the 1990s have all contributed to a strong awareness of the fluidity and arbitrariness of nationality. Although this awareness has not destroyed an underlying belief in 'real' national identity as something imposed on us by birth or early circumstances and remaining essentially unchanged thereafter, it has undoubtedly helped fuel the analytical trend among scholars to treat such beliefs as mythical, and to strive instead to understand identity as something we construct and negotiate throughout our life.

A consistent theme within studies of national identity over the last four decades has been the central importance of language in its formation. As we shall see, a number of prominent historians, sociologists and political scientists have argued that the existence of a national language is the primary foundation upon which nationalist ideology is constructed. Others, however, have paid more serious attention to the evidence compiled by linguistic historians showing that national languages are not actually a given, but are themselves constructed as part of the ideological work of nationalism-building. To take the example of the British Isles (a term which is itself offensive to Irish nationalists but for which no alternative has been established), for centuries their linguistic pattern was a patchwork of local dialects, Germanic or Celtic in origin. Only in modern times did individuals motivated by nationalistic ambitions of various sorts set about to establish 'languages' for the nations of England, Ireland, Scotland and Wales, as well as for Cornwall and other smaller regions (which often constitute 'nations' in the eyes of their more fervent partisans).

In the case of Scotland, where two separate national languages emerged (Gaelic and Scots, of Celtic and Germanic provenance respectively), their coexistence has not favoured the development of linguistic nationalism, but has impeded it, as partisans of the two languages have focused much of their energies on combating the rival claims of the other, rather than the hegemony of English. Although this makes Scotland sound like a failure in national linguistic terms, the vast majority of Scots do not see things this way; they consider the strategic economic value of using a world language as greatly outweighing the political, cultural and sentimental value of the 'heritage' languages. A case might be made that the eternal struggle between Gaelic and Scots is an intelligent way of keeping the nationalist flame burning while making sure that it does not set fire to the bank.

As the Scottish case shows, there are no 'universals' where language and national identity are concerned. Even the concepts of 'language' and 'nation' themselves are subject to local variation. We can, however, find certain patterns running through the linguistic construction of national identity worldwide, and they provide the matrix within which the vicissitudes of local construction can be read and compared.

When did nationalism begin?

As with many 'doctrines' which represent the articulation of something that has already been put into practice for some time, it is debatable where the beginning of nationalism should be located. This chapter will survey modern scholarly opinions that have placed it anywhere from the late eighteenth to the late nineteenth century. But even if it is true that nationalism underwent a sea change at some point in the last 250 years, it did not arise from nowhere. Modern nationalism certainly exhibits important continuities with national identities that extend all the way back to the beginning of recorded history.

The Old Testament records the oral traditions of the Hebrew nation concerning its origins, beliefs, relations with neighbouring nations, reduction to slavery and estrangement from its homeland, followed by its return to the homeland as prelude to its golden age. It was not written merely as a historical chronicle, but also to manifest and assure the nation's ongoing existence. Developments in nationalism in the eighteenth, nineteenth and twentieth centuries were all interpreted via their refraction through the biblical texts, the common base of European culture across national and social divides. Nations make their first appearance in Genesis 10. The chapter lists the names of the sons of Shem, Ham and Japheth (the three sons of Noah), together with the places where they dwelt, sometimes with precise specification of borders. Each of the three sets concludes with a passage like the following: 'By these [seven sons and seven grandsons of Japheth] were the isles of the Gentiles divided in their lands, every one after his tongue, after their families, in their nations' (Gen. 10: 5). Land, tongue, family . . . nation. All laid down in the Book of Genesis – according to believers, by the hand of God Himself.

Genesis 10 is a genealogical interlude between the story of the Flood (Gen. 6–9) and the account of how the descendants of Noah were subsequently spread across the world (Gen. 11). At the beginning of Genesis 11 we revert to a time when 'the whole world was of one language, and of one speech' (Gen. 11: 1), and the whole tribe of Noah, journeying westward, finds a plain in the land of Shinar and dwells there. They decide to build 'a city and a tower, whose top may reach unto heaven', plus one thing more: 'and let us make us a name, lest we be scattered abroad upon the face of the whole earth' (Gen. 11: 4).

Implicit here is the belief that, unless they have a shared name – which is to say, a national identity – they will inevitably scatter. An identity must be constructed for the nation to cohere, for its members to be mutually interdependent and form cities, rather than disperse, each to seek his own patch – a dispersion into rural space that in time would come to be characterised as 'natural', in opposition to the 'artificial' formation of urban spaces.

The ancient empires of the Mediterranean basin were well aware of the nations they overlay. In more modern times, English nationalist sentiments are obviously present in Shakespeare's history plays from the end of the sixteenth and start of the seventeenth centuries – but to call them 'nationalist' is, arguably, anachronistic, if the whole concept of nationalism as a general doctrinal position does not appear until two centuries later.

There is wide agreement that the American Revolution of 1776–81 and the French Revolution of 1789–93 were cardinal events in establishing the modern concept of nation as a political reality. But in a book that may be said to have got the contemporary scholarly discourse on nationalism under way, Elie Kedourie (1926–92) identified the crucial change as having taken place at the start of the nineteenth century, triggered by the Napoleonic aftermath of the French Revolution. His book begins with an intentionally provocative opening sentence:

> Nationalism is a doctrine invented in Europe at the beginning of the nineteenth century. [...] Briefly, the doctrine holds that humanity is naturally divided into nations, that nations are known by certain characteristics which can be ascertained, and that the only legitimate type of government is national self-government. (Kedourie, 1960, p. 9)

Most prior work on nationalism, including comprehensive studies by Deutsch (1953) and Shafer (1955), had focused on its twentieth-century manifestations while assuming that the nation itself, as a social structure, had existed in its modern form at least since the Renaissance, with nationalism as its inevitable ideological accompaniment. Moreover, having become the basis of political and social organisation worldwide, nations and nationalisms doubtless always would exist – unless, of course, Marx was right, and the nations of the world would fall one by one, like ripe apples, into communist internationalism.

Karl Marx (1818–83) had not invented the constructedness of nations. He was already able to quote from Thomas Cooper (1783–1839), writing in 1826, that 'The moral entity – the grammatical being called a nation, has been clothed in attributes that have no real existence except in the imagination of those who metamorphose a word into a thing [...]' (in Marx, 1955 [1847], §3a). Unsurprisingly, Marx interpreted that reification of the concept of nation in class terms, as a means whereby the bourgeoisie protects and maintains its interests. The existence of nations was, like religion and capitalism, merely a necessary phase in the historical development of mankind toward socialist perfection.

The fact that Marx's analysis was tied to a revolutionary programme aimed at bringing a quick end to those less than perfect phases probably made it more difficult than it might otherwise have been for non-Marxists (especially anti-Marxists) to accept the key notion that the concept of the nation was a historical product. A powerful non-Marxist case to this effect was made in 1944 by Hans Kohn (1891–1971), who argued that nations are a modern concept dating back not earlier than the mid-eighteenth century, and that 'Nationalism is first and foremost a state of mind, an act of consciousness, which since the French Revolution has been more and more common to mankind' (Kohn, 1944, pp. 10–11). In the immediate context of the Second World War and the struggle against Nazism (from which Kohn was a refugee) this was a position that found a ready audience in the English-speaking world, but with the onset of the Cold War, the old division whereby antinationalism was equated with Marxism fell back into place.

Another difficulty with Kohn's argument lay with its being grounded in an essentialist dualism between a 'voluntaristic nationalism', characteristic of England and France, versus the 'organic nationalism' of Germany and Central European nations – tied, of course, to the empiricist philosophical tradition of the former and the rationalist one of the latter. His positive portrayal of voluntaristic nationalism and criticisms of organic nationalism played well to the wartime audience, but lost relevance when, after the war, the key dualism came to be that of Marxist antinationalism versus any nationalism at all. Deutsch (1953) tried to fill the void in typical modernist fashion by reimagining nationalism in social science terms, starting with his redefinition of a people as a 'community of social communications', and seeking a quantitative methodology for pinning down what nations really are – a desire that, today, seems almost poignant in its hopelessness.

Kedourie (1960) presented a more purely constructionist view than Kohn's, replacing nationalism as 'act of consciousness' with nationalism as doctrine, unambiguous in its conventionalism, and pushing its beginnings forward by a few decades. By placing the concept within a historical context in which Marx simply did not figure, he made it possible for political scientists, historians and other scholars to treat nations and nationalism as historical contingencies without having others automatically classify their work as partisan. As we shall see, some of the most important work to benefit from this shift would begin by disagreeing vehemently with Kedourie on various particulars, though still acknowledging his key role in setting the discourse in motion, and for drawing attention to a thinker who, whenever one takes nationalism to have begun, was one of its most original and robust theoreticians, Johann Gottlieb Fichte (1762–1814). Fichte, who put language at the centre of his definition of the nation, will be discussed in detail later in this chapter, but first we need to go back five centuries to the grandaddy of all linguistic (proto)nationalists, Dante Alighieri (1261–1321).

Constructing national identity and language: Dante's *De vulgari eloquentia*

It has long been apparent that one of the first and highest obstacles that has to be overcome in establishing a national identity is the non-existence of a national language. The 'nation-state myth' – that basic view of the world as consisting naturally of nation-states – is bound up with an assumption that national languages are a primordial reality. Whatever difficulty we might have in determining the borderlines of who 'the Germans' are, whether the German-born children of Turkish immigrants are German for instance, or whether certain Alsatians are French or German, the German language is going to figure significantly in the equation. Hitler attempted to justify his initial invasions of neighbouring countries on the grounds that these German-speaking peoples were inherently part of the German nation; and, as Hutton (1999) has shown, his policies of oppression and ultimately extermination of the Jews were underpinned by the argument that, although their language, Yiddish, was a form of German, they had the perverse racial peculiarity of not being able to have a 'mother tongue'. They therefore did not belong to the German body politic but were a parasite within it (see further below, Chapter 7, pp. 171–2).

But whether Bohemian, Austrian, East Prussian and Yiddish dialects were part of 'the German language' were not facts given in advance, nor even ones that a linguist could establish scientifically. The reason is that 'the German language', like every national language, is a cultural construct. It dates from the sixteenth century and is generally credited to Martin Luther (1483–1546), who, in translating the Bible, strove to create a form of German that might unite the many dialect groups across what until the late nineteenth century was a patchwork of small and large states, linguistically very diverse. This story is itself a part of the cultural construct, and while not false, it is considerably oversimplified.

In order to shape up as a proper 'hero' myth, it ignores or marginalises the work of many other individuals in forging a 'German language', and encourages us to forget that Luther could have accomplished nothing without broader cultural changes under way since the late fifteenth century, including the invention of movable type and the beginnings of the nationalistic sentiments that would make thinkable a break from Roman religious monarchy.

The prototype of the modern national language was Italian, which may seem surprising given that Italy did not become a political nation until 1860, with full unification coming in 1870, just a year before that of Germany. Or perhaps it is not so surprising – the political divisions of the Italian peninsula may have been precisely what motivated the creation of cultural unity through linguistic means. In the Romance-speaking world during the thousand years from the fall of the Roman Empire to the Renaissance, 'language' meant Latin, used for all official and written purposes, though what people spoke in non-official contexts was a local dialect, historically related to Latin though significantly different from village to village.

There was, then, no 'Italian language'. That concept and its realisation are credited – heroically, and again only semi-mythically – to Dante, author of the *Divina Commedia.* Dante's treatise *De vulgari eloquentia* (*DVE*) (*c.*1306), not published until 1529, lays out the process by which he claimed to *discover,* not invent, the national language of a nation that would take five and a half centuries to emerge politically.

The task as Dante saw it was to discover this *vulgaris,* or Italian vernacular, and put it to use in place of Latin, the official language of the Western Christian world:

> [W]e call vernacular speech that which children pick up from those around them, when they first begin to distinguish words; or putting it more briefly, we say that vernacular speech is that which we acquire without any rule, by imitating our nurse. (*DVE* 1.1, my translation)[2]

He contrasts this kind of language with *gramatica* 'grammar', by which he means the official language, the language of writing, what we would now call the standard language. Again, for the Western Christian world that language is Latin – as it happens, the very language in which Dante is writing:

> We afterwards have another, secondary speech, which the Romans called grammar. The Greeks and others, though not all, also have

> this secondary form. Few actually arrive at its use, because only with much time and assiduous study do we learn and master it. (Ibid.)[3]

'Secondary' appears at first glance to have simply the temporal meaning that this type of speech is acquired second. But Dante then states that the classical standard is also second in *nobility* to the vernacular:

> Of these two the nobler is the vernacular, because it was the first used by the human race; because the whole world uses it, even if it is divided into different words and utterances; and because it is natural to us, whereas the other is artificial. (Ibid.)[4]

Latin is the language of the Church, a sacred language, and it would seem to border on heresy to suggest that the vernacular is nobler. But Dante makes his appeal to the 'natural' as opposed to the 'artificial', what is made by art. Artfulness is usually a positive quality in this period. Yet art is human, after all, while nature is divine.

Dante surveys the various Italian dialects to determine which of them is best suited to serve as the *volgare illustre*, the vernacular that is both illuminated and illuminating and that will be the best possible vehicle for poetry in a pan-Italian context. His verdict is that none of the actually existing dialects is suited to this end. Instead, the *volgare illustre* is an *ideal* language that will have to be found not with the ears, but with the mind:

> Since we have come through all the heights and pastures of Italy and have not found that panther we are trailing, let us track it down more rationally, so that with skilful striving we might net completely in our grasp this beast whose scent is everywhere yet which appears nowhere. (*DVE* 1.16)[5]

The way in which this can be done is to find among the dialects what is their 'elemental', the simplest member of their class:

> Everything becomes measurable by something in its class, by that which is simplest in its class. Thus with regard to our actions, in however many kinds they be divided, it behoves us to find this standard by which they may be measured. [...] In what concerns our acting as Italian people, we have certain elemental sign-marks of customs, clothing, and speech, by which our actions may be weighed and measured as Italian. (Ibid.)[6]

Without specifying anything about what these sign-marks of Italianness are, Dante declares somewhat abruptly that the search is now complete:

> Of those actions which are Italian, the noblest are those specific to none of the towns of Italy, but common to all. Among these we can now identify that vernacular we were seeking earlier, whose odour wafts through every city but which makes its bed in none [...]. (1.16)[7]

He has not actually demonstrated that the noblest Italian actions are those common to all the towns, which however appears here to be the conclusion of a long deductive chain. But Dante is confident that we have identified the illustrious vernacular we were seeking, by deducing that it must be the one which is specific to none of the towns of Italy but common to all. Now, there is an actual language which fits this description: *gramatica*, Latin, but it is ruled out by definition. It is not noble enough, because although common to all the cities of Italy it is not common to all the people. We want something common to all the people but specific to none of the towns; what all of them do, yet not what any one of them does.

To the modern reader this all seems a fiction, a pretence of discovery in what will actually be Dante's invention of an illustrious vernacular – which will in turn camouflage how much of it is actually based on his native Tuscan. But if invented it would have none of the features demanded by Dante, being neither original nor common nor natural, nor enjoying the nobility these features confer. On what grounds then could it possibly be preferable to Latin?

He proceeds as though toward the discovery of a natural element, which he will then use for his own art, never acknowledging that the element itself might in any way be the product of art. Whereas *gramatica* is artificial because it is the product of human history, the *volgare illustre* is the product of *anti*-history. For what is common to all the people of Italy yet what none of them do is *their past*, what they were when they were one. Of course they were one in the time when Latin was formed, but that oneness also included what would become the Spanish, the French, the Occitans and so on. Dante's panther is found by reversing history just far enough to reach a specifically Italian oneness. History is what has undone the common Italian language, and the *volgare illustre* will be found precisely by taking away what history has added to each local dialect as a superfluous deformation. For Dante, the problem of history could only be compounded, not solved, by the use of a 'gramatica' which was itself a historical product – historical in the worst sense because artificial, a wilful distortion of nature, a sin of commission. The historical divergence of dialects is a sin of omission, the passive distortion of nature by failing to abide by the elemental signs. Dante's illustrious vernacular is anti-historical in its opposition both to dialectal diversity and to the classical standard language. It aims instead to establish an alternative history that is, inevitably, deeply mythical, creating a pan-national unity under the pretence of rediscovering and restoring it.

Taming and centring the language: Nebrija and Valdés

Dante's *volgare illustre*, as put into practice in his *Divina commedia* and in the works of his near contemporaries Petrarch and Boccaccio, became the template upon which other modern European standard languages were modelled. Although Italian national identity took centuries to find a political realisation, largely because of the strong papal and foreign interests in keeping the peninsula fragmented, other European national identities benefited much sooner from the linguistic model Dante had created. What he had proven incontestably was the possibility announced in the title of his linguistic treatise – the eloquence of the vulgar tongue. Into that concept of 'eloquence' was packed a huge range of assumptions about the nature of communication, knowledge, truth, beauty and, not least, what a 'people' had to be. So long as their 'natural' way of speaking was deemed unruly (which of course it was, in comparison with a Latin rendered artificial through centuries of regulation and rarefied usage), no legitimate claim to autonomy could be made for a people.

Already in the *Gramática castellana* (1492) of Antonio de Nebrija (*c.*1444–1522), the first important grammar of a modern European language, the announced goal is to bring Castilian, the basis of the modern Spanish language, under control. The prologue to his grammar, addressed to Queen Isabella, famously begins: '[L]anguage has always been the companion of empire, and has followed it in such a way that they have jointly begun, grown, and flourished, and likewise the fall of both has been joined' (Nebrija, 1946 [1492]: 5–6, my translation).[8] There follows a series of examples of languages that have risen and fallen in tandem with great empires. Nebrija goes on to state why he is determined to *reduir en artificio* 'reduce to artifice' the Castilian language (p. 9):

> And, since my thought and desire has always been to aggrandise the things of our nation and to give men of my language works in which they can better employ their leisure, which now they waste reading novels or stories enveloped in a thousand lies and errors, I have resolved before all else to reduce our Castilian language to artifice, so that what is written in it now and in the future can follow a standard, and be extended for all time to come, as we see has been done in the Greek and Latin language, which, on account of having been subjected to art, remain in uniformity even though they have passed through many centuries.[9]

The three purposes Nebrija cites – to aggrandise the nation, better employ men's minds, and prevent the language from changing – are three of the central purposes of Renaissance linguistic thought generally. The phrases *reduir en artificio* and *debaxo de arte* mean the same thing – 'artificial' in this period still has the sense of 'made in accordance with art'. Nebrija conceived of writing a grammar of a language as conquering it, bringing it down and under control; 'reducing' it as one reduces an enemy, and reducing it in size by eliminating those elements that do not accord with logic and regularity. Therein lies the 'art' of grammar. Toward the end of the prologue, Nebrija tells Isabella (p. 11):

> [S]ince Your Majesty has put under her yoke many barbarian peoples and nations of exotic languages; and with the conquest they were obliged to receive the laws which conqueror imposes upon conquered, and with them our language; through my *Art* they may come into the knowledge of the latter, just as now we ourselves learn the art of Latin grammar in order to learn Latin.[10]

Nebrija's grammar will allow the Queen's newly conquered subjects to learn Castilian, so that the laws of Spain can be imposed upon them and the Spanish Empire can exist and function. The Empire will extend only so far as its 'companion', the Spanish language, extends. There is no sense here that Castilian 'belongs' to Castile or Spain in any natural sense, or that it embodies the Castilian soul. Nebrija's arguments are purely political and functional: Castile has conquered, and so her laws and language shall be imposed. Because the learning of Castilian by conquered peoples increases Spain's territorial dominion, the aggrandisement of language and empire go hand in hand.

The *Diálogo de la lengua* (1535–36) by Juan de Valdés (*c.*1495–1541) is typical of a genre of this period in which arguments are made in favour of a particular vernacular language, or, very commonly, asserting the advantages of one vernacular dialect over another as the basis for the nascent national language. The ultimate point of reference is always however Greek and especially Latin, as not only the sacred languages but the ones defining eloquence, setting the standard any vernacular would need to match. Although most people remained convinced that they could never be matched, Valdés was able to point to *toscano*, Dante's *volgare illustre*, as a modern idiom now generally accepted to have achieved at least a substantial measure of the sort of eloquence associated with the classical languages. By this time, too, there has been enough literary production in Castilian for it to be cited as evidence of the language's aesthetic qualities.

The debates over which language or dialect is best are also much concerned with questions of *purity*. The national language must not appear to have borrowed too much from its neighbours, especially if it has ever been under their rule. Valdés ties the presence of linguistic diversity directly to the absence of political unity and autonomy within a state, and to the inescapable fact that peripheral areas within a state have at least as much in common with neighbouring states as they do with the centre and the other peripheral areas of their own state:

Marcio [S]ince we take the basis of the Castilian language to be Latin, it remains for us to say how it came about that in Spain are spoken the other four types of languages that are now spoken there, namely Catalan, Valencian, Portuguese and Basque.

Valdés [T]wo things are usually the principal cause of diversity of languages in a province: one is that it is not entirely under one prince, king or lord, whence it proceeds that there are as many differences of language as diversity of lords; the other is that, since something always links provinces bordering on one another, it comes to pass that each part of a province, taking something from the neighbouring provinces, gradually becomes different from the others, not only in speech, but also in conversation and customs. Spain, as you know, has been under the rule of many lords [...]. This diversity of lordships has I think in some manner caused the difference of languages, although each of them conforms more with the Castilian language than with any other; because, although each one of them has taken from its neighbours, as Catalonia has taken from France and Italy, and Valencia has

> taken from Catalonia, on the whole you see that principally they draw on Latin, which is, as I have said, the basis of the Castilian language [...]. (Valdés, 1965 [1535–36], pp. 47–9, my translation)[11]

The belief that Castilian has undergone less outside influence than Catalan or Valencian strengthens its claims to be the national language in two ways: first, because its Spanishness has been less diluted, and second, being truer to the historical core of the language it is more likely to be understood by more Spaniards than any of the other, more 'eccentric' languages is. As for Basque and Portuguese, Valdés goes on to eliminate them from the equation by polarly opposed strategies: Basque, he says, is simply too far from the rest ever to be understood by them, while Portuguese basically is Castilian, with minor pronunciation and orthographic differences.[12]

Also part of the debate was how much 'purification' – i.e. Latinisation – the vernacular language should undergo. Such purification actually removes it from the 'naturalness' typically put forward as the principal argument in favour of its use, even by those most bent on taming it by such means. Moreover, what is being purified away is part of the dialect's *Spanishness* – and that raises the question of what precisely the 'origin' of the Spanish dialects is, and whether what has removed them from that original form has been something inessential and 'foreign'. For note that Valdés ties together borrowing of language with borrowing of *customs* from one's neighbours. This is as much as to put their very Spanishness into question. The centre, protected from outside influences by its geographical position, defines the essence of the national character and its linguistic manifestations.

Although rhetorically effective in arguing for a central dialect as the basis of the national language, the strategy of marginalising the periphery is quite the opposite of what political nation-building entails. The 'Spanish' (or Italian, or whatever) people is a construct based upon political boundaries, which are arbitrary in the sense that they are historically contingent, having lain elsewhere at other times. The political–cultural goal becomes that of fixing the boundaries to prevent them moving again (unless it is to expand). To do this, it is necessary to convince those living on the frontiers of the nation, near the borders, that they are one people with those in the centre, and not one with their neighbours just across the border. It is necessary as well to persuade those in the centre of the same thing, if they are to be motivated to pay for war to keep the nation's boundaries intact. The peasantry who in earlier times did the foot-soldiering may not have needed to be motivated to sign up for the army – they did so if their feudal lord told them to, the only possibility of escape being to leave his estate for an anonymous life in the city or overseas. In actual battle, however, a Christian soldier who had been brought up not to fear death but to yearn for a glorious afterlife might need motivation to give his all for the national cause.

The brilliance of the concepts of nation and national language for these purposes is that they are defined crucially by difference from one's closest neighbours, just as Tajfel's 'in-group'-based analysis would lead us to predict (Chapter 4, pp. 76–7). Anglophone Canadians know 'who they are' primarily through features that distinguish their culture and language from those of the United States; similarly for Scotland and England, the French regions vis-à-vis the centre, northern and southern China, and so on. This reliance on differences of a necessarily subtle order, given the proximity, endows even the smallest variation with huge cultural significance. The very essence of a nation can come to be seen as residing within some superficially insignificant idiosyncrasy – the retention of a guttural fricative within the phonetic system, the ceremonial wearing of a kilt or serving of a dish that the neighbours find so repugnant as to make a joke of it. There is little wonder that 'essentialism' came to be the usual scholarly mode of understanding national identity, given that such identity is so essentialist in its primary manifestations.

To recapitulate what was stated in Chapter 1 (p. 5), in semiology, following Saussure, a linguistic sign is the conjunction of a signifier (sound pattern) and a signified (concept). A national identity – 'Italian', for example – becomes the signifier of a signified that exists at first only as a desire. With sufficient motivation, this desire can come to be shared by a critical mass within the putative nation, and when that happens, the signified, the 'Italian people', becomes real, as real as any signified can be, given that they are concepts or categories rather than actual physical objects.

Language imagined as a republic: Du Bellay

The Italians and Spaniards may have produced the first treatises, dialogues and grammars asserting that their vernacular, or some particular form of it, could approach the eloquence of the classical languages, but the rest of Western Europe was not slow to get in on the act. Joachim Du Bellay (1522–60) wrote his *Deffence et illustration de la langue françoyse* (1549) with the intention of proving that French was as worthy and potentially capable of use in both literary and scientific writing as were Latin and Greek. Most of the arguments in the *Deffence et illustration* had been anticipated by Sperone Speroni (1500–88) in Italy, and by earlier sixteenth-century French writers like Geoffroy Tory (1480?–1533) in *Champ fleury* (1529). But this did not prevent Du Bellay's treatise from having an enormous impact in its time, and it remains to this day a staple of the French educational canon. Like Nebrija, Du Bellay presents the linguistic and political power of the nation as directly linked:

> Perhaps the day will come – and I hope it will, along with a happy destiny for France – when this noble and powerful Realm will in its turn take the reins of world dominance, and when our language (if it has not been entirely buried along with François I [d. 1547]), which is still just beginning to sprout roots, will burst forth from the ground and rise up to a height and size to rival even the Greeks and Romans [. . .]. (Du Bellay I.3, my translation)[13]

He recognises the paradox that, in order to achieve the requisite eloquence, French must take on elements and aspects of the very languages it is striving to equal. In the following passage he expresses this through a pair of metaphors, the first economic (our language can pay back what it borrows), the second agricultural (it will bear fruit for those who cultivate it), before tying all this directly to *love of country*:

> [O]ur French language is not so poor that it cannot faithfully give back what it borrows from others, so infertile that it cannot produce on its own any fruit of good invention through the industry and diligence of those who cultivate it, provided that some of them have enough love for their country and themselves that they will work at this. (I.4)[14]

The borrowing of words is almost an obsessive concern for Du Bellay, and understandably so, since the need for it admits the poverty of the language at the same time as it makes it possible to enrich it. Hence the endless search for metaphors whereby to justify borrowing – of which the most interesting is perhaps the following, in which he imagines the language itself as the equivalent of a nation, and individual words as immigrants which may or may not be fully naturalised, which is to say absorbed into the national identity ('family'):

> [T]ranslators should not worry if they occasionally encounter words which cannot be taken into the French family, given that the Romans did not insist on translating such Greek words as *rhetoric, music, arithmetic, geometry, philosophy* [...] and most of the terms used in the natural sciences and mathematics generally. Those words, then, will be in our language like foreigners in a city [...]. Thus, if the philosophy sown by Aristotle and Plato in the fertile fields of Attica were replanted in our own plains of France, this would not be throwing it into brambles and thorns where it would be sterile, but rather changing it from something distant into something near, and from a foreigner into a citizen of our republic. (I.10)[15]

Thus both language and culture are like 'republics', populated by words in the one case and ideas in the other.[16] Not every foreign element entering the republic will be granted citizenship, of course, but those offering some substantial benefit to the republic will be welcomed, and will, like transplanted seeds, not just thrive on French soil, but grow into French plants. It is interesting that Du Bellay says specifically 'foreigners *in a city*', cities being where populations were most mixed and foreigners most likely to be encountered, and indeed also where the national language would emerge – in part as a lingua franca for those coming to the city from various dialect areas, in part because the city was the locus of those institutions, legal, governmental, educational and communicational, that would play the lead role in the language's formation.

One of the key changes in European thought over the subsequent two and half centuries leading into the Romantic period would be a steady hardening of the belief that cities, on account of their strong foreign element, are not *really* a part of the nation at all. The authentic nation lies in the *country* – a belief inherent in the ambiguity of 'country' itself, a word that means either the nation or the opposite of 'city' (as is also the case with its congeners in a number of other languages). As we have seen, the question of *who the nation really is* was by no means absent from the linguistic debates of the Renaissance, but it functioned as one rhetorical topos among many within arguments aimed at expanding the functional sphere of a particular language or dialect. In the second half of the eighteenth century, that question took on a much greater centrality and significance, realised in America and France as revolutionary action, and in Germany, initially at least, as philosophical contemplation. Then, at the start of the nineteenth century, political developments moved it beyond the philosophical sphere for Germans and indeed for the whole of Europe. Somewhere within this complex of late eighteenth- and early nineteenth-century developments is where the modern concepts of 'nation' and 'nationalism' proper are held to originate, with the precise point of origin still much debated. Some of this debate was discussed above, notably with reference to Kedourie, one of whose own key figures, Fichte, is the subject of the next section.

Fichte on language and nation

General Napoleon Bonaparte seized control of the French government in 1799. In 1803 he became President of the Italian Republic as well, and in 1804 the French senate and people voted him their emperor. Over the next six years he expanded his empire to include most of Europe. It was in this period that German Romantic thinkers, many of whom had previously hero-worshipped Napoleon as the embodiment of the possibilities of the human will, now had to come to grips with the fact of having their own country defeated by him and themselves becoming his imperial subjects. From this experience arose the argument that such imperial rule was unjust, because it is natural for each nation to rule itself.

But what were the 'natural' boundaries of a nation? This was the key question, to which the answer seemed obvious to anyone in this period when the predominant definition of 'nation' was the extended one focused on the expanse of territory. The natural boundaries were the geographical obstacles, the sea coasts together with any mountain ranges or great rivers cutting the nation off from easy reach of its neighbours. But by that answer, there was nothing in principle to prevent 'Europe' being conceived of as a 'nation' rather than an empire composed of nations. None of the natural barriers within it was insurmountable (apart from the English Channel). In particular, for what most concerned the German Romantics, there was certainly no great land or water barrier defining their nation as distinctive from those of their neighbours to the east or west.

If the right of the German nation to autonomy was to be maintained by something more fundamental to the Romantic mind than mere historical difference, something non-geographical yet plausible as a primordial, 'natural' boundary had to be identified. One solution might have been to hark back to religious affiliation, on which the whole pre-modern edifice of dynasty had been defined. But all Europe was officially Christian, and however strong were the doctrinal differences within Western Christianity, particularly those separating Protestants from Roman Catholics, Germans in particular could not overplay them without weakening Western unity in the face of ever-present fears of Orthodox Slavs to the east. Moreover, in the wake of the Enlightenment, mainstream European thought was grounded in the secular. Arguments built upon a religious foundation had the air of belonging either to a bygone age or to the increasingly specialised domain of theology.

The most convincing answer was formulated by Fichte in an 1806 'address to the German nation', in which he argued that what defines a nation most clearly is its language:

> The first, original, and truly natural boundaries of states are beyond doubt their internal boundaries. Those who speak the same language are joined to each other by a multitude of invisible bonds by nature herself, long before any human art begins; they understand each other and have the power of continuing to make themselves understood more and more clearly; they belong together and are by nature one and an inseparable whole. (Fichte, 1968 [1808], pp. 190–1)

Epicurus notwithstanding, in the context within which Fichte wrote, language was by no means the obvious candidate to stand as the defining characteristic of nations. Most of the languages of Europe were understood to have descended from a common ancestor tongue, with the differences being merely the historical by-product of different subgroups of the original tribe having settled in different parts of the continent, separated by the geographical obstacles that were assumed to be the natural, primordial boundaries of nations, and remaining relatively isolated for long stretches of time. Fichte turned these traditional views on their head:

> From this internal boundary [of language], which is drawn by the spiritual nature of man himself, the marking of the external boundary by dwelling place results as a consequence; and in the natural view of things it is not because men dwell between certain mountains and rivers that they are a people, but, on the contrary, men dwell together – and, if their luck has so arranged it, are protected by rivers and mountains – because they were a people already by a law of nature which is much higher.
>
> Thus was the German nation placed – sufficiently united within itself by a common language and a common way of thinking, and sharply enough severed from the other peoples – in the middle of Europe, as a wall to divide races not akin [...]. (Ibid.)

Fichte's writings are given the principal credit for rousing Germans to rise up against Napoleonic rule. The point of view he espoused was by no means just a political one, though; it resonated so loudly just because it accorded so well with the idea system of German Romanticism generally. Neoplatonic in character, it was oriented toward the realm of eternal ideals, and located reality not in the world of mere superficial appearances and historical contingencies, but in the permanent, unchanging essence of things. In the case of a nation, its essence existed in purest form in its founder, and that essence that was in him persists throughout the whole history of the nation, providing the base of its language, culture, way of thinking and intellectual and artistic achievements. However, mixture with other nations means dilution of this essence:

> Such a whole [as the nation defined by language], if it wishes to absorb and mingle with itself any other people of different descent and language, cannot do so without itself becoming confused, in the beginning at any rate, and violently disturbing the even progress of its culture. (Ibid.)

This particular aspect of Romantic thought, which follows logically from its founding principles, would lead to the development of 'scientific racism' from the mid nineteenth to the mid twentieth century, with consequences more horrible than anything in the whole inhuman history of humanity. Whether any of those writing in this period foresaw such developments is a matter of interpretation and debate, but in the case of Fichte, one can be quite confident that his intention was to rescue the German nation, language and culture from what seemed at the time like an overwhelming domination by the French, with little if any thought that one day his own countrymen might invoke his equation of absorption with confusion as part of a rationale for genocide.

Renan and the Kedourie–Gellner debate

Halfway between Napoleon and Hitler occurred an event which put France in a position very like the ones Germans had felt themselves seven decades earlier. Between 1863 and 1871, Prussia, led by Otto von Bismarck, unified the nation of Germany under its own hegemony, through a series of victorious wars against Denmark, Austria and France. The culmination of the Franco-Prussian War with the siege of Paris in 1870–71 was a defining moment for modern nationalism in a number of respects: it ended with the proclamation of the German Empire – modern Germany as we know it – and the Empire's annexation of Alsace-Lorraine, territories which had repeatedly shuttled between French and German rule, where the local dialects were Germanic but the political allegiance of the populace was strongly to France. Paris continued to resist the new German Empire after the rest of France had surrendered, and for two months it was ruled by the Commune, a loosely organised proletarian 'communist' government that was finally crushed by the new French national provisional government formed in the wake of the treaties with the Prussians.

These events had a tremendous impact on the French psyche, comparable to that of Napoleon's victories on Germans at the start of the century, which produced Fichte's writings on nationalism among many others. Fichtean arguments about language defining a nation naturally were the mainstay of Germany's justification for the annexation of Alsace-Lorraine. So powerfully had this way of thinking shaped the modern European conception of nationalism that even Frenchmen who believed wholeheartedly that Alsace-Lorraine must be French could not find an obvious way to counter the linguistic argument. It was finally a linguist, Ernest Renan (1823–92), who produced a new conception of nationalism in response, and it was that conception that would become the basis for the Wilsonian principles by which the twentieth-century world map was redrawn at Versailles in 1919.

Renan's 1882 address 'Qu'est-ce qu'une nation?' is universally cited as a landmark. His conception of the nation starts from the Romantic idea of a shared *âme* (a word that means both 'mind' and 'soul'), as one would expect from someone whose approach to language, mind and race had crystallised in the 1840s under the influence of Herder (see Chapter 3, p. 44). But he passes beyond the Romantic when he breaks this *âme* down into its component parts: a heritage of memories, plus a will to continue validating that heritage of memories:

> A nation is a soul, a spiritual principle. Two things that are actually one make up this soul, this spiritual principle. One is in the past, the other in the present. One is the common ownership of a rich legacy of memories; the other is the present-day agreement, the desire to live together, the will to continue validating the heritage that has been inherited jointly. (Renan, 1882, p. 26, my translation)[17]

The nation, in other words, exists in the minds – the memories and the will – of the people who make it up. This is the conception that Anderson

(1991, p. 6) would return to in defining the nation as 'an imagined political community'. The 'legacy of memories' Renan pointed to would dominate future philosophical and academic attempts to analyse national identity. The other element, the collective 'will' of the people, would however have the deepest political impact, starting at Versailles. It has continued to be the assumed basis for the legitimacy of the political nation up to the present time.

Renan would turn up at the heart of the first great debate in the contemporary discourse on nationalism, which took place between two Jewish scholars in the years following the Second World War. Kedourie had grown up in Iraq, a country artificially created for British administrative purposes; he settled in the new state of Israel at the time of its creation, but was subsequently drawn to an academic career in London. Ernest Gellner (1925–95) had, like Hans Kohn, been a refugee from Nazi Germany, though to London rather than America. Gellner and Kedourie became friends, and each acknowledged the other as having played a key role in the formulation of their two fundamentally conflicting views of the nature of nationalism, views that reflect their different life experiences in interesting ways.

Two major differences separate them. The first is that, for Gellner, Kedourie's view of nationalism as 'a doctrine invented in Europe at the beginning of the nineteenth century' (p. 96 above) turned it from the natural, necessary, universal historical development it was generally assumed to be, into something 'utterly *contingent*, an accidental invention, a by-product of the scribblings of a set of thinkers in one particular historic situation' (Gellner, 1997, p. 10, italics in original). Gellner credited Kedourie with awakening him from 'dogmatic slumbers on this point – until I read his book, I continued to assume, or at least not to criticise with lucidity, the "naturalness" view of nationalism' (ibid.). But while taking Kedourie's point that nations are not an inexorable historical development for all people everywhere, Gellner rejected the further conclusion that nationalism is just an ideological accident that would never have come about if Kant and Fichte had not happened to write what they did:

> Nationalism is neither universal and necessary nor contingent and accidental, the fruit of idle pens and gullible readers. It *is* the necessary consequence or correlate of certain social conditions, and these do happen to be *our* conditions, and they are also very widespread, deep and pervasive. So nationalism is not at all accidental: its roots are deep and important, it was indeed our destiny, and not some

> kind of contingent malady, imposed on us by the scribblers of the late Enlightenment. But, on the other hand, the deep roots which engender it are not universally present, and so nationalism is not the destiny of all men. It is the highly probably destiny of some men, and the unlikely condition of many others. Our task is to single out the differences which separate nationalism-prone from nationalism-resistant humanity. (Gellner, 1997, pp. 10–11)

While not wishing to explain everything biographically, one can readily understand how urgent this task seemed to someone who had lost family members to the genocide of a fanatically nationalistic regime, and how to such a person the conception of nationalism as just an ideological abstraction might seem deeply unconvincing.

In any case, as Gellner set about the task he defined for himself, one of the most prominent factors that suggested itself to him as making people nationalism-prone was the very one Fichte had pointed to, the possession of a common language. As a result, contemporary scholarship on nationalism and national identity has tended, following Gellner, to assume language as a foundational factor, a tendency helped along by a general 'post-structuralist' ethos that sees all social structures as linguistic constructs. The Kedourian alternative, in which language is downgraded from primordial binding force of the nation to just one of several ideological sites within nationalist rhetoric, would find echoes in the arguments of those post-structuralists too wary of essentialisms to assign language or any other single factor a foundational role.[18]

Gellner's second major dissent was from Kedourie's Kantian conception of the nation as being modelled upon the Romantic ideal of the Individual. For Gellner, the nation is social in its constitution from top to bottom. In support of this he famously invoked Renan's (1882, p. 27) view that 'The existence of a nation is – pardon my metaphor – a daily plebiscite [...]',[19] as well as his description of the mental constitution of nations as being based not simply on shared memories, as was commonly assumed, but on shared *forgetting*, the putting aside of differences among groups constituting the nation, while also ceasing to remember that there was a time when they were not united as a nation (see next section).

There is a certain irony in Renan's now being so widely remembered for these rather modernist sounding statements, given that, as noted earlier, he was one of those nineteenth-century linguistic thinkers who developed the essentialist view of language to its highest point. In his celebrated early work on the origin of language, Renan followed the

German Romantic view, memorably articulated by Humboldt (see Chapter 3, p. 45) that the structure of languages must have been already fully fixed at the moment of their creation (Renan, 1858, pp. 105–6). Primitive man, Renan believed, created language effortlessly, like the child that he was (ibid., p. 98), not employing his will, but by letting language flow spontaneously and naturally from the structure of his faculties, physical and mental (ibid., pp. 92–3). In general Renan adheres closely to the views of Herder, but he rejects Herder's view that *reflection* was the key to the origin of language, and returns instead to something like the Epicurean idea of the language proceeding from the body – more precisely, from the ethnic body (see Chapter 3, p. 43). Like Fichte and Humboldt, Renan believed that 'The mind of each people is in the closest connection with its language [...]' (Renan, 1858, p. 190).[20]

Anderson's 'imagined communities' and Billig's 'banal nationalism'

The conjunction of Renan and Gellner would figure very prominently in Benedict Anderson's influential definition of the nation as an 'imagined political community':

> It is *imagined* because the members of even the smallest nation will never know most of their fellow-members, meet them, or even hear of them, yet in the minds of each lives the image of their communion. Renan referred to this imagining in his suavely back-handed way when he wrote that 'Or l'essence d'une nation est que tous les individus aient beaucoup de choses en commun, et aussi que tous aient oublié bien des choses'. With a certain ferocity Gellner makes a comparable point when he rules that 'Nationalism is not the awakening of nations to self-consciousness: it *invents* nations where they do not exist.' (Anderson, 1991, p. 6)[21]

As with the 'discovery' of a national language, a crucial part of this inventing or imagining of a nation is the creation of a belief that the nation has *not* been invented. Its invention must, in other words, be forgotten. For if invented, the nation might be perceived as merely artificial, arbitrary, contingent in character, thus making its validity seem very shallow indeed. Instead the myth must be made that the nation is a *natural* entity, with a deep-rooted authenticity that is being rediscovered. If the nation in question has not existed as a nation during the whole of recorded history, then the myth (or more usually, the complex of myths) will be extended back into prehistory as far as needed to establish its claim to legitimacy. Anderson goes on to explain that the nation

> [...] is imagined as a *community*, because, regardless of the actual inequality and exploitation that may prevail in each, the nation is always conceived as a deep, horizontal comradeship. Ultimately it is this fraternity that makes it possible, over the past two centuries, for so many millions of people, not so much to kill, as willingly to die for such limited imaginings. (Ibid., p. 7)

Both of the primary organisational structures which preceded the modern conception of the nation, the religious community and the dynastic realm, were vertical rather than 'horizontal' in arrangement. Authority flowed downward from God to the supreme human authority, whether religious or secular, and outward from there to the rest of the community. A hallmark of modern thought was that these vertical hierarchies came to be seen as mythical, serving the interests of those at the top and oppressing those at the bottom. And so they have come to be replaced, in part, by the 'horizontal' nation of which every citizen is, in a sense, an equal member. The fact of their inhabiting a contiguous territory becomes essential, overriding differences of religion, culture, class and so on. Yet how then to motivate people to fight, to the death if necessary, on behalf of the nation – often against other members of their own religion, for example? This is why the new mythologies were required.

Relying heavily on Seton-Watson's (1977) account of nationalism as being built upon linguistic difference, Anderson ascribes the construction of national myths, starting in the Renaissance, to a shift from

> the idea that a particular script–language offered privileged access to ontological truth, precisely because it was an inseparable part of that truth. [...T]he search was on, so to speak, for a new way of linking fraternity, power and time meaningfully together. Nothing perhaps more precipitated this search, nor made it more fruitful, than print-capitalism, which made it possible for rapidly growing numbers of people to think about themselves, and to relate themselves to others, in profoundly new ways. (Anderson, 1991, p. 36)

These profoundly new self-conceptions found a ready-made template from which to work: the national languages, which, Anderson believes, emerged in the sixteenth century 'as a gradual, unselfconscious, pragmatic, not to say haphazard development' (ibid., p. 42); 'in their origins, the fixing of print-languages and the differentiation of status between them were largely unselfconscious processes' (ibid., p. 45). The accuracy of these views will be brought into question in the next section of this chapter.

Nationality is not necessarily the identity people will be most willing to die for. Regional and local identities matter, as do social class identities, racial, religious and sectarian identities. Even linguistic identity can be an end in itself, though it tends to get transmuted into quasi-racial terms. Given their importance in defining who individuals believe they really are, one would expect identities to be founded in every case on an extremely profound basis, such as whole libraries of texts recording thousands of years of cultural tradition. This has usually been the case with the older organisational structures of religious communities and dynastic realms, but modern structures such as the nation are typically founded on much shallower, often purely symbolic grounds.[22]

Billig, mentioned in Chapter 4 as a colleague and collaborator of the late Henri Tajfel, has made a number of crucial expansions upon Anderson's position. The term 'imagined community' might suggest that the nation 'depend[s] upon continual acts of imagination for its existence' (Billig, 1995, p. 70). Instead it is the case that the original 'imagining' is *reproduced* – Billig takes the term from Bourdieu (see p. 75) – sometimes through purposeful deployment of national symbols, but mostly through daily habits of which we are only dimly aware or even unaware. Examples include the national flag hanging in front of the post office, or the national symbols on the coins and banknotes we use each day. Billig introduced the term *banal nationalism* to cover

> the ideological habits which enable the established nations of the West to be reproduced. It is argued that these habits are not removed from everyday life, as some observers have supposed. Daily, the nation is indicated, or 'flagged', in the lives of its citizenry. Nationalism, far from being an intermittent mood in established nations, is the endemic condition. (Billig, 1995, p. 6)

This idea was perhaps implicit in Anderson's invocation of Renan on the necessity of 'forgetting', but by not drawing out the implications, Anderson leads readers to associate nationalism strictly with what Billig calls the 'passionately waved flag', and to ignore 'routine flags', like the one hanging limp in front of the post office, which operates to reproduce banal nationalism precisely because it is a 'forgotten reminder' (ibid., p. 8) – its significance is 'forgotten' by the observer, yet remembered in the depths of his mind. Billig's point is that studies of nationalism have perversely paid attention to the strongly asserted nationalism that is typical only of a small minority of people, and ignored the banal nationalism that is part of everyone's everyday life (strong nationalists included). What is more, he argues that this is part of

> an ideological pattern in which 'our' nationalism (that of established nations [...]) is forgotten: it ceases to appear as nationalism, disappearing into the 'natural' environment of 'societies'. At the same time, nationalism is defined as something dangerously emotional and irrational: it is conceived as a problem, or a condition, which is surplus to the world of nations. The irrationality of nationalism is projected on to 'others'. (Ibid., p. 38)

In his view, which owes more to Bourdieu than to Tajfel, 'an identity is to be found in the embodied habits of social life' (ibid., p. 8), including, as we shall see in the next section, language.

One further aspect of national identity that will be highlighted in this chapter is not explored in any depth by Billig, although he points toward it by quoting Said's (1983) insistence that nations are 'interpretive communities' (borrowing Fish's concept as discussed on p. 65) as well as imagined ones, because what has to be created is not only a concept of the nation but an entire history, based on a particular interpretation of recorded events. In fact, as pointed out in Chapter 1, identities are not simply a matter of what their possessors (or would-be possessors) project, but of how such projections are received and interpreted. As a group of sociologists have asserted,

> National identities are not essentially fixed or given but depend critically on the claims which people make in different contexts and at different times. The processes of identity rest not simply on the claims made but on how such claims are received, that is validated or rejected by significant others. (Bechhofer et al., 1999, p. 515)

Nor, I would add, can we neglect the identities that others project onto us. However, it is important to note that, of all the claims which people make and receive about a national identity, none is more crucial or powerful than the claim that the identity *is* in fact fixed and given, *is* imposed on us by birth and *does* remain essentially unchanged thereafter. From the constructionist point of view, the mistake of an essentialist analysis lies in its failure to see past the myth that is embedded within the identity under study. At the same time, constructionists must take care to avoid a potential mistake of their own, by dismissing the 'myth' as mere fallacy, and therefore unworthy of analytical attention in its own right. It is a cultural construct that ultimately cannot be separated from the national identity as a whole.

De-essentialising the role of language: Hobsbawm and Silverstein

Although several years older than either Kedourie or Gellner, Eric Hobsbawm (b. 1917) turned his attention to nationalism some two decades after they had set the parameters of the current discourse. In common with so many modern writers on nationalism, Hobsbawm was born in Germany to a (non-observant) Jewish family and came to Britain in 1933, though not actually as a refugee. But unlike the others, he was a card-carrying member of the Communist Party from 1936 until 1991 and remains a committed Marxist. That his approach to nationalism downplays its status as an ultimate explanation of political developments and human behaviour, and ties it to deeper socio-economic factors, is therefore not surprising. But such are Hobsbawm's skills as a historian, particularly an economic historian, that his views are taken seriously even by those who dismiss other far-left scholars as partisan. What is more, his major reassessments of nationalism (Hobsbawm, 1990) appeared just at the moment when the old Cold War partisan divisions themselves became history.

For Hobsbawm, the discourse of nationalism, including the prominent role assigned to a national language, encodes other, deeper concerns, and it is a mistake simply to take the discourse at face value. No one disputes that when the modern concept of nation began to be asserted in the late eighteenth century, it was for political reasons, but when justifications were put forward on the basis of a people's natural right to self-determination, it was never *just* from hostile foreign powers that autonomy was being proclaimed, but at least as much from the ruling class of the people's own country:

> [W]hat characterized the nation-people as seen from below was precisely that it represented the common interest against particular

> interests, the common good against privilege, as indeed is suggested by the term Americans used before 1800 to indicate nationhood, while avoiding the word itself. Ethnic group differences were from this revolutionary-democratic point of view as secondary as they later seemed to socialists. Patently what distinguished the American colonists from King George and his supporters was neither language nor ethnicity, and conversely, the French Republic saw no difficulty in electing the Anglo-American Thomas Paine to its National Convention.
>
> We cannot therefore read into the revolutionary 'nation' anything like the later nationalist programme of establishing nation-states for bodies defined in terms of the criteria so hotly debated by the nineteenth-century theorists, such as ethnicity, common language, religion, territory and common historical memories [...]. (Hobsbawm, 1990, p. 20)

As for national languages, Hobsbawm agrees with earlier students of nationalism, culminating with Anderson, on their central importance within the discourse. But whereas Anderson takes the national language as a given, furnishing the foundation on which the rest of national identity can be constructed, Hobsbawm realises that the national language is itself a discursive construction:

> National languages [...] are the opposite of what nationalist mythology supposes them to be, namely the primordial foundations of national culture and the matrices of the national mind. They are usually attempts to devise a standardized idiom out of a multiplicity of actually spoken idioms, which are downgraded to dialects [...]. (Ibid., p. 51)

No one who has studied the history of any national or standard language (unless for partisan purposes) has come up with a different conclusion than this one. But historians of nationalism had not in general attended to the work of linguistic historians in the way Hobsbawm did; and as for the linguistic historians themselves, they were seldom aware of the broader implications of their own findings. Indeed, I do not think any linguist has ever provided quite as apt and succinct definition of the standard language as Hobsbawm does: 'a sort of platonic idea of the language, existing behind and above all its variants and imperfect versions' (ibid., p. 57). A 'mystical identification of nationality' then occurs with this idea of the language, an identification Hobsbawm believes 'is much more characteristic of the ideological construction of nationalist intellectuals, of whom Herder is the prophet, than of the actual grassroots users of the idiom. It is a literary and not an existential concept' (ibid., p. 57). Here I cannot fully agree: for while it may be *historically* true that the national/standard language is the property of nationalist intellectuals rather than of ordinary users during the period when it is initially being constructed, this ceases to be the case once it enters the educational sphere, and once education is widespread. The linguistic ideology then becomes common national property, as least as likely to find firm belief among the working classes who do not control it as among the upper classes who do. Indeed, in a subsequent chapter of his book Hobsbawm will place great stress on the fact that enthusiasm for linguistic nationalism has historically been a phenomenon of the *lower middle class*:

> The classes which stood or fell by the official use of the written vernacular were the socially modest but educated middle strata, which included those who acquired lower middle-class status precisely by virtue of occupying non-manual jobs that required schooling. (Ibid., p. 117)

These are also the people who become the mainstay of nationalism – not just by active flag-waving on symbolic occasions, but daily in the banal ways pointed to by Billig, including their use of 'proper language' and their insistence on its norms, for instance in conversation with their own children. Hobsbawm believes that 'national identity' in the sense we usually think of it really goes back to Victorian shopkeepers and clerks who envied the sort of class belonging enjoyed by both the upper classes, with their clubs and aristocratic titles, and the workers, who could locate their identity in socialism:

> If they already lived in a nation-state, nationalism gave them the social identity which proletarians got from their class movement. One might suggest that the self-definition of the lower middle classes – both that section which was helpless as artisans and small shopkeepers and social strata which were largely as novel as the workers, given the unprecedented expansion of higher education white-collar and professional occupations – was not so much as a class, but as the body of the most zealous and loyal, as well as the most 'respectable' sons and daughters of the fatherland. (Ibid., p. 122)

In other words, although their real identity was that of a social class, they masked it for themselves and others in a nationalistic guise. And the mask was double-sided: in their obsession with 'speaking properly' as a mark of respectability, they were contributing to the linguistic construction of their nation.

Gellner had already suggested that, even if is it true that nationalism begins as an ideology at the start of the nineteenth century, something transformative occurred with the events of 1870–71 and their aftermath. With Hobsbawm this later period becomes the truly cardinal one, as for the first time ideological notions about nation and language, heretofore restricted to intellectuals and the government elite, spread down through the general populace, eventually even reaching the working class. Hobsbawm points to one further development in this period that would have dramatic consequences. Prior to about 1880, the claims of a group of people to constitute a 'nation' would have been taken seriously only if their population met a certain unstated threshold. But from that time onward,

> *any* body of people considering themselves a 'nation' claimed the right to self-determination [...I]n consequence of this multiplication of potential 'unhistorical' nations, ethnicity and language became the central, increasingly the decisive or even the only criterion of potential nationhood. (Ibid., p. 102)

This seems to conflict with evidence we have seen of much earlier arguments using language to define the nation, notably by Fichte. What Hobsbawm leads us to consider, however, is the possibility that we read Fichte and others of his period through post-1880s lenses, finding implications that Fichte and his contemporaries would not have entertained, and that reflect the concerns of the later age that has effectively defined nationalism for us. Moreover, we perhaps overestimate the influence Fichte and his fellow intellectuals exercised on their countrymen, of whom, after all, a rather small proportion were actively engaged in these debates.

One development that certainly altered the intellectual climate at the start of the modern period was the rise and dissemination of belief in human evolution, associated in particular with the name of Charles Darwin. Among the many effects that Darwin never could have foreseen was that evolution theory was used to construct a 'scientific' basis for belief in racial differences of an intellectual and moral order. As such ideas diffused into popular culture, they subtly and gradually made it seem more and more like 'common sense' that ethnic differences were fundamental in nature, so that it was naturally right for distinct nations to define distinct states. One of the problems, though, as Hobsbawm points out, is that ethnic differences are not always so easy to detect on the physical level, at least not reliably (see Hobsbawm, 1990, pp. 65–7). Where language differences correspond with ethnic differences, they appeared to provide a more objective basis on which to draw dividing lines – this despite the insistence of leading linguists that language did *not* have any direct historical link with ethnicity. Evidence was in fact readily available to anyone that the two do not have to go together, so long as they had ever encountered someone bilingual (and it is difficult to imagine that they might never have done so). But again, such was the desire to construct national difference that what appeared to help would be seized on, and anything contradictory ignored.

Whether or not one is prepared to go as far as Hobsbawm does in locating class-based factors underlying linguistic nationalism, his work has had an undeniably salutary effect in counteracting Anderson's aprioristic approach to language within identity. A prominent linguistic anthropologist, Michael Silverstein, has recently launched a similarly spirited critique of Anderson's use of 'language in modeling the cultural phenomenology of nationalism' (Silverstein, 2000, p. 85). His critique, which relies heavily on his somewhat idiosyncratic reading of the linguistic ideas of Whorf, culminates in an assertion that Anderson has mistaken discursive for 'real' linguistic nationalism:

> [...] Anderson seems to mistake the dialectically produced trope of 'we'-ness for the reality. He seems not to see that the dialectical workings of political processes that construct the sharable space of realist reportage in standardized language are the facts to be characterized and explained. (Silverstein, 2000, p. 126)
>
> The regime of language on which such a dialectic depends is a frequently fragile sociopolitical order, seething with contestation that emerges from actual plurilingualism, heteroglossia, and like indexes of at least potentially fundamental political economic conflict. Such a regime of language is, however, energized and in a sense maintained by the ritually emblematized trope of 'we'-ness. It seems to have taken in Anderson, who buys the trope as a transparently imagined 'reality'. (Ibid., pp. 128–9)

Again, it would be hard not to agree with Silverstein's critique in so far as it implies that Anderson takes language too much for granted. That is, in order to explain his major variable, the construction of national identity, Anderson uses national languages as though they were a constant – when in fact they are just as much variables, constructs, 'imagined communities' as the national identities they are invoked to explain. In other words, Anderson's constructionist approach to nationalism is purchased at the price of an essentialist outlook on languages. It seems a bargain to the sociologist or political scientist, to whom it brings explanatory simplicity (not to mention ease). But to Silverstein, as to Hobsbawm, it is a false simplicity. National languages and identities arise in tandem, 'dialectically' if you like, in a complex process that ought to be our focus of interest and study.

Silverstein goes a step further, however, to assert that the only 'real' facts are the 'political processes' and 'political economic conflict' which underlie the discourse through which the national/standard language is battled into existence. The 'we'-ness on which the imagined national community is built is but one 'trope' produced out of this discourse. The fact that it is 'ritually emblematized' leads to the illusion that it is really real, when in truth it is only a figure of speech. What this means is that, contra Anderson, identity constructed in language is not the true locus of nationalism. Where nationalism really exists is in politics and economics, and what we see in language is only the reflection of that real nationalism. Anderson, in effect, has mistaken the image in the mirror for the thing reflected.

Hobsbawm does not go this far. On the contrary, he is alert to the danger of 'reduc[ing] linguistic nationalism to a question of jobs, as vulgar-materialist liberals used to reduce wars to a question of the profits of armaments firms' (Hobsbawm, 1990, pp. 117–18). Silverstein, in contrast, is close to a vulgar-materialist reduction when he insists that ideologies of language are merely a reflection of what is real, and have no reality in themselves. In doing so, he perpetuates the very error he has already criticised another aspect of in Anderson, namely an overly strong distinction between linguistic and political 'reality'. Anderson recognises that the two are *functionally* intertwined, but treats them as fundamentally different in their internal nature, language being a coherent given, and political identity a construct. Silverstein recognises that their internal natures are more alike than Anderson assumes, but he denies that they are functionally intertwined except in the relatively trivial sense that the one reflects the other.

Here I believe Anderson has it right. Silverstein's mistake, to borrow his own terms from the first quote above, is to assume that what he calls 'we'-ness is a 'dialectically produced trope' rather than part of 'the dialectical workings of political processes' themselves. For this assumption demands a strict and transparent division between what is 'in language' on the one hand and what is 'political' on the other. In the absence of such a division – and in my view that division could only be illusory – Silverstein's relegation of 'we'-ness to the category of mere 'trope', on which this part of his critique of Anderson depends, is nothing more than an axiomatic declaration, and an unjustified one. This 'we'-ness, and the national identities and imagined communities founded upon it, are neither more nor less real than 'the dialectical workings of political processes' or 'political economic conflict', because they are in fact an inseparable part of them.

Comments by Silverstein elsewhere in the paper lead me to suspect that he might wish to invoke here a principled difference between 'standard' languages that involve political construction in the way I have suggested, and 'non-standard' languages or dialects, which have not been politically constituted in the same way. Although I myself accepted the existence of this difference when setting out to problematise it in Joseph (1987), I have ultimately ceased to be convinced that any language or dialect, standard or non-standard, can be constituted by anything other than a form of the same political processes (see Joseph, 2000b). But even if one accepts the distinction, the 'we'-ness of which Anderson and Silverstein write is clearly and unambiguously a matter of political construction. The fact that it overlaps with a first-person plural pronoun shared by non-standard dialects does not somehow remove it from the political sphere, either by making it 'natural' or by making it 'metaphorical'. It does, as Hobsbawm and Silverstein correctly recognise, contribute to an *essentialising* of national identity. As I argued in Chapter 4, that essentialism is an important fact that we need to explain, hopefully without letting it seep into our explanation. In so far as Anderson's treatment of language in a quasi-essentialist vein opens the way for such seepage, Silverstein has made a useful contribution to stopping it.

Studies of the construction of particular national-linguistic identities

My earlier work on language standardisation (Joseph, 1987) surveys the literature on national languages as it stood at that time. In much of that literature, the concept of 'national identity' is implicitly present, but since then, many studies have appeared in which that concept has been pushed into the foreground. This section surveys a wide global range of such studies, with an emphasis on those that have appeared in the last decade.

Europe

In recent years the thrust of scholarly attention in the European context has been toward the 'emerging' national languages – often called 'minority' languages – of peoples who live within some more inclusive state. In the 1990s, following the break-up of the USSR and Warsaw Pact and the consequent re-emergence of nation-states that had not existed as such since 1939 or even 1919, the momentum seemed to be strongly in the direction of the dissolution of larger polities in favour of a Europe of small nation-states united by the European Union. Certainly the policies of the European Commission were wholly geared toward this end, but they steadily came into conflict with the European Parliament and the governments of the individual states, in some of which the erosion of national autonomy had become a serious election issue. Attempts at a *vue d'ensemble* of the linguistic situation can be found in Baggioni (1997), Barbour (1996), Bellier (2002), Tony Crowley (1996b), Haarman (1995), Hoffman (1996), Parry et al. (1994), Tabouret-Keller (1999) and most synthetically in Wright (2000, 2004). Escalle & Melka (2001) bring together historical studies of the construction of a range of European national linguistic identities.

In the United Kingdom, the revival of the Scottish Parliament and the creation of the Welsh Assembly, with a wide range of domestic policy matters devolved to each, have proved surprisingly effective in satisfying the nationalist aspirations of a core plurality of the electorate. Language policy in Northern Ireland, the Republic of Ireland and Scotland is surveyed in 23 papers compiled in Kirk & Ó Baoill (2001), as well as by Williams (1999). Görlach (1997) and Turville-Petre (1996) look back over the role linguistic identity has played in the development of English, while the papers in Frantzen & Niles (1997) focus more specifically on 'Anglo-Saxonism'. The work of Tony Crowley (1996a) has been centred on the contrasting ideologies of British and Irish English, especially in the nineteenth century, while Maley (1994) has extended the perspective back to Spenser. Among the papers in Tristram (1997) looking at 'Celtic Englishes', that by Payton considers the highly interesting case of Cornish, a language that reputedly died out in the eighteenth century but is looking increasingly alive and well, in conjunction with the identity to which it corresponds. I myself have examined the status of Scottish linguistic identity in Joseph (2000b), while Hardie (1996) has focused specifically on Lowlands Scots.

On the western end of the continent, much attention has gone to Catalan as the best success story of a national language re-emerging after deliberate suppression within Franco's Spain (see e.g. Siebenmann, 1992). Archilés & Martí (2001) look at the situation in neighbouring Valencia, while Conversi (1997) contrasts Basque, Catalan and Spanish national ideologies, with much attention given to the role of language. Alvarez-Caccamo (1993) examines the current state of Galician national linguistic identity, a case made especially interesting by the fact that Galician, although subsumed politically within Spain, is much closer linguistically to the language of a neighbouring country, Portugal, and by the fact that Galician national identity is constructed partly on a memory (perhaps mythical) of Celtic origins (see below, Chapter 8, pp. 214–15). Iglesias Álvarez (2000) studies the consequences of internal migration for Galician sociolinguistic identity, and Millán-Varela (2000) looks at Galician identity from the perspective of translation.

For France, an important study of national linguistic identity comparing it with the case of Sweden can be found in Oakes (2001), and an overview of the contemporary situation in Safran (1999). Among minority languages in France, the genuinely Celtic linguistic identity of Breton has received the most attention, for example in Jones (1998), Kuter (1992, 1994) and Press (1994), while Provençal identity has been examined by Blanchet (1995), and the Corsican situation by Jaffe (1999) and Jensen (1999). For Belgium, Francard (1998) studies the Francophone communities of Wallonia and Brussels, while Berré (2001) looks back at the interaction between national identity and pedagogy in the teaching of French in late nineteenth-century Flanders.

For Italy, Strassoldo (1996) has assessed the status of Friulan, while Jahn (1998) examines the situation in Istria. Bivona (2001) discusses the construction of Italian national identity in school textbooks. The role of Italian language identity on Malta is studied by Covino (1999), and Friggieri (1998) investigates the overall situation of linguistic identity on Malta.

Within the Germanic language family, an overview of Scandinavian linguistic identities is given by Huss & Lindgren (1999). The Faroe Islands have been the subject of a study by Nauerby (1996), and Icelandic linguistic identity has recently been examined by Jónsson (2000) and Kristinsson (2001). Bucken-Knapp (2003) studies the role of language in Norwegian identity politics. Stevenson (1993) and the papers in Gardt (2000) focus on German language and national identity construction in a range of countries. Newton (1996) looks at the role of Letzgeburgisch in the national identity of Luxemburg, and Menke (1996) at Dutch in northern Germany. Cillia (1997), Stubkjaer (1997) and Wiesinger (2000) focus on Austria, as do, from a discourse perspective, Wodak et al. (1999). Nation and language in Switzerland is the subject of Grossenbacher-Schmid (1998) and Koller (2000).

At the Germanic–Slavic frontier, Blanke (1999) considers the national identity of 'Polish-speaking Germans' in the Masuria region, Hannan (1996) looks at Teschen Silesia, Rohfleisch (2000) at Poland and upper Silesia. Kamusella (2001) examines the situation of linguistic identity in Central Europe generally.

The papers collected in Sériot (1996) and Lord & Strietska-Ilina (2001) assess the situation in the former Eastern bloc generally. Gorham (2000) studies identity and language debates in the USSR and Russia from 1985 to 1999. Kreindler (1997) investigates the effects on identity of multilingualism in the successor states of the USSR, while Laitin (1998) looks at the formation of linguistic identities among Russian speakers in the post-Soviet diaspora, and Dollerup (1995) more specifically at Uzbekistan. Holman (1995) focuses on post-Soviet Estonia, and Spires (1999) examines the symbolic role of the cult of antiquity in Lithuanian linguistic nationalism. Sayer (1996) is a historical survey of national linguistic identity as manifested in one city, Prague, from the late eighteenth century to the end of the First World War. Stefanink (1994) studies the role played by linguists in establishing Romanian national identity in the mid-nineteenth century.

In the Balkans, Levinger (1998) looks at Bosnia-Hercegovina, Belaj (2000) at Croatia, and Garde (1996) at both of these plus Serbia. Jahn (1999) examines the linguistic identity situation in the upper Adriatic. Friedman (1999) studies the case of Macedonia in the context of the dissolution of Yugoslavia, while Nihtinen (1999) interestingly compares 'Macedonian' linguistic identity with that of Scots. The interrelationship of Bulgarian and Romanian identity is studied by Steinke (2000). Samara (1996) examines the situation in Albania, and Frangoudaki (1997) that in Greece. Gutschmidt & Hopf (1999) attempt an overview of the Balkan situation.

Asia

National linguistic identities in continents other than Europe are often complicated by the ongoing presence of former colonial European languages in prestigious functions. This is not to deny that 'internal colonialism' exists in Europe, or indeed within Asia, with Chinese and Japanese, for example, standing in the way of the development of other potential national languages. But English in particular has been largely unavoidable as a factor in South Asian and East Asian linguistic nationalisms, as French has been in Indochina, and Arabic through the whole great swathe of South-East Asia where Islam is dominant.

Starting on the western end of the continent, in the Arab world, the work of Suleiman (1994b, 1996, 2003) has led the way in understanding linguistic nationalism (and pan-Arabism) in linguistic terms. For Lebanon, I have added my own contributions in Ghaleb & Joseph (2000) and Joseph (forthcoming c), as well as in Chapter 8 of the present book, to a literature that includes Dagher (1994), Der-Karabetian & Proudian-Der-Karabetian (1984) and Gordon (1985). Cyprus is the focus of Sciriha (1995). The symbolic value placed on the Central Asian provenance of the Turkish language in the formation of Turkish national identity is probed by Alici (1996), while Berger (1998) compares Turkey with Israel in their development of a national language ideology. Ben-Rafael (1994) is a study of Hebrew linguistic identity in Israel as it has developed in the presence of a wide range of immigrant tongues, as well as Palestinian Arabic.

For South Asia, Guneratne (1998) has studied Tharu identity in Nepal. Pandian (1997) focuses on Dravidian identity among Tamils, Ramaswamy (1997) on attempts both to Indianise and Dravidianise Tamil as part of identity-based nationalism projects. Van Bijlert (1996) examines the role of Sanskrit in constructing Hindu national identity in nineteenth-century Bengal. Kachru (1996) discusses the construction of South Asian identity in English.

In East Asia, Rowley (1997) looks at linguistic identity in Meiji Japan, while Hong Kong is studied by Bolton & Kwok (1990), Bolton (2003b), Joseph (1996, 2000c) and the following chapter of the present book. The history of 'Chinese Englishes', focusing on Hong Kong, is the subject of Bolton (2003a). Mawkanuli (2001) examines Tuva linguistic identity within the People's Republic of China. Taiwan is the focus of Huang (2000) and Tse (2000).

In South-East Asia, Winichakul (1994) examines Thailand, Longmire (1992) Cambodia. Rastorfer (1994) looks at the role of Kayan identity in Myanmar. Keane (1997) studies linguistic identity in eastern Indonesia, while Errington (1998) examines the effects of language shift on linguistic identity in Javanese Indonesia, and Kuipers (1998) the effect of shifts in religious identity on the use of traditional ritual speech on the Indonesian island of Sumba. Omar (1998) considers 'image building' as part of Malay language policy in Malaysia, and Sercombe (1999) analyses the linguistic identity of the Iban communities on either side of the Malaysia–Brunei border on Borneo. Singaporean linguistic identity is studied by Chew (2000) and Hvitfeldt & Poedjosoedarmo (1998), while Omoniyi (1999), despite its title, focuses on the Malaysia–Singapore border.

Africa

The comments on the presence of former colonial languages made at the start of the section on Asia apply here as well. Blommaert's (1999a) study of state ideology and language in Tanzania is of great interest because of the role of Swahili in constructing both a national and a pan-African identity. Tanzania is also the focus of Ngonyani (1995). In a volume devoted to shifting African identities, Garuba (2001) examines language and identity in Nigeria, where the role of English has also been studied by Adekunle (1997), and that of Igbo by Van den Bersselaar (2000). Ehret (1997) considers the situation of Krio in Sierra Leone, which is also the locus for Breitborde's (1998) investigation of the construction of class and ethnic identities in local languages, ex-colonial languages and creoles in the urban West African context.

In the southern part of the continent, Alexander (2001) considers language politics in South Africa. Chennells (1998) studies the case of Zimbabwe, and Stroud (1999) looks at the post-colonial role of Portuguese in linguistic identity in Mozambique.

For the African countries which continue to be part of 'Francophonie', Woods (1995) examines the situation in the Congo, and McLaughlin (1995) looks at Haalpulaar identity in Senegal. Canut (1997) analyses the identity value of the names given to languages in Mali. Hylland Erisken (1990) studies the construction of linguistic identity on Mauritius. In North Africa, Redouane (1998) considers bilingualism and identity in Morocco, while Kaye & Zoubir (1990) examine the role of language and literature in constructing national identities in both Morocco and Algeria. Ennaji (1999), despite its title, is also focused almost completely on these two countries.

Americas

In North and South America, studies of linguistic identity have focused either on the tension between indigenous and (ex-)colonial languages (English, French, Spanish and Portuguese), on struggles between pairs of ex-colonial languages (particularly English and French in Canada) or between creoles and either indigenous or ex-colonial languages, and on the minority language identities of other immigrant communities from the late nineteenth century to the present. For Mexico, Cifuentes (1994) offers a historical outlook, while King (1994) takes a more contemporary anthropological approach that concentrates on the role of literacy. Erfurt (1997) studies linguistic identity in the Francophone diaspora of Canada, while Carey (1997) conducts a still broader review of bilingualism, multiculturalism and identity in Canada. Scacchi (1999) examines the co-development of American dialects and national identity in (what would be) the United States from 1760 to 1831. Lo Bianco (1999) considers the identity ramifications of contemporary attempts to have English declared the official language of the United States.

For Central America and the Caribbean, linguistic and social identity in Barbados is examined by Blake (1996), in Belize by Bonner (2001), in Cuba by Ashley (2002), in the Dominican Republic by Toribio (2000), in Puerto Rico by Morris (1996), Centeno Añeses (1999) and Clampitt-Dunlap (2000). Le Page & Tabouret-Keller (1985), a study already discussed in Chapter 4 for its theoretical import, takes up a number of Caribbean Creole situations.

Linguistic identity construction in South America as a whole is the subject of Barros et al. (1996). The link between ethnic and sociolinguistic identity in Guyana has been studied by Haynes (1997). Paraguay is the focus of Solé (1996), while Orlandi & Guimaraes (1998) analyse the role of grammars in the creation of Brazilian linguistic identity.

Australasia and Oceania

A brief overview of this part of the world can be found in Lotherington (1999). Among national governments worldwide, Australia has been in the forefront in developing and executing a vigorous policy for constructing a multilingual and multicultural identity. An overview of issues there can be found in Clyne (1997), while Turner (1997) focuses exclusively on the development of 'Australian English' as a locus of identity, and Delbridge (2001) more precisely still on the role of lexicography. Linguistic identity in New Zealand has been the subject of two studies by Bell (1997, 1999). Duranti (1994) examines the politics of language and identity on Western Samoa, and Terry Crowley (2000) that on Vanuatu.

6
Case Study 1: the New Quasi-Nation of Hong Kong

This chapter is devoted to an in-depth look at a linguistic situation in which distinctive identities are in the relatively early stages of emerging. There is a good chance that, in the long run, they will prove not to have emerged at all, given that potent social, cultural and (supra-) national forces are ranged against any such emergence. Yet comparable forces have been in play in the history of every national linguistic identity, successful or unsuccessful. For that reason, Hong Kong provides a valuable insight into how the process of linguistic identity construction is played out.

Historical background

Hong Kong was a British colony from 1841 until 1997, at which time it became a semi-autonomous Special Administrative Region (SAR) of the People's Republic of China (PRC). By terms of the treaty negotiated between the UK and the PRC in 1984, Hong Kong is to retain SAR status until 2047, when it will be fully incorporated into the PRC. Both Chinese and English continue to be co-official languages in Hong Kong, with official documents published in both languages. Prior to 1 July 1997 the English document was the 'controlling' version, the one which prevailed in the case of any discrepancy between it and the Chinese version. Since 1 July 1997, the Chinese document is the controlling version.

What makes the case of Hong Kong linguistically intricate has partly to do with the use of English, but at least as much with what is covered by the word 'Chinese'. Although there is a relatively unified *written*

Chinese that literate people throughout the Chinese-speaking world share,[1] the spoken 'dialects' differ so much from one another that linguists classify them as separate languages. There is little mutual comprehensibility between Putonghua, the 'official' spoken language based upon the northern dialect called Mandarin, and southern dialects such as Hakka, Hokkien, or the dialect that is mother tongue to over 90 per cent of Hong Kong residents, Cantonese. The linguistic distance between Putonghua and Cantonese has been compared to that between English and Swedish.

When it became a British colony, Hong Kong Island (which was the whole of the original colony) had only a small population of fisher people. The colony developed trading relations with wealthy south Chinese merchant families, and this led to the growth of a local population brought in from neighbouring Canton province to work in trade-related industries. The population spilled over to the mainland area of Kowloon, just across the strait from the island, and this area was ceded by treaty to Britain in 1860 following another conflict with China. Then, in 1898, the 'New Territories', a large rural expanse extending up to the mountains, was leased by the colony for 99 years. It was the forthcoming expiry of this lease in 1997 that led Britain in 1984 to decide that the colony would not be viable without the New Territories, and that it should be returned to Chinese sovereignty.

The population growth was reasonably steady until 1949, when the Kuomintang government of General Chiang Kai-Shek was overthrown by the Communists led by Mao Zedong, and forced to retreat to Taiwan.[2] From that point on, great masses of people from China began seeking refuge in Hong Kong, until the British government imposed limits on immigation. The Chinese government supported such limits, and has strengthened them since the return of Hong Kong to Chinese sovereignty.

The last British governor of Hong Kong, Christopher Patten, attempted to introduce democratic institutions into the colony from 1992 onward, but these attempts met with a mixture of hostility and indifference from Beijing, which considers its own style of oligarchic rule to be 'democratic' and has tried, with partial success, to impose it upon the Hong Kong SAR. However, the SAR administration was forced as early as 1998 to bend its policies in the face of popular protests, one of the first and most powerful of which was over language policy. The government's proposal to shift from English to Cantonese as the language of instruction in government-run schools met with vehement opposition from parents, who contended that their children would be put at a disadvantage in their future careers by not being taught in English from the elementary level onwards. They took to the streets in protest, until the government retreated to a compromise position. As a result, it is likely that English will play a significant role in Hong Kong culture and society for many decades at least.

The political situation in Hong Kong has remained extremely tense. In the summer of 2003 popular demonstrations forced the SAR administration to withdraw 'security' measures Beijing was trying to impose, which would have significantly restricted civil liberties. Beijing seems not to have anticipated that the ethnically Chinese population of Hong Kong, once free of British influence, would be prepared to stand up against the same sort of iron-handed rule it exerts on the mainland. The fact that they are provides ample evidence that Hong Kong culture is distinctive from mainland Chinese culture in more than superficial ways.

Hong Kong people do not see themselves as 'a people', but as part of the Chinese people, and, in certain contexts (discussed in a later section) as part of the southern Chinese people. This corresponds with the linguistic situation: Hong Kong people consider their 'language' to be Chinese, of which their spoken Cantonese is a 'dialect'. The social hierarchy of Hong Kong is however defined in significant part by bilingualism with English. For the senior managerial generation, brought up in the 1950s and 1960s, fluent, quasi-RP-accented English is the hallmark of their being products of the 'glory days' of colonial education, helping to define them as the upper echelon of Hong Kong society. For the younger generations, native-like proficiency belongs almost exclusively to those sent overseas for their education. Many of these have come back to Hong Kong, while others have remained overseas, but in any case the returnees are greatly outnumbered by those who stayed in Hong Kong for their university education. For this much larger group, the hallmark of their identity is their ability to code-switch, relentlessly and seamlessly, between Chinese and English (see Gibbons, 1979).

The 'myth' of declining English

The public discourse about English in Hong Kong has been studied by Joseph (1996) and Lin (1997). Starting around the late 1970s it progressively became centred upon the notion of a deterioration in English standards, with the predominant metaphor that of 'decline' or 'falling'. Here is just one of many examples cited by Lin, this one from the front page of the leading Hong Kong economic publication:

> The falling standard of English in Hong Kong is starting to pinch corporate pocketbooks.
>
> As the territory's burgeoning service businesses boost demand for English speakers, there are signs that the English proficiency of university and secondary-school graduates entering the work force is dropping, forcing local companies to fork out large sums on remedial language training. [...] (Lotte Chow, 'Drop in English Standard Hurts Hong Kong Business', *Asian Wall Street Journal Weekly*, 12 June 1995, p. 1, cited by Lin, 1997, p. 428)

Commissions were set up to study this problem, generously funded bodies established to address it, and dozens of linguists hired from outside to counteract it. Some of the linguists have echoed the perception of a decline in English standards, particularly when participating in a public forum, where to do otherwise would be perceived (rightly or wrongly) as being out of touch with reality and abrogating professional responsibility. However, in professional discourse, it is rare for linguists to speak in terms of declining English standards. Instead, the view has tended to be that the supposed linguistic deterioration is the product of a false, or at least skewed, perception.

The notion of linguistic decline depends upon a concept of 'good' and 'bad' in language which linguistics has rejected as 'prescriptive' since the nineteenth century.[3] Following the views of Bourdieu and Billig discussed in the preceding chapter, we can see this rejection as merely superficial, with the activity and discourse of 'descriptive' linguistics being ultimately inseparable from that of 'prescriptivism'. Nevertheless, the distinction is crucial to the ideology under which most linguists operate. To say that a language situation is deteriorating carries implications about language quality that linguists are trained early on not to entertain. Further complicating the case of Hong Kong, the 'good' situation of the past is one in which university students were (or are imagined to have been) solidly bilingual and biliterate in Chinese and English, the colonial language. Western linguists sometimes appear to be suggesting that a change from colonial-plus-native-language bilingualism to native-language monolingualism is desirable, or on the contrary that it is undesirable. Either way, the argument presents serious problems, quite apart from the fact that the data (some of which are given below) do not support the belief that Hong Kong is moving toward monolingualism. The positive value judgement implies that monolingualism and monoliteracy are preferable to multilingualism and multiliteracy, a view that linguists are constitutionally disposed to reject, and that Hong Kong people too are generally disinclined to accept. The negative judgement could be taken to mean that English is better than Chinese, a proposition any linguist would reject immediately as nonsense if applied to the structure or 'inner logic' of the language (since we have no independent criteria by which to measure the quality of languages, even relative to one another), and would likely steer clear of even if 'better' simply has the sense of 'more useful' (since 'usefulness' has many more aspects than are immediately apparent).

For these same reasons it has seemed to many linguists that the idea of a decline in standards of English in Hong Kong is logically untenable. But more than that, it is directly contradicted by empirical research. Table 6.1, cited from a Hong Kong language survey project by Bacon-Shone & Bolton (1998), shows the number of English speakers in Hong Kong *increasing by 50 per cent* between 1983 and 1993. Bacon-Shone & Bolton have found a steadily accelerating rise from the 1930s to the present in both the proportion and the sheer numbers of Hong Kong people proficient in English, certainly giving the lie to any statement to the effect that 'Hong Kong is a monolingual (Cantonese-speaking) and ethnically homogeneous (ninety-eight per cent Chinese) society' (So, 1987, p. 249), or even this slightly tempered version: 'Hong Kong is essentially a monolingual Cantonese-speaking society where English is used in only a restricted number of domains' (So, 1992, p. 79).[4]

Table 6.1 1993 survey of languages spoken and understood by whole population of Hong Kong (%)

	Understand	*Speak*	*(Speak: 1983 survey)*
Cantonese	91.5	91.9	98.5
English	68.6	65.8	43.3
Putonghua (Mandarin)	61.9	55.6	31.9
Chinese	7.3	6.6	(not in survey)
Hakka	7.4	6.0	7.5
Chiu Chau	7.0	5.2	9.3
Fukien	4.2	4.1	4.2
Sze Yap	3.2	3.3	6.3
Shanghainese	3.7	2.7	4.1
Cantonese dialects	3.5	2.5	4.7
Other Chinese dialects	1.5	1.5	(not in survey)
Other European languages	1.9	1.8	(not in survey)
Others	0.4	0.3	3.6

Adapted from Bacon-Shone & Bolton (1998, pp. 68, 74).

Table 6.2 Responses to the question 'How well do you know English?' (%)

	1983	*1993*
'Quite well' / 'Well' / 'Very well':	5.1	33.7
'Not at all' / 'Only a few sentences' / 'A little':	92.8	66.3

Adapted from Bacon-Shone & Bolton (1998, p. 76).

Bacon-Shone & Bolton's study also shows a marked increase between 1983 and 1993 in the proportion of people claiming to know English with considerable proficiency (Table 6.2). Among the public at large, then, one finds a substantial shift of perception of how well English is spoken in Hong Kong, in the opposite direction to that maintained by the discourse of decline. In order to understand what is going on, it is useful to consider how the perceptual shift came about historically.

Until 1995 the territory had two universities, the University of Hong Kong, founded in 1911, and the Chinese University of Hong Kong, founded in 1963. Between 1994 and 1997, five colleges/polytechnics/institutes were upgraded to university status and one wholly new university created. The number of university student places tripled in less than three years. At the same time, the number of school-leavers going abroad for university education, mainly to the UK and North America, had been on a sharp upward curve in tandem with the territory's growing affluence since the late 1980s. Families who can afford to do so send their children overseas, which means that the higher-ranking local universities (the older ones, particularly the University of Hong Kong) get the cream of the poorer families. Twenty or 30 years ago this was not so. In those days the well-off went to the then very British University of Hong Kong, while middle-class students might get a place in the Chinese University if they were lucky. But as recently as the early 1970s, only 2 per cent of secondary-school graduates in Hong Kong went on to university. By 1997 the figure was 20 per cent.

In 1972, the secondary-school graduates in the top 3–18 per cent ranking of their class mainly took up jobs as clerks and secretaries, in which they dealt extensively with the public. Management jobs were not immediately open to them; the executive sector, like the economy, was much smaller and dominated by expatriates. When one visited a government or business office downtown, the receptionist or the clerk behind the window may well have been from the top 5 per cent of their graduating class, highly educated and with excellent English. By today, with more than 20 per cent of graduates going to university and from there to management jobs on an executive ladder, the receptionist or clerk at the window downtown will not even have come from the top quarter of their graduating class. In that sense, there has been a decline in standards, but it has come about as part of a great increase in educational opportunity – a very good thing even in the eyes of those who complain about poor English.

These changes have made Hong Kong in many ways like the Victorian Britain described by Hobsbawm, with a large 'exam-passing' class moving via education from being hourly wage-earners or small shopkeepers into the lower ranks of the middle class. Their use of language (particularly English) is closely bound up with the urban institutional structures (schools, universities, testing agencies, employment offices) responsible for hierarchising them. In every act of speaking or writing, through the particular forms of Chinese and English they speak – often intermittently within a single sentence – they enact their identities as Hong Kong Chinese who have reached the top of the educational ladder. To speak Standard British or American English would not be desirable, as it would mark them as outsiders; to speak no English would be even less desirable, marking them as uncosmopolitan, uneducated, undesirable as marriage partners.

When people talk about a decline in English standards in Hong Kong, they are reacting to the most readily perceptible aspect of a major social change. This point was already made by Lord (1987):

> In Hong Kong, over the past two decades, English has changed from being a purely colonial language whose use was largely restricted to government circles, the law, high-level business, and a few other sectors, to becoming an indispensable language of wider communication, for a growingly large range of people, all the way down from top brass to clerks, from taipans to secretaries...Not unnaturally, it has *seemed* to many that standards of English are falling. (Lord, 1987, p. 11; italics in the original)

By italicising the word 'seemed', Lord suggests, as many other linguists have done, that the decline is mythical. This is not entirely wrong. It is not as though some entity called the English language exists in Hong Kong and used to be better but now is worse. Whatever we mean when we talk about 'English' – whether we have in mind a set of words and rules existing independently from speakers, a form of knowledge in the minds or brains of speakers, or a way of behaving in communicative discourse – it is clear that what has happened in Hong Kong is that *more* people have obtained access to English, not fewer. As is typical when a privilege of the few becomes open to the hoi polloi, it is no longer perceived as having the same quality as before.

From this point of view the 'myth' of declining English in Hong Kong is a type of linguistic snobbery. That helps explain one aspect of my own experience as Professor of English at the University of Hong Kong in the mid-1990s – the fact that, without exception, the people who complained to me in vociferous and emotional terms about the decline of English in Hong Kong were ethnic Chinese. Westerners sometimes mentioned it, but with a resigned shrug. Ethnic Chinese Hong Kong people who themselves are highly proficient in English continue to get very worked up, insisting that this is an urgent issue, a crisis situation that must be got under control. Then they inevitably add that not only is the university students' English terrible, but their Chinese is just as bad – a complex comment given the Chinese language situation as described earlier, but mainly reflecting anxiety over 'code-mixing', the use of English words within ostensibly Cantonese conversation (see p. 134 above on the identity value of such code-mixing). Actually I do not think that they say these things entirely out of snobbery, and shall elaborate further on what else I believe is behind it. But through such discourse, they establish the value of the kind of English which they and other university graduates of their generation possess, and which is increasingly rare among today's students.

The first thing they would deny is that they speak something that ought to be identified as 'Hong Kong English'. With few exceptions, it is linguists who talk about this language. Its speakers scoff at the notion that there is anything other than 'good English' (represented by the overseas standard) and the 'bad English' of their compatriots. In this respect, Hong Kong English is in exactly the same position as every modern Romance language was in the early stages of its emergence vis-à-vis either Latin or some other Romance language (with further, Slavic complications in the case of Romanian).

It is almost certainly the case that the perception of a decline in English standards is tied in part to the emergence of a syntactically distinctive Hong Kong English with clear interlanguage features. Recognition of a new 'language' depends on three sets of factors: linguistic form, function and status (see Joseph, 1987). The following sections present samples of Hong Kong English, then consider it in the light of these three criteria, beginning with form.

Samples of Hong Kong English

In order to give readers at least an initial sense of what Hong Kong English is like, I offer three texts, each in a different genre. The first is drawn from *Hong Kong Voice of Democracy* (3 September 2003). It is a purely written text, only semi-formal in nature, inviting readers to a group hike the following weekend. I have highlighted features which do not follow the British or American standard, differentiating among them as follows. Those features which are, in my view, idiosyncratic to the text at hand are in ***boldface italic***. Those features which are more generally shared by speakers and writers of Hong Kong English, and are likely to be part of the distinctive form of that language if and when it emerges, are in **boldface roman**:

> Dear Members / Friends of 7.1 People Pile
> ***The below*** plse have a look **of** the details of the hiking event held this Sunday.
>
> Democracy heading to Lion Hill
>
> Time: 7th September 2003 (Sunday)
> Gathering time: 1:30pm
> Gathering place: Hang Seng Bank of Wong Tai Sin MTR station (group of bright orange polo **shirt** as identification)
> Transport: NO.18 Mini-bus
> Route: Shatin Pass Estate → Shatin Pass → Unicon Ridge → Lion Rock → pavilion → Amah Rock → Hung Mui Kuk
> ***Characteristics***: To observe the development of Kowloon and Shatin and have a close look **to** Amah Rock
>
> Distance: around 7.5 km
> Time: around 2.5–3 hours
> Difficulty: level 2
> Facility: None
> Time of departure: 5:30pm
> Departed place: barbecue
> Transport: There are buses available in Hung Mui Kuk going to Kowloon or Shatin.
> **For alternative**, we can walk 20 minutes to Tai Wei KCR station
>
> *Remarks:
> 1) Bring enough food & water (700–1000 ml). **Prepare enough** transportation fees

2) **Under the sun**, should **prepare** umbrella, sun-block products, sweat-shirts and towels

Among the 'regular' features of Hong Kong English in this text we can note the following:

- flattening of count noun vs mass noun distinction, reflected in use of singular for Standard English plural and in different distribution of definite and indefinite articles (e.g. *group of [. . .] shirt, for alternative*).
- highly distinctive distribution of prepositions
- semantic differences in individual lexical items (e.g. *prepare* meaning 'have available, bring')

The second text, also drawn from the *Hong Kong Voice of Democracy* (1 June 1998), consists of excerpts from the transcript of an interview with Szeto Wah, a prominent pro-democracy politician and Chairperson of the Hong Kong Alliance in Support of Patriotic Democratic Movement of China:

Q The Alliance has raised a lot of money from the citizens through its activities all these years. What is the financial picture now? What if **all the money are** spent? Will the Alliance accept foreign sponsorship?

A As of April, we still have three million Hong Kong dollars in the bank. We have been trying our best to cut all unnecessary expenses. I think this year we'll have no problem. And every year, especially during the commemoration activities, we receive a lot of donations from the citizens. However, as Hong Kong **is going through** an economic down turn **recently**, we shall have to see. If we can raise a million and a half this year at the commemoration activities, it will be okay. Last year **we have raised** more than two million Hong Kong dollars. Money is a problem, but not the major one. We will adjust to work with what we have. We will never seek foreign sponsorship. All our past resources **are** based on the money donated to us directly **from** the citizens.

[. . .]

Q Last May, a debate **has been** successfully motioned in the Legco to call **for** Beijing for rectification of the June 4th massacre. Of course the act itself was symbolic rather than substantial. That Legislature has been disbanded. But now, many of you have been re-elected back to the council; do you think another similar motion can trigger the attention of both the public and **the authority**, thus **exercising** media pressure?

A The LegCo system of motioning is quite different now. Some are newly elected legislators. The voting set-up of the council will not permit that kind of motion to take place. Without the written permission of the Chief Executive, such a motion will never arrive at the discussion agenda. The possibility of such an action is quite bleak. We can of course repeat the application to motion in order to attract media coverage, but it will never lead to the kind of debate and influence ***as before***. Even **for** the last debate, it was just a record for the expression of opinions from the LegCo members. It **is** never anything with judicial authority.

In addition to the features noted in the first text, we find here several instances of another characteristic of Hong Kong English, namely its different distribution of verb tenses from Standard English (e.g. *is going through [...] recently, last year we have raised*). Although many 'world Englishes' exhibit such differences from the Standard, there does appear to be some distinctiveness among them that may be traceable to the mother tongue 'substratum'. For instance, native speakers of Germanic languages have a strong tendency to overuse the progressive forms from the point of view of Standard English (e.g. *Where are you coming from*? vs Standard *Where do you come from*?), but this is not a tendency one finds in Hong Kong English.

The final text samples come from papers written by two students of mine for the course Language in Society at the University of Hong Kong in autumn 1996. I include them here not only as samples of emerging Hong Kong English as produced by top-level university students in the second half of the 1990s, but also in order to allow the voices of Hong Kong English speakers themselves to say what they think about the language situation:

Multilingualism **becomes** more common and popular **among** the countries [...]. According to Ramirez, multilingualism appears to be a characteristic of most **human**. There are already many countries **recognize** two or more languages **are** their official languages. As the technology **is** largely improved in recent decades [...] multilingualism is ***need*** for a country to develop trade/communication with other countries [...]. **Besides, people** with ***multi-linguistic*** people **are** able to communicate with other countries, **that** serve global needs and shorten the gap between nations.

In Hong Kong, people are exposed to written Chinese **in the** most of the time as it is the mother language for over 95% of the population. Problems of written Mandarin/Cantonese are **concerned**. Students in Hong Kong are taught **of** written Mandarin and it is commonly used. However, written Cantonese can represent spoken Cantonese syllable by syllable, and all people in Hong Kong can fully understand [...]. Hong Kong has a smaller percentage who cannot read Chinese **while comparing** with Singapore. For English, Hong Kong has a lower standard **comparing** with Singapore as **it** can be expected as **language** mainly used in Singapore is English (to communicate with other races) while Chinese is used in Hong Kong.

The quality of teacher directly **affect** the performance of the students. In Hong Kong, most teachers [...] have the problem of ***the using*** of English themselves. **Then** some teachers [...] will teach in half English and half Chinese **that** make students neither good at English nor Chinese [...]. When the children are in **the** primary, they use their Chinese language logic to study English. This is the reason that primary students ***make*** Chinese style English like 'Do you think you can pass me the salt?' instead of 'Can you pass me the salt?' [...].

Many parents in Hong Kong have **strong desire** to have their children learning in English. It is because ***having*** higher English can have better job opportunities [...].

Although most of the features have already been discussed following their appearance in one of the earlier samples, the fifth sentence of the first extract above ('Besides, people with multi-linguistic people are able to communicate with other countries, that serve global needs and shorten the gap between nations') contains three noteworthy features:

- The use of *Besides* as a sentence opener, corresponding to Standard English *Furthermore* (similarly with *Then* in the second extract).
- The first occurrence of *people* would in Standard English be *a people* ('people with multi-linguistic people' = a people with a multilingual population), and would be followed by a singular rather than a plural verb, so both features of the count–mass flattening are present here.

- The use of *that* as a pronoun of broad reference – the Standard English equivalent here would be something like 'an ability which' or 'a situation which'.

Of all these features, the most characteristic – to the point of having long been a locus for caricature of Chinese speakers of English – are undoubtedly those related to the flattening out of the count–mass distinction in the noun phrase. They will be the focus of attention in the next section.[5]

The formal distinctiveness of Hong Kong English

As Kloss (1978) noted, the first requirement for a new language to be recognised is simply that it differ in form from the already recognised variety. Kloss used the term *Abstand* to designate the required linguistic distance. Of course, difference always exists – no form of language, no matter how narrowly defined, is free of variation, and at the level of 'a language' there is bound to be variation that will cause a certain amount of disruption in communication among speakers. As we have seen, there is no preset threshold of difference that a distinct 'language' must reach. If the desire for a distinct language to be recognised is strong enough, the most minor differences will be invested with the ideological value needed to fill the bill.

One marker of Hong Kong English that regularly occurs in discourse samples is the lack of the Standard English distinction between count noun phrase and mass noun phrase. In this respect the simple noun phrase (NP) in Hong Kong English has the structure of its equivalent in Chinese, as shown in Figure 6.1, where CNP stands for 'common noun phrase', CL for 'classifier', CL-P for 'classifier phrase', and X for 'to be determined'. Hong Kong English speakers, including master's students I have taught who are English teachers and some of the best local

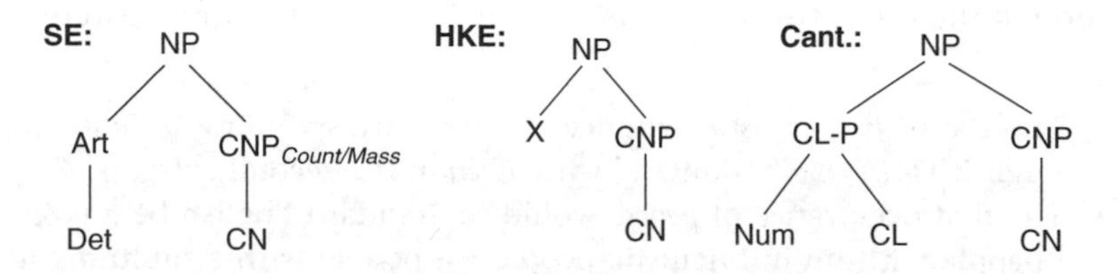

Figure 6.1 Structure of simple NP in Standard English (SE), Hong Kong English (HKE) and Cantonese (Cant.)

university English graduates of the last two decades, have invariably been astonished to learn that *noodle* is a count noun rather than a mass noun in Standard English, and that one does not say **bowl of noodle* in parallel with *bowl of rice*. A current student of mine from Hong Kong reports having been strongly rebuked by a teacher for saying *bowl of noodles* in lieu of the 'correct' *bowl of noodle*. The nouns *faahn* 'rice' and *mihn* 'noodles' take the same nominal classifier in Cantonese, *wún* 'bowl'.[6]

SE:	**HKE**:	**Cant.**:
a. a bowl of rice	a. a bowl of rice	a. yāt wún faahn
a′. *a bowl of rices	a′. *a bowl of rices	(one bowl rice)
b. *a bowl of noodle	b. a bowl of noodle	b. yāt wún mihn
b′. a bowl of noodles	b′. *a bowl of noodles	(one bowl noodle)

In Chinese, every common noun selects a particular classifier, so that in Cantonese 'a book' is *yāt* ***bún*** *syù*, 'a university' is *yāt* ***gàan*** *daaih-hohk*, and so on. Chinese learners of English implicitly expect that if two nouns select the same classifier in Chinese, their English equivalents will show identical syntactic behaviour. Although with many, perhaps most, structural contrasts between the two languages, proficient Chinese learners of English do not bring a similar expectation to bear, *bowl of noodles* sounds just as strange to my highly proficient master's students as **bowl of rices* does to them or to me.

The syntactic structure of these noun phrases can be represented as in Figure 6.2, with Standard English and Cantonese on the left, and on the right, Hong Kong English represented as an interlanguage continuum.[7] The NP consists of an article, *a*, and a CNP, whose head is the common noun (CN) *bowl*. This CNP selects a phrase headed by the preposition *of* as its complement. The complement of that phrase is another CNP which will always be specified as count or mass. If it is a count CNP, then it will be further specified as singular or plural, whereas the mass CNP does not have this specification.

Looking now to (c), we find that the Cantonese equivalent of these two NPs is a single structure, consisting of a CL-P and a CNP. The CL-P consists of the number *yāt* and the head, the classifier (CL) *wún*. The CNP is headed by a noun for which there is no evidence to suggest that it is syntactically marked as count or mass. Chinese has no direct singular or plural marking of nouns or verbs. Demonstratives show interesting number phenomena, but here too there is no real evidence of a count–mass distinction in Cantonese. The other main difference between the English and Cantonese phrases is that in English *rice* and

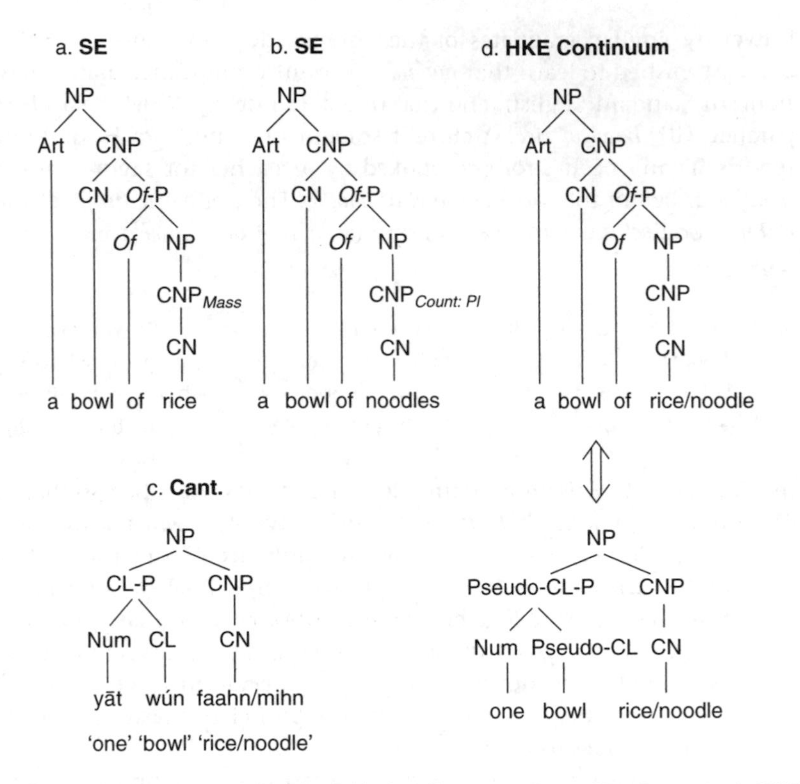

Figure 6.2 Structure of *bowl of rice/noodle*-type NP in SE, Cant. and HKE Continuum

noodles are not the head of the highest CNP, whereas in Cantonese *faahn* and *mihn* are. English structures like *a lot of rice* seem to show something closer to the Chinese structure, with *a lot of* behaving like a compound quantifier and *rice* like a head noun; but that is not actually crucial to the analysis at hand.

For Hong Kong English in (d), at the top end we have virtually the Standard English structure, at the bottom virtually the Chinese one. This is not to say that Hong Kong English lacks a singular–plural distinction; on the contrary, that distinction exists and functions as a marker of *where individual speakers lie on the continuum of interlanguage variation*.

But in the Standard English noun phrase, singular–plural is a secondary distinction, applying only when count rather than mass has been selected. Even speakers at the top end of the Hong Kong English continuum have little or no sense of the count–mass noun distinction, even if they have a well-developed proficiency with singular and plural markers. Instead, as I have noted, there is a strong implicit sense for these speakers that nouns selecting the same classifier in Chinese should show the same syntactic behaviour in English. That is the main reason for my labelling *bowl* here as a pseudo-classifier. My suspicion is that the presence of what we might term a 'pseudo-classifier effect' even at the SE end of Hong Kong English is responsible for the non-standard subject–verb agreement one finds even in those highly proficient speakers.

It is more than 30 years since the notion of 'interlanguage' in applied linguistics established that second-language speakers do not simply make random errors. To be precise, they *do* make random errors, just as mother-tongue speakers do, but the great bulk of the features that set their interlanguage apart from the standard version of the target language are systematic in nature. Hong Kong English speakers make the same 'errors' (from the point of view of Standard English) in regularly recurring patterns, many of them traceable to the influence of Cantonese. Given this regularity of structure, it makes sense from a linguist's point of view to speak of Hong Kong English as an emerging 'language'. The second point is that the 'emergence of Hong Kong English' and the 'decline of English standards in Hong Kong' *are one and the same thing,* looked at from two different points of view. In some ways two opposite points of view, because 'emergence' implies that English is in the process of becoming a language of Hong Kong (using 'of' in the strong sense of 'belonging to'), whereas 'decline' implies that Hong Kong is losing English. There *is* in fact a sense in which Hong Kong is losing English, and it can be expressed precisely thus: the British or American or other foreign standard of correct spoken English has ceased to be the majority norm for Hong Kong. Likely more people than ever before speak 'correct' British English in Hong Kong, yet as a proportion of the Hong Kong English-speaking population, they have never been smaller.

This development was inevitable once universal education, all or largely in English, was instituted in the territory in the late 1970s. Given the massive numbers of students involved, there would have been no way to prevent the development from ensuing that is simultaneously the emergence of Hong Kong English and the decline in English standards. If it seems paradoxical that the spread of education should be connected with a decline in standards, that association is made routinely in the contexts of North American, British and Western European education. People there have come slowly and painfully to realise that, given inequalities in the home environments from which students come and the limitations on human and economic resources which societies can deploy toward education, choices have to be made between being bound to traditional academic standards and educating the masses. No one has yet shown how to achieve both, and rare indeed are the voices ready to call for abandoning the masses for the sake of the standards.

The status of Hong Kong English

In the context of English in Hong Kong, if history teaches us anything it is that the 'decline' in externally imposed standards *must* occur if English is to survive in post-colonial Hong Kong (see Harris, 1989). New 'internal' standards must replace them – and that is precisely what has been happening with the emergence of a distinctive form of English. If Hong Kong English shows regularly occurring patterns traceable to the influence of its speakers' mother tongue, it was by just such a process that the Romance languages came into being – an emergence that was at the same time a crumbling of the standards of Latin measured against the external criterion of Virgil and Cicero, and not a random crumbling, but one connected to the other languages spoken in the former Roman Empire. In the Middle Ages, the Romance dialects were already taking on their distinctive forms, but it was only over the course of many centuries that they came to be recognised as distinct 'languages' (see Wright, 1982). Particularly where writing was concerned, but also in prestigious spoken registers, there was good Latin, conforming to classical standards, and bad Latin, where those standards were giving way to the influences of the vernacular language. With the Renaissance and the spread of the modern idea of nationhood, the *status* of this 'bad Latin' changed into something and people began to think of it as something else, their language. In the case of France, by the eighteenth century it became an *idée fixe* that French was the most rational of all human languages, an opinion which continues even now to be widely held in French culture.

The status of Hong Kong English today is somewhat comparable to that of 'bad Latin' in the later Middle Ages, though there is a twist. The typical pattern in the recognition of a new language or form of a language is that a group of partisans within the native population begin asserting linguistic autonomy, and there ensues a struggle for international recognition. In the case of Hong Kong English, international recognition has come in the almost total absence of local assertion.

Hong Kong English is, for example, one of the forms of English under study in the massive International Corpus of English (ICE) project. The lack of any positive recognition of Hong Kong English in the local public discourse is perhaps not surprising, given that the emergence of other Englishes, including American, Australian, Canadian, Indian, New Zealand and Singapore English, as well as Quebec French, Venezuelan Spanish, Brazilian Portuguese and the like have always been post-colonial phenomena in the most literal sense (for fine studies of the post-colonial emergence of new Englishes in Singapore and Malaysia, see Platt & Weber, 1980; in Sri Lanka, Parakrama, 1995; and for an overview, Platt et al., 1984 and Brutt-Griffler, 2002). In some cases the emergence took a few years, in others entire decades, after the withdrawal of the colonial power. We do not find cases of local varieties of a language attaining official or social recognition as distinct 'languages' during the time of colonial rule. So it may be that the best we can expect is that Hong Kong English will be a future development. That is, although in terms of linguistic form it is well along the path of emergence, in terms of status we could not, projecting from historical evidence, reasonably expect it to attain recognition until well after 1997, other than from linguists focusing on its formal distinctiveness.

This is not to say that initial steps toward the creation of that status are not discernible. University students in Hong Kong are by and large oblivious to any sense that their English is 'bad', and this fact in itself constitutes strong evidence that Hong Kong English is at an early stage in the development of language status. These students have, after all, been studying English since the age of four or five, and if they have been accepted into university, they have likely been in the upper ranks of English users in their peer group. They are quite befuddled, sometimes even amused, to arrive at university and encounter expatriate and foreign-educated teachers telling them that the English they have been consistently praised for is deficient. One does not see them heading in panic to the English Centre to 'improve' their English, unless specifically ordered to do so. Again, these are signs that a 'local' standard is in operation, even if that standard has as yet no recognition or status within the local discourse about English.

If the emergence of a formally distinctive English in Hong Kong, also known as the decline in English standards, was inevitable once universal education was instituted in 1978, the eventual recognition of this 'new English', the accordance to it of the status of 'Hong Kong English' within the public discourse as well as within the specialised discourse of linguists, if and when it comes to pass, will appear in hindsight to have been inevitable once the end of British colonial rule in Hong Kong was decided upon in 1984. Again, history leads us to expect that Hong Kong English will not be publicly recognised until well after 1997, and that its attainment of public status will be closely connected with its use in particular linguistic *functions*, to be discussed in the next section. This is the real wild card, because the future distribution of languages in official and non-official functions in the Hong Kong SAR depends crucially on still developing policies of the Beijing and Hong Kong governments, and on the development of a Hong Kong identity, all of which are far from predictable.

The functions of Hong Kong English

While the attainment of language status depends upon the use of a language in certain functional spheres – what Kloss (1978), focusing on literary functions, calls its *Ausbau* – it is also the case that use in those spheres depends on a certain status having already been attained. Status and function are intertwined in a dialectical fashion. The account in Joseph (1987) says or at least implies that language status begins with a group of native-speaking partisans who, having learned standard-language functions in the colonial language, then begin using the new language in those functions, sometimes increasing the formal differences in the process. By this means the new status spreads to the population at large and ultimately gains national and international recognition.

Again, this is what has been observed regularly in post-colonial situations, as well as in the emergence of standard European languages in the Renaissance and after. But Hong Kong has not exactly moved into a post-colonial situation, at least not the typical one where a colony is granted independence. Rather it has been turned over to another power, the PRC, which did not exist until more than 100 years after Hong Kong became a British colony. The PRC has its own standard spoken language, Putonghua, and written language, for which it uses simplified characters rather than the traditional ones still in use in Hong Kong. The majority first language of Hong Kong, Cantonese, does serve in some spoken standard-language functions in the PRC – though at this point the discussion becomes extremely complex, because in those functions a special form of Cantonese is used which is itself in a diglossic relationship with 'colloquial' Cantonese dialects.

With colloquial Cantonese, standard spoken Cantonese, formal spoken Cantonese, spoken and formal Putonghua, written Chinese in traditional and simplified characters, and a distinctive written Cantonese already available, what functions could possibly be left for Hong Kong English to fill? It will remain a co-official language, and so long as the territory remains part of the common law tradition, English will not be far distant from legal usage and status even when proceedings are superficially in Chinese. In addition, there is a widespread feeling in Hong Kong that English is the language of international business and tourism, as well of science, and that there will therefore remain economic and educational imperatives for learning and using it. And from a different sort of 'functional' perspective, there is the fact that language mixture, or code-switching, is so widely attested in ostensibly Cantonese discourse in Hong Kong that the borders between the languages are becoming ever more nebulous, despite the great structural gap between them. But again, even that gap is narrowing, based on what we saw for Hong Kong English in Figure 6.2 above, and arguably in the other direction too, as discussed in Joseph (1996).

Chinese identities

Part of the problem for China is the global techno-culture of which English appears to be the chief language. Since at least 1919 Chinese intellectuals have struggled with what Tu (1991, p. 6) has called 'the May Fourth intellectual dilemma: the intertwining of nationalism (patriotism) and iconoclasm (antitraditionalism)'. How was it possible to be both Chinese, with all the weight of cultural tradition that identity implied, and modern? The genius of Mao was to offer an answer that convinced so many for so long: real Chineseness lay with the peasantry, working the soil, and modernity lay in the first instance with the overthrow of the ruling classes, so that the peasantry would rule. In both cases the peasantry, as it turned out, was personified in him (see further Tu, 1991, pp. 24–5).

Mao's Cultural Revolution was in some sense a semantic revolution, a redefinition of *Chinese* such that its old opposition with *modernity* was not merely undone, but reversed. Whatever was not modern would henceforth be unpatriotic, hence un-Chinese. As Wang (1993, p. 72) puts it, Mao launched this revolution 'by putting on parts of a Chinese face, invoking features of authority and power'.

That all things un-modern would be unpatriotic did not imply that all things modern would be patriotic. Much of the liberalisation of the mid-1980s was based on an assumption that Deng Xiaoping's economic modernisations, patently capitalistic even though labelled as 'socialism with Chinese characteristics', meant an opening of doors to all the hallmarks of the modern – products with international brand names, rock and roll, and Western-style liberal democracy. Even *patriotism* was appropriated for the neo-modernist cause:

> The millions of democracy demonstrators in the spring of 1989 dubbed their movement 'patriotic', in contrast to a regime which they found had wasted the people's hard-earned wealth on imported luxury items such as Mercedes-Benzes for a parasitic ruling caste. (Friedman, 1993, p. 1)

(Apparently at least *one* international brand name, Mercedes-Benz, was beyond the pale.) On 4 June 1989 the central government made a definitive semantic clarification of the meaning of patriotism, when it broke up the democracy demonstrations using all necessary force, including murdering university student protestors.

It came as a shock to Chinese and non-Chinese everywhere, though a shock of a particular kind to Hong Kong people, whose fate had been delivered into this government's hands five years earlier. For the whole of Hong Kong's colonial history, and ever more intensely since the anticolonial riots of the late 1960s, *Britain* had stood in semantic opposition not only to *China* but to *self-rule* and *democracy*. Unlike what was the case for many Chinese elsewhere, *China* seemed to represent not the past, but the future, because for Hong Kong, *Britain* meant the past. Locating their own identity with the Chinese 'mother country' was an easy choice for both ethnic and political reasons, a choice of a democratic future with themselves as subjects, in the Hegelian sense, over a colonial past in which they were objects. When it became clear that China was rejecting any such alignment as a threat to its internal stability, the choices for Hong Kong identity no longer seemed to make any coherent sense.

Friedman (1993) and Siu (1993) both stress the renewed importance of *south* Chinese identity in opposition to Chinese identity in the current politically and culturally ambiguous context. Mao successfully created a mythical history in which the rise of the Chinese nation is credited entirely to the northern 'Han' people and their superior civilisation, and all later heroic events too are the work of northern Chinese peasants (see Friedman, 1993, pp. 2–4). This was not the prevalent view before Mao. 'At the outset of the twentieth century, Chinese patriots often identified the hated, conquering Manchus with an alien North and a backward Czarist Russia, while identifying patriotic Chinese (not Han) with the South' (ibid., p. 6). Since Mao, the mythical Han history has crumbled in the south and something like the old identity has re-emerged. With the south's economic boom, 'Beijing is ridiculed as a backward town of mere talkers who live off the people's wealth and contribute nothing to wealth expansion. Northerners are mocked as people who would not even recognise money lying in a street' (ibid., p. 10). By the 1990s, 'Even in Beijing, people understood that the future was coming into China from the commercialized South and the trading coasts. Cantonese language and culture spread. Even farther north, traders hired Cantonese tutors' (ibid., p. 11).

It is not implausible that south China – as opposed to Hong Kong specifically or China generally, or in addition to them – could emerge as a locus of Hong Kong people's identity in the years or decades ahead. This prospect has language in its favour, the Cantonese tongue which links Guangdong and Hong Kong culturally despite their vastly different modern histories. There is geography and economics as well. The dyad of *north* and *south* might replace the old one of *Britain* and *China*, with all the negative attributes transferred wholesale from Britain to Beijing, along something like the lines shown in Figure 6.3. Obviously

Pre-1989 oppositions

Britain	***China***
The past	The future (and the *glorious* past)
Colonial rule	Self-determination
Self-serving oppression	Democracy
Good business and management	Good business/management *potential*

Post-1997 oppositions

North China	***South China***
The past	The future (and the *glorious* past)
Colonial rule	Self-determination
Self-serving oppression	Democracy
Bad business and management	Good business and management

Figure 6.3 Pre- and post-1997 identity oppositions in Hong Kong

Beijing would prefer not to see a pan-south Chinese identity emerge as a locus of loyalty for people throughout this thriving region. They would prefer to win Hong Kong hearts and minds to Beijing's definition of Chineseness, thus encircling Guangdong and forcing it back into line. But how to win those hearts and minds?

Constructing colonial identity

In approaching the question just posed, it is instructive to look back at how the British colonial adminstration tried to do it, at a point when sovereignty was, potentially at least, in crisis. The pair of texts which follow are from a volume entitled *Proclamation by H. E. the Governor, Sir Alexander Grantham, G. C. M. G., Queen Elizabeth II Coronation Celebration N[ew] T[erritories] H[ong] K[ong]* (Hong Kong: The Times News Agencies, no date), held in the Hong Kong Collection of the University of Hong Kong Library. Actually this pair is part of a set of three texts, the first being the Hong Kong New Territories District Commissioner's Speech at the Coronation Dinner, 5 June 1953, the second a Chinese text that corresponds closely enough to it to be considered a 'version' of it, though not a translation in the usual sense, and the third an English translation of the Chinese version. That the last text should have been produced and published at all is rather extraordinary, and it and the first text are the ones I here reproduce and discuss.

Version for British audience:

> **District Commissioner's Speech at Coronation Dinner,** ***5.6.53***
>
> The Coronation of Her Majesty Queen Elizabeth II is an occasion for celebration and rejoicing in Britain and throughout British Territories all over the world.
>
> This rejoicing is not only an expression of loyalty and affection for the new Sovereign: the Coronation also provides a special opportunity for people everywhere in British Territories to reaffirm their deep conviction and belief in the ideals of freedom and democracy. The unity of this belief throughout the British Commonwealth and Empire is symbolised by loyalty to the Queen who is voluntarily recognised as the head of the commonwealth.
>
> During the past few days we have all been much impressed by the spontaneous rejoicing and happiness which has marked Coronation celebrations in the New Territories. The Government has given you some encouragement and help, but the organization and preparation have been yours, and I am pleased at the efficient and orderly

way in which everything has been conducted. I offer you my congratulations, and also my thanks to those whose generosity has enabled the poorer people to share in the general rejoicing.

The opening of a new reign is a good time to remember our duty to help and serve others. No one works harder for the good of her people than the Queen, and we should all follow her example. Most of you here are members of Rural Committees or are village representatives. You have been appointed at the wish of the people in your districts, and you should continue to work unselfishly and energetically for the good of the majority. Many of you have already served for several years as the representatives of your villages or towns, and have earned the respect and gratitude of the public.

We have already drunk the health of the new Queen. Let me now take the opportunity of this great occasion to wish you, one and all, happiness and prosperity in the days which lie ahead.

Version for Chinese audience:

Respectful Congratulations on the Great Occasion of the Coronation of Her Majesty Queen Elizabeth II.

2nd June 1953 is the Coronation Day of Her Majesty Queen Elizabeth II.

All under heaven celebrate together and all beyond the seas rejoice.

All Her Majesty's servants and subjects leap and dance with joy.

Long have we been numbered as her subjects and have been deeply grateful for Her Majesty's protection and benevolence. Like palm trees inclining to the sun, we bow in splendid ceremony toward her.

In pure, heartfelt devotion, we, for two hundred thousand New Territories' inhabitants, send rejoicings to the Maple Palace.

Heaven bestows its wisdom on Her Majesty; in ability and virtue she excels all contemporaries.

She has won the admiration of both heaven and earth for her wisdom and good fortune.

Her star shines with brilliance and inspires the poets to song. Her virtue towers to the sky, and in happiness today we see the Dragon flying.

Following in the footsteps of her ancestors, she brings peace to the nations. Governed in virtue and wisdom, her dominions extend far and wide.

As we travel through the imperial realms we recognise the true qualities of a sage. She is clad in virtue and benevolence; the people are given new strength.

Those who come to pay homage to the Crown climb over mountains and sail across seas; eight hundred nations gather within the glittering walls. Those who enjoy the Queen's bounty pledge their wisdom in utmost devotion: millions of people swear everlasting loyalty.

Gazing at the palace door thousands of miles away, we all yearn to go there. We are treated without distinction, and our love is deepened.

We burn incense in the midnight and pray for Her Majesty's health; as we go along the road we sing good wishes for the Commonwealth's prosperity.

What is happening in the transition from the British-audience to the Chinese-audience version of the text is the construction of a hybrid Hong Kong New Territories Chinese British-colonial identity, centred upon the traditional Chinese national identity focus, devotion to the monarch. On one level, the original text has been 'translated' into the 'target culture' of the New Territories inhabitants, who were and to some extent still are the 'most Chinese' of the people of Hong Kong, their lives in their remote mountain villages having received far less impact from the British colonial administration and Western settlements than did Hong Kong Island or Kowloon.

But what has been lost in the translation is quite extraordinary. Where the first version (for a British audience) confines the celebration to 'Britain and British Territories all over the world', in the second version (for a Chinese audience) it is a universal celebration of 'all under heaven and all beyond the seas'. There is no mention of Britain or British Territories, only of 'the Commonwealth'; it is as though the text is speaking of the monarch of the world, or indeed of a goddess. And whereas in the second version it is the wisdom and virtue of the Queen that are praised, in the first it is simply her hard work on behalf of her people. That is perhaps British empiricism coming into play: virtue and wisdom are not directly observable, but everyone in the British audience will have seen pictures of Princess Elizabeth steadfastly at work on her official African tour, then having to abandon it and return to Britain as Queen upon her father's death. Meanwhile, in the last paragraph of the two versions, the British are characteristically drinking, while the Chinese are out burning joss sticks in the midnight.

The 'ideals of freedom and democracy' invoked in the first text have no counterpart in the second; and where the Queen 'is voluntarily recognised as the head of the commonwealth' – which is rather an unusual use of the word 'voluntarily' (does anyone remember who the other candidates were?) – in the second everyone is bowing toward her 'like palm trees inclining to the sun'. The closest thing to democracy in the second text comes in the penultimate paragraph, where 'we all yearn to go' to the 'Maple Palace' (Buckingham Palace?), and in this dream of desire we arrive to find that 'We are treated without distinction'. The ambiguity of that last phrase is all too apt; it is hard to imagine any New Territories inhabitant, or any other British subject for that matter, turning up at the Palace and being treated as anything other than a very undistinguished visitor indeed.

One of the most intriguing features of the Chinese-audience text is that it never mentions 'the new Queen', as the other version does. Apart from the word 'coronation' – which a New Territories inhabitant might or might not understand as occurring toward the beginning of the reign of a new sovereign – the rhetoric is entirely of continuity, above all in the sentence 'Long have we been numbered as her subjects and have been deeply grateful for Her Majesty's protection and benevolence.' *Her Majesty* and the *her* in 'her subjects' refer of course to the Crown rather than to the present monarch; the New Territories had at that point been subject to the British Crown for some 55 years (actually not all that long in Chinese dynastic terms), but to Elizabeth II for only a matter of months. Yet a few paragraphs down, *Her Majesty, her* and *she* are being used in a way that makes sense only with personal reference to Elizabeth II: for example, 'in ability and virtue she excels all contemporaries'. Thus the person of Elizabeth II is wedded rhetorically to the permanence of the Crown in a way that effaces the newness of her reign. Further confusing the issue was the fact that there had already been a Queen Elizabeth (subsequently the Queen Mother) on the throne since 1936. Might it have been she who was being crowned upon the death of her husband the King? Certainly the second text would make more sense if she, rather than her untested 27-year-old daughter, had been the Queen in question.

The effacing of the change of monarch in the hybrid text highlights the fact that the continuation of a reign means stability, and the end of a reign is inherently a moment of crisis. In opinion polls conducted in the UK, many of those who say they support ending the British monarchy add that they do not believe that this should happen during the reign of the present Queen. Rather, they opine, after her death or abdication no successor should be crowned. Other proposed changes to constitution or long-standing protocol should, respondents again say, be considered only after the reign of Elizabeth II is completed (for many years the Queen Mother's lifetime was frequently given as the period in which no major changes should be undertaken, but her death in 2002 has not so far been followed by any wave of political reaction). The change of sovereign is, in principle at least, a moment when the relationship between the people and the Crown, which remains central to national identity, can be negotiated without fear of seeming disrespectful or ungrateful to the present monarch. Our Chinese-audience text is an attempt to assert a hybrid identity at just such a moment of crisis. In the absence of any record of the details of its production, one assumes that it was created by one or more high-level Hong Kong Chinese interpreters in the civil service, possibly working in collaboration with a British 'old China hand', and no doubt sincerely convinced that the need for political stability in Hong Kong, in the wake of Mao's revolution in China and the Korean War, overrode any concern for the virtues of freedom and democracy espoused in the British text, or for making it clearly understood that they were celebrating the coronation of a relatively inexperienced young woman who was obviously a dedicated, hard worker, but whose wisdom, ability and virtue had yet to prove themselves.

The present and future roles of English

Beijing's position on language in Hong Kong universities has been clear and consistent for a decade or more: it does not support any movement toward teaching in the 'mother tongue', Cantonese, nor does it support making Putonghua (Mandarin) the main teaching language. China is full of Mandarin-language universities, in the PRC's view, and it needs Hong Kong as its English-speaking bridge to the rest of the world.

This policy has not been disagreeable to the senior Hong Kong leadership, most of them graduates of the University of Hong Kong and all of them bilingual with a very high level of English. But it was unsatisfactory indeed to a large segment of the Hong Kong leadership class, particularly those agemates of the most prominent leaders who never quite made it to the top of the colonial hierarchy *just because* their English was not good enough. And among people in the 45–50 age range who were themselves students at the time of the 1960s riots and led what Choi (1990) has called the 'search for cultural identity' in the students' movement of the early 1970s, there are many who have dreamed ever since of an *independent* Hong Kong, throwing off the colonial language entirely and functioning exclusively in their mother tongue, Cantonese. Many of them are having difficulty coming to terms with the fact that Hong Kong is *not* independent. It will be interesting to see what happens when, ten years from now, they take over as the senior leaders – unless Beijing's policy of virtually lifelong tenure will be extended to the present Hong Kong leaders, which is not beyond imagining.

The future of English in Hong Kong depends on the future direction of Hong Kong identity. If Beijing continues to see the major threat to national stability as residing in movements for regional autonomy, it would not be surprising if active efforts were made to promote the use of Putonghua over Cantonese in Hong Kong. Today, when Cantonese is the first language to more than 90 per cent of the population, it may seem unthinkable that the language could ever be weakened. But in fact the figures cited back in Tables 6.1 and 6.2 suggest otherwise. Most Hong Kong people are bilingual or trilingual, and that is the first stage in the demise of a language. There are plenty of historical cases of large populations largely or entirely losing their language in favour of another one within a relatively short span of time – one has only to think for example of a place like Wales, where this occurred when education, communications and opportunity for travel were only a fraction of what they are now. If the Beijing government wanted to, and went about it in the right way, they could significantly increase the spread of Putonghua in Hong Kong at the expense of Cantonese (despite the protestations of Yau, 1992). The people of Hong Kong might equally well find their primary identity within the common language of China.

But if Hong Kong people were to strengthen and intensify their non-mainland identity – that is, regardless of any question of their loyalty to the Beijing government, if they were to want to manifest their historical and cultural differences vis-à-vis the rest of China rather than what they share, and particularly if Cantonese were to undergo suppression of the sort discussed above, then they might in a sense 'remember' that the majority of them also know English. That memory of English, even if it does not take the form of everyone in Hong Kong being fluent in the language – i.e. if it is only a memory of having known it, as is sometimes the case with ethnic identities in the USA – could form a part of Hong Kong linguistic identity, for those people who wanted to assert it. In so far as the history of other peoples is a guide, it is when this identity function emerged, and only then, that one could expect a recognition of 'Hong Kong English' to become a part of the public (non-academic) discourse. This possibility is further bolstered by the ongoing emergence of a global postmodern identity in which English plays the predominant linguistic role, and by the widespread (though not necessarily accurate) perception of English as the international language of the global economy (see Lau, 1997, pp. 123–5).

The changing patterns in the use of English in Hong Kong can best be understood within a historical perspective which takes account of similar developments in other times and places while remaining aware that the particular circumstances of Hong Kong are unique. The perception of a decline in English standards, which dominates the public discourse, and that of the emergence of Hong Kong English, which dominates the specialised discourse of linguists, are actually two sides of the same coin, two ways of looking at the same phenomenon.

Linguists risk having only a very partial understanding of the linguistic situation if we dismiss the popular perception outright because it is contradicted by our 'scientific' data. We would do better to think in terms of 'stories': linguists have a different story concerning language in Hong Kong than the one that has emerged in public discourse. Both matter in respects so different from one another that it makes little sense to compare them; but in any case surely the last thing we want to say is that the story in public discourse does not matter. It matters very much indeed. It is through such stories that a society constitutes and maintains itself, determines the direction in which it will develop, and creates an identity and, when necessary, a resistance.

What people are reacting to as a decline in English standards in Hong Kong is, at one level, a tremendous rise in social opportunity, that has produced a democratisation of the language, allowing a distinctive Hong Kong English to emerge, as such Englishes have already emerged in Singapore, India and various other places around the globe. The idea of such a language is not one which Hong Kong people take seriously – not yet, anyway. But the cultural identity crisis constantly threatens to deepen if Beijing plays the cultural unity and stability card too strongly and suppresses the vibrant written Cantonese literature, mainly in the form of comic books and popular newspapers which the mainland government undoubtedly considers vulgar and subversive. Then the possibility that Hong Kong English might find its functional niche and become a locus of cultural identity and expression no longer seems far-fetched at all.

As noted above, at present, if one mentions 'Hong Kong English' to Hong Kong people, they assume one is using the term in derogatory fashion, to identify their 'mistakes' vis-à-vis Standard English. This is less overwhelmingly the case in Singapore, where books like *Singapore*

English in a Nutshell (Brown, 1999) present this 'new English' in a positive light. But in his introduction Brown notes that the usual Singapore English term for Singapore English itself is *Singlish*, which does not carry such positive connotations. Nevertheless, recognition of the linguistic distinctiveness is the necessary precondition for the development of a sense of local identity within the English language itself. Historically, this development has never happened until some decades after the end of colonial rule. Whether it will continue to progress in Singapore or ever begin in Hong Kong, I do not venture to predict. But if the conditions shape up in a way that favours the location of a Hong Kong identity in English, the key to it happening will be the hybrid culture of the classroom. Although our understanding of the role of linguistic identity in second-language learning is still in the early stages (see especially Norton, 2000), this much is clear: only if and when teachers come to recognise that the 'errors' in Hong Kong students' English (at least the regularly occurring ones) are precisely the points at which a distinct Hong Kong identity is expressed in the language, will a Hong Kong English genuinely begin to emerge, and to be taken as a version of Standard English rather than as a departure from it.

7
Language in Ethnic/Racial and Religious/Sectarian Identities

Ethnic, racial and national identities

However tightly they are bound up with national identities, languages are no less potent a force in constructing identities concurrent with and often resistant to the national. As this chapter enquires into other such identities, the focus, in the constructionist spirit, will be less on the product (identities as labels or categories) than on the process. While national identities are already arbitrary in their construction, they at least develop an institutional status through such practices as the issuing of passports, the coinage of money and the production of other talismans through which 'banal nationalism' is effectuated. This tends to set the national apart from other identities, while at the same time creating a temptation to treat other identities as though their own status were on a par with the national. The most salient example is the Marxist treatment of 'class' identities, which is based upon unsustainable Romantic reifications – ironically, reifications of the very sort which Marxist linguists are quick to denounce in the 'post-structuralists' whom they now treat as their principal enemies.

'Ethnic' identity is sometimes used as a synonym of 'national' identity – indeed, it was formerly common (and still is in some languages) for 'racial' identity to be used in the same way. But it is more useful to maintain the distinctions that are most often made or at least implied by the different terms, where

- *ethnic* identity is focused more on common descent and on a cultural heritage shared because of common descent, than on political aspirations for autonomy;

- *national* identity is focused on political borders and autonomy, often justified by arguments centred on shared cultural heritage, but where the ethnic element is inevitably multiple;
- *racial* identity – now a concept virtually taboo in American discourse (and this taboo itself represents an identity phenomenon in need of interrogation and discussion) – focused, like ethnic identity, on common descent and cultural heritage, but conceived on a grander scale, for example 'black' identity as opposed to Wolof identity.

There are also *regional* and *local* identities which, if they do not qualify as ethnic or national by the criteria identified above, will not be treated here, yet can nevertheless function as central foci of identity and belonging, complete with linguistic manifestations. In a community imbued with 'campanilismo', identity on the most narrowly local level, linguistic forms gain particular value for their incomprehensibility to people from the nearest villages. In such a setting, national identity rarely has any salience except in times of calamity – changes of regime, and above all, war.[1]

'Racial' and 'ethnic' identities sometimes come into conflict, for example in the movements known as 'pan-Slavism' and 'pan-Arabism' which arose in the nineteenth century and had adherents until well into the twentieth. Their proponents maintained that ethnic divisions (sometimes coinciding with national or religious ones) needed to be overcome for the greater good of the 'race' as a whole, which could be restored to its original, unified glory. But strong partisans of particular ethnic identities within the larger 'races' saw this as no less a danger to their interests than foreign conquest or international socialism represented. Kohn (1965) juxtaposes a pair of extracts, the first of which is from the pan-Slavist Nikolai Danilevsky (1822–85):

> The political independence of the race is the indispensable foundation of culture, and consequently all the Slav forces must be directed towards this goal. Independence is indispensable in two respects; without the consciousness of Slav racial unity, as distinct from other races, an independent culture is impossible; and without fruitful interaction between the Slav peoples, liberated from foreign powers and their national divisions, diversity and richness of culture are impossible. (Danilevsky, 1869, cited from Kohn, 1965, p. 154)

The second extract, from Danilevsky's close contemporary, the Czech journalist Karel Havlíček Borovský (1821–56), shows however how statements like the above tend to be read by those committed to specific ethnicities within the 'race':

> The Russians ([...]) have taken up the idea of Pan-Slavism. [...] The Russian Pan-Slavs believe that we and the Illyrians would like to be under their domination!! They are firmly convinced that they will one day control all Slav lands!! They now look forward with joy to their future vineyards in Dalmatia. These gentlemen have started everywhere to say and write Slav instead of Russian, so that later they will again be able to say Russian instead of Slav....
>
> [T]he Slavs are not one nation but four nations as independent and unconnected as any other European nations. [...] It is impossible then for all Slavs to use one literary language, and therefore all efforts in this direction are meaningless, and, as a waste of time, harmful. (Havlíček, 1846, cited from Kohn, 1965, pp. 158–9)

Within individuals, ethnic and racial identities can coexist harmoniously, though conflict is possible here as well. To take up the example cited on p. 163 under 'racial identity', a given individual might have the ethnic identity of a Wolof, the racial identity of a black, and the national identity of a Senegalese. He or she might then move to the USA, and over time experience a shift such that, in certain contexts at least, their national identity becomes American, their ethnic identity Senegalese-American (or Wolof-American) and their racial identity African-American, or possibly Black African, if they want to distinguish themselves from 'indigenous' African-Americans.

An intriguing such shift has been reported by Perta (2003) among the Albanian (Arbëresh) communities that have been established on the Italian peninsula since the sixteenth century. Throughout that time they maintained a strong sense of distinctive identity as ethnic Albanians, and were extremely resistant to the construction of Italian national identity leading up to and following upon the creation of the Italian state in the 1860s. The 'Italians', as far as the Arbëresh were concerned, were those 'other' people surrounding them. They themselves were not Italian, even if, as would increasingly be the case in the second half of the twentieth century, Italian rather than Arbëresh was their dominant (or only) language.

However, this situation appears to have undergone a drastic shift following the influx of new Albanian immigrants into Italy since 1990. These 'New Albanians' have become associated (rightly or wrongly) in the popular press with crime and prostitution. The old Arbëresh communities, rather than embracing them as their own, have kept their distance. Although they would not deny their kinship on the grander, quasi-'racial' level, they have asserted an ethnic distinction on the basis of 'old' vs 'new', and most importantly have shored this up by, for the first time, declaring their own national identity to be Italian. In a sense, they discovered their Italianness when their Albanianness became problematic.

Perta reports as well that, although the Italian government has opened the door to Albanian-language education in the Arbëresh communities, in the spirit of European Union recommendations passed in 1999, the communities themselves, which a generation ago would undoubtedly have embraced such a move, have become markedly ambivalent towards it in the wake of their recent ethnic/national identity shift.

The Iberian peninsula is a virtual textbook of configurations of ethnic and national identities:

- the obvious 'nation-states', the Republic of Portugal and the Kingdom of Spain;
- a 'state without a nation', the Principality of Andorra;
- the 'nations without states' existing within Spain, with strongly held feelings of difference toward it, namely, the Catalans and the Basques;
- 'nations without states' with a considerably more moderate, though still strong, separatist identity, such as Galicia;
- regions where separatist identities exist but are not presently such a strong cultural force, such as Valencia and Andalucia.

In explaining why Basque identity is strongly opposed to the Spanish identity of the 'nation-state', it would be difficult not to have recourse to the fact that the Basque language is unrelated to the Romance dialects spoken throughout the rest of the Iberian peninsula – a fact which lies behind Basque claims to form a wholly distinct people ethnically. There is also the fact that the Basque language community traverses the Spanish–French national border. So does the Catalan language community, and even though Catalan is part of the Romance family, its distinctiveness as a 'language' in its own right, rather than a dialect of Spanish or Provençal, owes something to its 'international' status, and something to a centuries-long tradition of creative writing in it that has included writers of world renown, such as the Majorcan Ramon Llull (1232–1316). This literary 'building out' is what Kloss (1978) refers to as *Ausbau* (see p. 150 above). Still, the main factor has been the sheer determination of its speakers for its distinctiveness to be recognised.

Valencian and Andalucian also possess centuries-old written literatures, but neither crosses a national border, has a world figure comparable to Llull, or is spoken by a population largely inclined toward insisting that it is a different language from Spanish rather than a dialect of it. The case of Galician is complicated by the fact that, if it is a dialect of any other language, that language is Portuguese. Its closer linguistic affinity to Portuguese than to Spanish has been much exploited by those seeking Galician independence from Spain. On the level of ethnic identity, they have also constructed and maintained an account of their supposed Celtic origins, the evidence for which ranges from archaeological artefacts to a tendency toward light hair colour and other purported affinities with Celtic cultures.

It will become clear in the next chapter just how far-flung Celtic is as an ethnic identity constructed and deployed for political purposes. The Celtic identities within the British Isles, Irish, Welsh and Scots (and more weakly Cornish, Manx and others) have developed not only an ethnic and a linguistic but also a religious-sectarian dimension. We shall see in a later section of this chapter how religious identities, which usually predate national ones, can have their own linguistic markers and manifestations, often including the maintenance of a language or form of language no longer used in secular contexts. Although of more recent date, sectarian divisions have generated their own identity patterns, including linguistic ones. Irish Gaelic, for example, has had strong associations with Irish republicanism since the late nineteenth century, and Irish republicanism has strong associations with Roman Catholicism. While it functions as a symbol of Irish national identity for Irish Roman Catholics, in Protestant areas of Ireland (and a fortiori in Northern Ireland), it functions instead as a symbol of republicanism, and in some contexts of militant republicanism (see O'Reilly, 1999). Scots Gaelic, in contrast, is closely linked with the Free Church of Scotland, whereas the identity of members of the established Church of Scotland (Presbyterians) is more bound up with Scots. The case of Lebanon, in which religious and sectarian differences have led to the imagining of ethnic ones, will be looked at in depth in the next chapter. In many post-colonial situations, fluency in the former colonial language can be a reliable indicator of education in Christian schools. It does not denote that an individual is a practising Christian, but is at least interpreted as suggesting that the person's parents were not strongly tied to indigenous religious beliefs. In all the cases mentioned in this paragraph, language choice, code-switching and formal/discursive/rhetorical variation all play a part in linguistic identity.

From communities of practice to shared habitus

This leads us to the question of whether language can be culturally 'neutral'. Voloshinov (see pp. 49–51 above) argued that it cannot be, not even at the level of the individual linguistic sign: 'Wherever a sign is present, ideology is present too' (Voloshinov, 1973 [1929], p. 10). In the context at hand, we can say that individuals use language in such a way as to signal – or more precisely, to create – their cultural identity, making language culturally 'loaded'. But a given language is capable of sustaining more than one culture. Even the Arabic language, with its intense cultural bonds to Islam, has sustained Christian cultures for centuries, and has the potential to sustain any number of cultures. The same is true of every language, and in that sense language is culturally 'neutral'. Even if, historically, it has developed within a particular culture, it does not *in itself* spread that culture to other people who learn the language. The language must be embedded within the cultural habitus in order to function as the vehicle in which the culture will be acquired. Transferred to a different habitus, the language will mould itself to that habitus, rather than the other way round.

As sociolinguistically based identity research has moved further away from notions of class compatible with the Marxist ones, the concept of communities of practice (see p. 65 above) has emerged as a basis for understanding how groups of people develop, deploy and recognise their own linguistic recognition markers formed around any set of shared beliefs. This approach has largely supplanted earlier attempts to account in a broader way for notions of sexual or generational identity in language. These were never wholly satisfactory, the most difficult case having been that of 'women's language' (later reidentified as 'powerless language'), a concept that arguably brought into existence the very category it purported to identify, and exacerbated the very problems it purported to remedy. Looking at communities of practice, on the other hand, can help us to find what there is in common in the production of shared linguistic features among groups of workers or scientists or lawyers, children in a particular school, just the Asian children in that school, and so on.

Still, despite its usefulness for heuristic purposes, we need to remember that not every group of people who constitute a 'community of practice' as that term is commonly defined will behave in the same way where language and identity are concerned. Indeed, not every community of practice will manifest itself in a linguistic identity. This is where the notion of the habitus becomes useful. We can expect a community of practice to manifest a linguistic identity in just those cases where the practices around which the community is formed enter into the habitus of the individual community members. This happens most powerfully when the individuals grow up performing the practices as part of their everyday routine. When the practices are something to which they are introduced in later life, they will not necessarily become part of each individual's habitus, only of certain individuals, and in varying degrees.

Criticisms have been made of constructionist approaches to language and identity on the grounds that they put 'casual' identities on a par with the sort of identities for which people go to war. In fact there is no clear dividing line between the sorts of identity that go with being a member of the Scottish Nationalist Party, the Free Church of Scotland or the Scotch Malt Whisky Society – except that only in a farce could one imagine the banner of the Scotch Malt Whisky Society being carried into battle – and if sociologists and sociolinguists studying identity have levelled the distinctions, it is in order eventually to arrive at a fuller understanding of them. We are still a fair way from such an understanding, but in my view it will be helped along by an approach to linguistic and other cultural identities that is grounded in the notion of *shared habitus*, with 'communities of practice' serving as a general model for understanding and analysing how the 'shared' dimension of the habitus comes to be, and to be maintained.

The particular power of ethnic/racial identity claims

Of the two main types of identities investigated in this chapter – ethnic/racial and religious/sectarian – the first is the one most directly bound up with the national identities discussed in the two previous chapters. It is also, rhetorically, the most powerful type of identity claim that one can make. As a result, claims of national, religious/sectarian and even social class identity are often shored up with claims of ethnic difference, so that the boundaries between them become blurred. (An example of this will be analysed in Chapter 8.)

When considering why ethnic/racial difference should possess such power, it is worth recalling Epicurus' letter to Herodotus, discussed in Chapter 3 (pp. 42–3), and the long tradition of belief that the human body – visibly differentiated from ethnos to ethnos, such that we imagine ourselves able to read the ethnicity of another person off their skin colour, body shape, facial features and, by no means least, their voice – gives rise directly to differences in culture and language. Such beliefs are very much a double-edged sword, giving coherence and positive identity to the in-group, but also producing the sort of over-reading that engenders ethnic stereotyping and prejudice. Moreover, Young (1995) has argued powerfully that racism and the perceived need for racial segregation are motivated by the naturalness of cross-racial *desire*, the appeal of the exotic and the proverbial attraction of opposites. Historically, exogamy – marriage to a partner who does not belong to one's own 'in-group' – has been much more widely practised than endogamy, though of course there has been wide variation on how the in-group is defined. In so far as racism and segregation are about reinforcing group boundaries, such reinforcement is only necessary when the boundaries are threatened from within. But here again we find the paradox that cross-racial desire demands a recognition of separate racial categories at the same time as it contributes to the blurring or erasure of those categories.

In some circumstances the motivation for ethnic/racial identification can be so strong that categories are not so much blurred or erased as shored up, multiplied and complexified. A truly extraordinary record of such balkanisation of racial identities is the *Dictionary of Latin American Racial and Ethnic Terminology* (Stephens, 1999), an 825-page compilation of terms by which people classify themselves and others, for purposes ranging from the informal to the official, across the Spanish, Portuguese, French and Creole-speaking areas of Latin America. As a sample, the word *chino* (literally, 'Chinese') is recorded as having 32 meanings, expanding to 68 when submeanings are included. Some of these follow:

- Indian (i.e. Amerind: general Spanish American)
- Goajiro Indian (Colombia)
- a Goajiro Indian who happens to look Chinese (Venezuela)
- offspring of a mulatto and an Indian; 25 per cent white, 50 per cent Indian, 25 per cent black (Peru)
- offspring of a *saltatrás* and an Indian (Mexico) [*saltatrás* = 'jump back (from white)', 43.75 per cent white, 50 per cent Indian, 6.25 per cent black]

Chino and *china* are also associated in various regions with domestic servitude, low social class and prettiness. There are a range of subdivisions of *chinos*, such as *chino cholo* 'offspring of a black and an Indian', and *chino prieto* 'offspring of a black and a *chino cholo*' (Peru). These terms give evidence of an intense cultural sensitivity to slight degrees of racial difference, which get charged with symbolic significance because of how they are taken to function as the 'text' off which can be read a person's origins and background, and by extension their character.

Again, this is the double-edged sword of, on the one side, racial prejudice that works unfairly against individuals, and on the other, the ethnic/racial identity that binds individuals together in a way that enriches them with cultural unity and, potentially, enables them to counteract oppression.

The importance of language in this regard is by no means restricted to the names that get attached to people to indicate their ethnic belonging, but can extend to the way they speak generally. In the USA, working-class blacks and whites have markedly divergent dialects, even in cases where they and their forebears have inhabited the same cities for over a century and have worked side by side in the same factories since the end of workplace segregation some 40 years ago. During this same period, the growing black middle class has integrated linguistically with their white counterparts, but those below them on the social scale have not, probably because of the strong sense of ethnic solidarity and cultural distinctiveness they maintain. It would be unfair to the black middle class to suggest that they lack ethnic solidarity because they do not speak 'Black English', or do not speak it exclusively; accommodation to the 'White English' norm is necessary for entry into certain middle-class domains, and it must surely be possible to shift one's social standing without necessarily being a traitor to one's ethnicity. But one is always suspect. Nor is this situation restricted to ethnic and racial identities – it pertains to anyone who aspires to a higher social standing within a stratified society, though it is perhaps especially strong, and understandably so, in cases where there is a historical legacy of slavery or colonial rule that lends great force to the feeling of class treachery when a descendant of the oppressed takes on the identity of the former masters.

Racial categories continue to exert a strong hold over our minds, even in cultures that have made significant efforts to move beyond denying civil rights to those not of the majority race. As was discussed in Chapter 1 (pp. 6–7), a claim to have changed one's religious affiliation would tend to be believed today, even in cultures where such a change would not be readily accepted; and so too with a claim to change of gender, particularly where surgical confirmation of the claim is readily available. A claim to change of racial category, on the other hand, is viewed with deep suspicion, as though one is trying to disguise one's true identity. Moreover, efforts by governments to undo a legacy of racial preference by 'affirmative action' – giving preference in hiring, university selection and so on to races or ethnicities previously underrepresented in the relevant sectors – however justified it may be in certain cases, obviously depends on a faith in the physical reality and accuracy of racial categorisation no less strong than that which underpinned the earlier negative prejudices.

A great deal of research on language and identity over the last decade has focused on a phenomenon called 'crossing', whereby people who belong to one ethnic group adopt the identity signals of another group of lower social status (inevitably, otherwise it would not attract the attention of the linguistic anthropologists who study it). While much of this work, notably Rampton (1995), is superb for the data it presents and the original ways it analyses them, it embodies a paradox related to that discussed in the preceding paragraph. Descriptions of 'crossing' tend to reinforce conservative views of the power of the categories people are supposed to 'stick' to. My own working assumption – perhaps influenced by my own interethnic, trans-sectarian, international background – is that 'crossing' is less remarkable a phenomenon than is the perception that there are categories rigid enough to be crossed.

In one of the great ironies of modern history, the most convincing denial of the physical reality of racial categories was produced by German anthropologists and ethnographers of the Nazi period who had in fact set out to endow those categories with scientific rigour. As Hutton (1999) relates, their research steadily falsified the premises from which they had started. They did not hide the negative results from the party and government officials who had set their research tasks, but informed them that no scientific criteria existed for physically distinguishing a Slav from a German, or indeed a Jew from a German. Rather, the distinctions were essentially cultural – and in a German culture nurtured for 150 years on the Romantic views of Herder, Fichte, Humboldt et al., the natural place to turn to for locating that cultural essence was language.

Thus it developed that linguists' theories of ethnic/racial historical development and 'mother tongue' belonging came to form the 'scientific' bedrock for the Nazi policy of genocide. The supposed inferiority of Slavic peoples was embedded in a linguistic structure that was both the product and producer of low intellectual power. This still made for a problem where the supposed inferiority of Jews was concerned, since the principal language of the Central European Jews was a German dialect (Yiddish). The approaches to Yiddish taken by both German and Jewish linguists of the Nazi period are complex (see Hutton, 1999, pp. 188–232). Many built upon the widespread perception of Yiddish as a 'mixed' language, to argue that its 'inner form' was not actually German. But Peter Heinz Seraphim (1902–79), identified by Hutton as the 'strategically most important scholar of Eastern European Jewry in National Socialist Germany' (ibid., p. 223), developed a still more alienist view, according to which Jews are anomalous in having no 'mother tongue' at all, hence no true linguistic identity. They are able parasitically to take on the appearance of the linguistic identity of whatever country they inhabit, but their real identity is always that of their 'freely willed desire to be set apart from other peoples' (ibid., p. 229, citing Seraphim, 1938, pp. 396–7). The idea was not original with Seraphim: the composer Richard Wagner had said essentially the same thing in an essay on 'Judaism in Music' which he published anonymously in 1850.

We have here plummeted to the nadir of the evil done in the name of ethnolinguistic identity, so unspeakable as to make it impossible still for many people to contemplate the topic at all.[2] Yet analysing and understanding what was done in using linguistics to construct such a strong view of racial/ethnic difference is our best hope of stopping it from happening again. The next section, on 'Religious/sectarian identity', is only mildly less depressing reading, and of course the case of Jewish identity just discussed is one in which religion and ethnicity are tightly bound together. But it must be pointed out that across the long centuries in which Jews have been persecuted in Christian realms, a Jew who converted to Christianity was 'saved', both religiously and temporally. Only when the doctrine of racial/ethnic difference of Jews was developed in its strong form from the mid-nineteenth to the mid-twentieth centuries – and, as we have seen, came ultimately to rely on belief in linguistic identity – did a genocidal Holocaust ensue.

Religious/sectarian identities

Ethnic and religious identities concern where we come from and where we are going – our entire existence, not just the moment to moment. It is these identities above all that, for most people, give profound *meaning* to the 'names' we identify ourselves by, both as individuals and as groups. They supply the plot for the stories of our lives, singly and collectively, and are bound up with our deepest beliefs about life, the universe and everything. Moreover, in most cultures ethnic and religious identities are bound up with reproduction, in the sense that they limit who one can marry, whether endogamy or exogamy is the cultural norm. That, of course, gives them an evolutionary dimension.

In Europe, for over 1000 years beginning in the fourth century after Christ, religion was the primary focus of people's identity. With the fall of Rome in 453, there ceased to be a 'Western' and an 'Eastern' Empire, and was again just one Empire, ruled from Byzantium. The various Germanic kings who actually controlled the territory in continental Europe still considered themselves bound politically to the Emperor, as well as religiously to the Pope. The political situation would change in the eighth century as Charlemagne unified his Holy Roman Empire, a few decades after the religious situation had begun to change as distance grew between the Pope and the Emperor, particularly with the proclamation of the doctrine of iconoclasty by the Emperor, Leo III the Isaurian, in 725–6. By Christmas Day 800, when the Pope crowned Charlemagne Emperor, the transfer of allegiance was all but complete, even though the official split between the Roman and Eastern (Orthodox) churches did not take place for another 254 years.

Throughout these long centuries, any strangers wandering through countryside or village, if asked to identify themselves, only in rare cases could have cited a 'national' identity, but would have claimed to be Christians (or Jews) from such and such a parish (or town). The obvious exception was in times of war between Christian armies, and of course such wars, great and small, were very numerous in certain parts of Europe. Identifying where strangers were from, based on the sort of Latin they spoke (or did not speak), was a matter of life and death. So the groundwork for later identity differences among Christian sects after the Reformation in the late fifteenth century was already there to be built upon, even in the time of the unified church and of a Latin language that was still officially unified (though regional and local differences had always existed in some degree).

Somewhat paradoxically, then, religion functioned as a linguistically unifying force, but also as a divisive force. Religion bound Christian Europe to Latin, the Islamic world to Arabic, and Jews to Hebrew. Yet when Christianity underwent an East–West split the use of Latin vs Greek became its most potent symbol. The islands of Christians within the western Asian lands ruled by Muslims pegged their identities to Syriac, Chaldean and other languages. Hebrew loan-words helped mark out the forms of German and Spanish spoken by Jews from those of other German and Spanish speakers. Sectarian splits in Islam came to be associated with dialectal differences in Arabic, just as splits within Christianity would do. It is extremely unlikely that any of these alignments in belief and language were accidental. Members of the various sects needed and wanted to be able to recognise one another, and to identify members of other sects, and they adopted various ways of doing this, from circumcision, to distinctive clothing and ornaments, to rituals such as the sign of the cross or bowing to the east for prayers. In such a semiotically charged context, language could hardly fail to play its part.

Chapter 8 will focus on language and religious identity in Lebanon, where bilingualism has come to play an important signifying role. In some cases, however, religious differences actually come to be built into the grammar of the language, and personal pronouns seem to be a preferred locus for such difference. A famous example is the retention of the familiar second-person pronoun *thou* and its related forms (*thee, thy*, etc.) by dissenting sects such as the Quakers, long after their disappearance from general spoken English. In a number of European languages which, unlike non-Quaker English, have retained a formal–informal pronoun distinction, Roman Catholic and Protestant sects differ (or have differed) in which of the two they use to refer to God – a choice seen as having profound theological implications about the relationship of human beings to the divinity.

But its more immediate effect is to mark the different identities of the sects that use the divergent forms, and to mark the identity of an individual as belonging to one or the other sect. In this latter regard it serves a double function: to inform the out-group of one's membership of the sect; and also, in many cultures, to allow in-group members to assess one's status within the religious system. This status can take the form of 'full membership', as when the young Jewish male signals his bar mitzvah status by his knowledge of Hebrew, or the young Muslim by his knowledge of Koranic Arabic; or it can be a matter of depth of religious piety, as measured through repetitions of formulaic invocations of the deity (and avoidance of 'vain' invocations of the divine name), or through general linguistic *purism*, using whatever language the religious identity is bound to in its most 'proper' form. This is the religious equivalent of the behaviour of the nineteenth-century lower middle classes as described by Hobsbawm (cited above, Chapter 5, p. 121), where they signalled their identity as the most 'proper' members of the nation through their proper use of language. An extreme example of linguistic purism tied to religious identity will be discussed in the next chapter (pp. 200–3), which details how early Islamic scholars sought to prove that every word of the Koran is 'pure Arabic'. In a comparable way, extremely conservative Protestant Christian sects such as the Amish and Mennonites in the USA try to live in accordance with the Bible to such a degree that they shun modern inventions and use a form of English that, in so far as possible, does not depart from that of the King James Bible. Among Southern Baptists as well, exceptional piety is 'performed', by preachers in particular, through the use of archaic biblical formulae and frequent quotations of scripture even in secular contexts.

A still more all-embracing system of signifying religious belonging is found in Malayalam, spoken by Christian, Hindu and Muslim communities living side by side in southern India. Asher & Kumari (1997, p. 451) note that

> Dravidian kinship terminology is complex, and perhaps nowhere more so than in Kerala, where, apart from dialect variations, there are terms which are restricted to one or another of the major religious communities – Hindus, Christians and Muslims.

The examples they furnish of such terms include (but are not restricted to) those shown in Table 7.1.

As kinship terms are regularly used as terms of address in the language, there is a connection in this regard to the personal pronoun phenomena described above. Since it is impossible to hold a conversation with an elder of one's family without making constant use of these words as terms of address, every conversation is a public manifestation or 'performance' of religious identity for a Muslim speaker of Malayalam.

Table 7.1 Distribution of kinship terms by religion in Malayalam

	Hindu	*Christian*	*Muslim*
Elder brother	jyeeştan/ceettan	ceettan/ muutta aaŋŋala	ikka
Elder sister	jyeeştatti/ceecci	ceecci	itta/taatta
Father	pitaavə/acchan	appan	uppa/baappa
Mother	maataavə/amma	ammacci	amma
Father's elder brother	val(i)yacchan	valyappan/ peerappan	muuttaappa
Father's father	acchacchan	appaappan/ valyappan	valyuppa/ uppuuppa
Father's mother	acchamma	ammaamma / valyamma	valyumma
Mother's father	muttacchan/ muttaššan	appaappan/ valyappan	valyuppa
Mother's mother	ammamma/ muttašši	ammaamma/ valyammacci	ummuumma/ valyumma
Grandson	pautran/peeramakan	koccu moon	moon
Granddaughter	pautri/peeramakal	koccu moolə	moolə

Adapted from Asher & Kumari (1997, pp. 452–4).

In Western Europe, one of the most striking social phenomena of the last 40 years has been the decline of Christian identities, in contrast to the great strengthening of religious identities taking place in the rest of the world. The most dramatic of these have been the rise of 'militant Islam' and the resurgence of Christian worship and identities in Eastern Europe and Asian countries where they had been suppressed or banned outright until the fall of communism.[3] Christianity has also made steady gains in parts of Africa and South-East Asia where Islam or forms of Buddhism had previously been dominant, and its presence in American cultural life has grown rather than receded. Western European societies, however, experienced massive secularisation in the last third of the twentieth century. In the UK, where government subsidies for churches is limited, vast numbers of urban church buildings have been abandoned or given over to other uses, and a majority of people under the age of 60 have become extremely reticent about proclaiming a Christian identity, because they associate religion with conflict, strife and war. The 30 years of 'troubles' in Northern Ireland have contributed their share to this association; but younger people throughout Europe display similar antipathy to traditional religious identities, preferring instead to locate their belonging and their spirituality elsewhere, in 'New Age' spiritual practices, popular music or other secular pursuits – or nowhere at all.

Personal names as texts of ethnic and religious identity

With national, subnational, ethnic and regional identities, it is clear that difference and confrontation play a central role in calling them up and sustaining them. Individual identities are rather different. They start with a *personal name*, and the desire to give meaning to that name. In the case of one's own name, its meaning consists on one level of the deictic function of 'identifying' the individual. But when asked about the meaning of their names, most people are able to unravel long, complex, deeply felt narratives about their personal history, the people they are a part of, the aspirations of their parents and their own aspirations (for an example see Nkweto Simmonds, 1996). On this level, which is particularly important in certain cultures though absent in none, the meaning of one's name is tantamount to the meaning of one's life.

The importance of names as carriers of identity has only recently attracted the attention of linguists, who have long relegated names to the marginal area of 'onomastics'. The reason for this has to do with the conception of language that has long dominated linguistics, in which any aspect of an individual's wilful choice is not to be considered part of language, but of speech. Names are chosen by individuals – parents usually, though increasingly people are choosing new names for themselves for use in Internet chat rooms, as Internet code words and the like.

In the summer of 2000 I undertook some research among students from a range of South-East Asian countries studying on a diploma/ master's course in Singapore, asking them to tell me about their names, including any significance or stories they attached to them. The results were not only surprisingly voluminous, but revealed a great deal about how their names function for them as texts of ethnicity, religion and family history, as well as personal identity.[4]

Peck Sim was one of only two Singapore Chinese in the class who did not go by a Western name (the renaming of students is a practice with its own very interesting linguistic identity dimensions). It turns out that 'Peck Sim' *is* her Christian name. As she relates:

> Peck means 'pure' while 'Sim' means 'heart'. My father had never explained why he had given this name to me, except to say that he wanted his daughters to be given decent names. [...A]ny Chinese with some knowledge of dialects will be able to tell that I am Hokkien and a female. [...]
>
> Despite my father's good intentions, my Chinese name has proved to be a source of vexation to me. Some close friends and relatives had out of humour, distorted the pronunciation of my name 'Peck Sim' to 'Kek Sim' – a Hokkien word which means 'to worry'. This upsets me as it seemed to hint at my greatest fear – that indeed, I was a 'worrier'. I worried a lot (I still do). I worried about real or imagined problems concerning my work, self and family. [...]
>
> Upon looking back, I realise that I had never liked my name at all. In school, I used to wish that my dad had given me a better sounding name, like Mei Ling or Siew Yen [...]. It was with so many reasons that I decided to have a Western name. It was also in keeping with a trend in those days for teenagers and adults to adopt a Western name, perhaps for the sake of convenience. Besides, I have always been inclined to Christianity (I have believed in God since primary two) so a Western name would surely identify me as a 'Christian'. As I wanted to be different, I sought the assistance of my cousin's sister who came up with a name 'Viona'. Initially, I was delighted with the name as it was an uncommon one.

'Viona' became my adopted name as I broke out of my turbulent adolescence and embarked on my passage into adulthood. I was caught up in a heady swirl of socializing – dating, partying, going discos and fine dining. 'Viona' became synonymous with that party creature in me. [...]

My identity crisis ended when my life path took off in another direction. I enrolled in the university for my first degree and later, I became a converted Christian. During baptism, for some unexplained reasons, I was reluctant to be baptised under my Western name. Perhaps I realised that it was not a scriptural name and subconsciously, that name also reminded me of my frivolous party days. [...] I was eager to close up that chapter of my life forever. As I could not think of any suitable biblical names, I finally chose to be baptised with my Chinese name. I had come a full circle.

Now I am very proud of my Chinese name. I've come to treasure it as I become increasingly interested in emphasising my 'Chinese-ness'. I take pride in my Chinese roots (but not all its traditions of idol worship, etc.) [...]

Finally, my Chinese name has added a new and significant dimension to my identity. If my Pinyin name, 'Pi Sing' means 'pure heart', then it has assumed linguistic connection and scriptural connotation in the context of the Beatitudes (Matt. 5: 8) – 'Blessed are the pure in heart, for they shall see God'.

Another of the subjects tells a story that would be repeated often, of an intergenerational family squabble erupting over the naming of a child. In this case the squabble was centred upon religion and ethnicity – her traditional Chinese grandfather objected to her parents giving her a Christian name. So she was given both; but paradoxically, today it is in her *English* name (or truncated forms of it) that she locates her *Chinese* identity.

[...] My family members call me 'Nie' which is the second syllable. I suppose it sounds a little more Chinese while my friends call me either 'Win' or 'Winnie'. The English name, 'Winnie' was chosen by my parents who named me after a Sunday School teacher in a Methodist church here in Singapore. [...] However, my paternal grandfather [...] objected to my English name. He came from China in the thirties and was very proud of his heritage. Because of his strong objections, I have 'Siew Choo' as my Chinese name today. Ah Kung was adamant about giving all the eldest grand daughters on

> his side of the family, the same 'root' name which is 'Choo', meaning pearl in the Chinese language. Thus, my female cousins are called 'See Choo', 'Ming Choo', and 'Swee Choo'. Strangely though at the end, he called me 'Nie' like everyone else in the family except that he would add 'Ah' in front – 'Ah Nie'. [...] Today, I'm called more by my English name, 'Win'. However, in written form, I would sign off my name as 'Wne', a balance between 'Win' and 'Nie'.
>
> [...] An interesting episode occurred in Canada when I was studying there. On registration day, I got confused because the school registrar had put my last name/surname at the end of all my names. I realized then that that was how all western names were normally called. Anyway, I soon got used to it. [...]
>
> So my present identity is embodied in 'Wne', but pronounced 'Win'. In that name, the two main categories that I'm represented by is found in that three letter word. Although, it sounds English, the 'e' is part of my Chineseness, short for 'Nie'. Thus, even though I'm very English educated (my degree is in English literature), I'm also very Chinese.

A similar identity 'crossing' is reported by another Singapore Chinese female. Here again, as in the earlier discussion of Malayalam kinship names (p. 175), a crucial cultural component is the taboo against using the actual name of an older relative in addressing that relative, out of respect.

> [...] Now my niece calls me 'Biggy' which is her version for 'big auntie'. [...] Thus although the word 'Biggy' is English, it reminds me of my culture – the practice that one should not call one's senior by his/her name. Therefore 'Biggy' is very 'Chinese' to me. [...]

Christian and Chinese identities are of course not the only ones in which such conflicts occur. Oktavianus, from Indonesia, reports that his unusual name is problematic for him because it does not signal his Muslim identity. It is further exoticised by containing a sound that is relatively foreign to his home dialect. He is regularly confronted about the apparent religious discrepancy, and is clearly bothered by the mystery surrounding the actual giving of his name. It seems as though a satisfying story about why the name was chosen would resolve at least some of the identity conflicts it provokes.

[...] I began to question my name when the teacher at my senior high school asked why I was named Oktavianus. My mother told me that when I was born, my aunt, the teacher at the junior high school, named me with that word. Sometimes, in August 1990, I tried to ask her the meaning of my name. At that time, the only answer I got was that because I was born on October. [...] Nevertheless, it seems to me that the reason is weak because *okta* 'octav' can mean eight, so that people can interpret that I am the eighth child in my family. In fact, I am not the eighth child but the older [i.e. eldest] one. Then, I asked her if she was inspired to name me in that way by her experience as the teacher, she just smiled. However, I believed that her background as the teacher influenced her choice of giving me the name.

In my home town, the people of my generation mostly took the name from Arabic language. It happened because one hundred percent of them are Moslem. Thus, it is quite strange for people to identify me with the name Oktavianus. Then, since my name contains the sound /v/, it seems that it is difficult for people in my hometown to pronounce it. They replace the sound /v/ with /f/ because the sound /v/ is not common both in Minang and Indonesian language.

[...] Furthermore, usually when I introduced my self to the foreigners, and they knew that my name is *Oktavianus*, for the first time I noticed there was misinterpretation about me. The assumed that I was a Christian and I was not Minang man. They would rise the question to me why I was named *Oktavianus*. Then, I told them my real identity that I am a Moslem, from Padang (Minang) and I speak Minangkabau language. They surprised. [...]

Finally, a male subject from Cambodia has the most disturbing tale to tell, one in which his ethnicity, entangled with social class difference and encoded in his birth name, became a death sentence during a period of genocide. His father's family were ethnic Chinese, and his belonging to what was perceived as a socially privileged community in Cambodia was signalled by his name, which was not only transparently Chinese but included the word Kim 'gold', with all the aristocratic and capitalist connotations of that metal. His story includes no fewer than three changes of name.

[...] Since I was born my father gave a very special name to me, 'KIM LENG'. This name sounds like Chinese name. My father's

> parents were from China and my mother's parents were Cambodian. He gave me this name because KIM LENG means the gold dragon [...]. My family name, [...], derived from [...], Chinese word. I do not know what it means as I cannot contact him [my father]; he passed away during Pol Pot time. The reason why my family name was changed because when my older sister attended school, the register recorded the wrong spelling. This comes to our present.
>
> In 1975, the most tragic event happened. The new government came. Kampuchea under the label of Democratic was under the leadership of POL POT. All kinds of people had to work as workers, farmers and even slaves. This affected my name. 'KIM LENG' sounds that I lived in the upper-class family and the government was likely to kill the upper-class people. So my name was changed to aa Leng instead. The way they pronounced my name was obviously not so soft and sweet as they did in the past.
>
> Again, after our country was liberated from Pol Pot regime, we returned to the city. It was the time I started my school. The new government was still strict with names sounded like Chinese. If I had not changed my name, I would not have been able to attend school. Then, my name was completely changed to 'CHAN NARITH' the present name I have used officially. The second part of my official name sounds completely Cambodian. [...]

In view of evidence such as this it would be difficult for any socially inclined linguist not to take ethnic/religious identity seriously as a topic or to refuse to move beyond the traditional exclusion of names from linguistic inquiry on the grounds that they represent acts of individual will. At the very least they represent texts for linguistically informed textual analysis, and indeed ones of extraordinary power for the people who possess them.

Language spread and identity-levelling

Press reports about linguistic matters rarely have much in common with academic discourses on language. But in the last decade the two have come together to form a consensus about the global spread of English and the loss of diversity it is thought to be bringing about, in terms of both linguistic and cultural identity. The topic merits discussion here because the languages and identities thought to be in jeopardy are not national ones for the most part, but the sort that would be described as 'ethnic' by the criteria laid out in the opening section of this chapter, and also 'religious', because the spread of English is bound up with a 'modernity' widely seen as eschewing traditional beliefs in favour of a faith in technology.

The spread of English is held to be connected with 'globalisation', a sort of economic imperialism that entails not just linguistic homogenisation but cultural levelling as well. When the economist Richard G. Harris (1998) says that 'The general presumption of many observers on international use of language is that English is the de facto lingua franca of the global economy', the observers he refers to include linguists, anthropologists and sociologists whose work includes direct observation of language use, as well as pundits, reporters and business people who draw their conclusions from personal experience – less systematically recorded, though not necessarily less real.

The various groups react differently to these developments. Business people are the most likely to see them as facts of life that educational systems must adjust to if the interests of students and the wider community are to be served. Anthropologists, while perhaps wishing for the perceived loss of cultural diversity to be slowed down, are nonetheless used to the notion that cultures are never stable.

Linguists, on the other hand, tend toward more extreme negative reactions. The writings of Tove Skutnabb-Kangas have spread the message that 'Languages are today being killed and linguistic diversity is disappearing at a much faster pace than ever before in human history' (Skutnabb-Kangas, 2000, p. ix). She identifies the perpetrator as 'globalisation', which she calls 'a killing agent'. Education is also to blame: 'Schools are every day committing linguistic genocide' (ibid., p. x). The politics surrounding this issue are very nebulous. Marxists like Holborow (1999) reject Skutnabb-Kangas and Phillipson as reactionaries trying to shore up the linguistic nationalisms that stand in the way of class solidarity. For liberals like Davies (1996), their undisprovable Gramsci-derived notions of 'hegemony' represent far-left dogmatism at its worst; while for Pennycook (2001), Davies, Skutnabb-Kangas and Phillipson all fall into one of his rejected categories, as either 'emancipatory modernists' or 'liberal ostriches'. In any case, the basic premises upheld by Skutnabb-Kangas and Phillipson have entered mainstream applied linguistics through work such as that collected in Graddol and Meinhof (1999), and even the critics named here contest only their attributions of blame and proposed solutions, not the reports of unprecedented language shift themselves, for which the evidence seems overwhelming.

But in an area like this one, evidence is not neatly separable from interpretation, and it is important to scrutinise our data and subject our interpretations of them to rigorous interrogation, including considering the possibility of alternative interpretations. We can say with reasonable certainty that the dominance of English as the preferred second language of study, already well established in much of the world throughout the twentieth century, has increased since the end of the Cold War in 1989–91. This increase has been at the expense of the other European 'world' languages, especially French, German and Russian, with Spanish and Portuguese, and to a lesser extent Italian and Dutch, figuring significantly in certain parts of the world. In the 1990s English also clawed back some of the popularity that had accrued to Japanese and Arabic since the emergence of Japan and some of the Middle Eastern oil-producing countries as major economic powers in the 1970s – though the position of Arabic as the language of Islam has meant that its study as a second language would always grow so long as Muslim populations grow and spread.

However, these changes – the ones we have some reliable statistics for (for instance those collected by Crystal, 1997, pp. 55–60) – are not the ones that most of the worry is about. The spread of English that is the source of so much anxiety is one in which what is being replaced or at least eroded are *mother tongues, native languages, first languages* (I shall use these terms interchangeably), along with the ethnic identities and associated cultures of which they are a part. The extent to which this may be happening is much harder to pin down, for a number of reasons:

1 What is meant by 'mother tongue' is ambiguous. It is generally understood to mean the dialect or language that one grew up speaking in the home. But in the discourse about the spread of English, it is often used to refer not to the home dialect, but to another regional or national language that is learned at school.
2 Mother-tongue use, unlike second-language use, has as its principal domain the home and other private spaces and contexts which are the least penetrable to objective observation.
3 When people talk about the erosion or degrading or loss of a language, the data they give tend to be extremely partial and superficial, instances of English words being inserted into what is otherwise a mother-tongue utterance. Such code-switching behaviour is probably universal among bilingual people; it does not necessarily mean that they are losing their awareness of which language is which, or allowing one language to cannibalise the other.

4 Those who write about the spread of English and its effects on culture and education fail surprisingly often to consider the role of other languages, either European ones or indigenous regional and national languages, which may be partly or wholly responsible for the effects in question over a given population.

Point (1) means that two distinct questions need to be asked about the encroachment of English: to what extent does it affect *mother-tongue* use of other languages and dialects, and to what extent the use of regional and national languages (not 'mother tongue' in the strict sense) in education? The distinction is a crucial one, because facts about one's mother tongue do not automatically transfer to regional or national languages, even if sometimes treated as though they did. If the regional or national language is being used in the education of students who did not grow up speaking it at home, then the encroachment of English will be displacing not the mother tongue, but the language which itself displaced the mother tongue. In that case, the notion of English being a 'killer' of languages and cultures is considerably weakened – indeed, there are situations in which English, by displacing the national language that is the immediate threat to the mother tongue, makes it possible for the mother tongue to be used in a greater range of functional domains. Such is the case, for example, in Hong Kong, where the presence of English as the 'international language' blocks any attempt to impose Mandarin Chinese in place of the native Cantonese in education, government and other areas of public life (see Chapter 6 above).

The essential distinction between the mother tongue and any other tongue relates directly to what in modern times have traditionally been identified as the two essential functions of language, namely, communication and representation. Language is our means of understanding the world and representing it in our minds, as well as of communicating with others. Despite recurrent debates about which of the two is primary, such as Vygotsky's critique of Piaget or Hymes's critique of Chomsky, few have questioned that both functions are of fundamental importance. Yet this is only necessarily the case with our mother tongue, or tongues if we are deeply bilingual. When we do not claim mother-tongue competence in a language with which we are nevertheless able to communicate, we are saying something about the limitation of that language in the representational function for us.

Of the hundreds of millions of speakers of English as a second language, how many use English in communicative functions only, and how many in representational functions as well? This is a further complication to the difficulties already cited in determining the depth, along with the breadth, of the spread of English, since it means trying to decide objectively what language someone is 'thinking in' when they speak. One can think of tests for this much more easily than one can muster the confidence that what the tests show would be consistently true for the speaker tested, let alone for others.

Of course, the other important fact that must be borne in mind about the relationship between mother tongue and speaker is that the mother tongue is central to the construction of the speaker's linguistic identity. The mother tongue is itself a 'claim' about national, ethnic or religious identity (or any combination of the three) that speakers may make and hearers will certainly interpret. But as has been made clear by the Communication Theory of Identity (see above, Chapter 4, pp. 80–3), we all have many layers of linguistic identity, and it is also the case that second languages can play a significant role in one's linguistic identity. Still, the mother tongue has a very special role, bound up as it is with representation, which is to say with the way we think. This is not to assert a Whorfian view, at least not a strong one, but only to say that we have a particular attachment and allegiance to the languages in which we think, classify, interpret, imagine and dream.

Another fact we can feel reasonably sure about, unfortunately, is that many 'small' languages and dialects, i.e. with relatively few speakers, are not being actively used by the grandchildren of people who themselves typically represent the last monolingual generation in those dialects. The grandchildren usually still have considerable passive knowledge of the language, and understand their grandparents even though their active use of the language is halting and mixed with their first language. This is mainly, but not entirely, the result of the general rural-to-urban population shift which has been taking place in the so-called 'developed' world steadily for 150 years,[5] and is now accompanying 'development' elsewhere. Perhaps 'accompanying' is the wrong word, for the creation of urban centres is itself an integral part of the complex of processes identified as 'development'.

This is the form of language loss with which the Foundation for Endangered Languages is concerned. In 2001 they announced a forthcoming conference on 'Endangered Languages and the Media', concerned with 'the shrinking of the world's minority languages'. The Foundation noted that this would be its first conference 'outside the English-speaking world'. But then it declared that 'The language of the conference will be English'. I e-mailed the Foundation's President, Nicholas Ostler, to ask whether there was not perhaps some cognitive dissonance between the conference theme and its language policy, to which he replied saying, nonsense, English and French are not the problem at all, it is the medium-sized languages like Berber that are swallowing up all the little dialects. This is clearly a different position from Phillipson's, whose 1992 book deals strictly with *English* linguistic imperialism. Skutnabb-Kangas (2000, p. xi) takes a more ambiguous position, in which the forces of homogenisation are 'dominant languages and cultures, and maybe specifically English'. No matter: the debate over what language is driving the shift only serves to draw attention away from the need to sift more carefully through its results.

The loss of small local and tribal languages is both real and lamentable. It represents a cultural loss not only for their living speakers but for their descendants yet unborn, and strong support should go to efforts for helping these speakers preserve their languages by creating resources that will help their children to be bilingual in their traditional language and whatever bigger language is pushing it aside, rather than just monolingual in the bigger language. I do not however agree that denying them the choice of education in the bigger language is a legitimate answer. The believers in linguistic imperialism argue that the economic hegemony which drives such choices makes them not choices at all. Again I disagree, based on my experience of many cultures (including that of my own family) in which individuals have made different choices, some following the economic tide and others swimming directly against it, and can fully articulate their reasons for doing so, in a way that gives the lie to any suggestion that they are not exercising their will in conscious awareness of the 'power' structures in the world, but are merely its pawns – a dehumanising suggestion if ever there was one.

The other truism I dispute is that the loss of linguistic diversity we are seeing now is unprecedented. The fact that inevitably gets pushed aside in the discourse of linguistic homogenisation is one that no linguist would think of denying: the expansion of the population speaking a language through absorption of speakers of other languages and dialects introduces huge new diversity into the language. Historically this is how unified languages have broken up – how Latin, for example, gave way to the thousands of the Romance dialects spoken at least through the early decades of this century, when the great linguistic atlases of France, Italy and later Spain were drawn up.

The effect we are witnessing, I believe, is this: situations of language shift which produce greater dialectal diversity can be perceived, while they are happening, as instead producing less diversity, if they are also producing increased intercomprehension and communicability.[6] Now, how do we measure 'greater' and 'lesser' dialectal diversity? Was Europe more linguistically diverse before the spread of Latin and the retreat of various pre-Indo-European and Indo-European languages than it was after the break-up of Latin into Romance dialects which in part reflected the structure of those earlier substratum languages? The linguist is inclined to say as a knee-jerk reaction that the prior situation was one of more diversity because the languages involved showed a larger typological difference from one another. Yet degree of typological difference does not really mean much to ordinary speakers of the language, for instance to two medieval peasants from Bologna and Florence who could not understand one another's dialect, although their Etruscan ancestors might well have understood each other perfectly a few centuries before.

What we as linguists must bear in mind is that, although the break-up of Latin into a panoply of dialects may have been inevitable, the emergence of subsets of them as new 'languages' was not. Romance-speaking Europe was conceived of as linguistically unified for centuries after the dialectal fragmentation was complete. Only the political–cultural changes of the Renaissance – in particular, the rise of (proto-)nationalism – led to the recognition of dialectal difference as language difference. And that change was driven by a need on the part of various Romance-speaking populations to identify themselves as distinct peoples.

In 1907, in response to an earlier wave of concern about the spread of English and the loss of diversity (on which see further Joseph, forthcoming d), W. J. Clark, a proponent of the artificial international language Esperanto, represented as follows the position to which he was opposed:

> Jingoes are not wanting who say that it is unpatriotic of any Englishman to be a party to the introduction of a neutral language, because English is manifestly destined to be the language of the world. [...] The interests of English-speaking peoples are enormous, far greater than those of any other group of nations united by a common bond of speech. (Clark, 1907, p. 36)

Clark then explains why he thinks this view is wrong-headed:

> But it is a form of narrow provincial ignorance to refuse on that account to recognize that, compared to the whole bulk of civilized people, the English speakers are in a small minority, and that the majority includes many high-spirited peoples with a strongly developed

> sense of nationality, and destined to play a very important part in the history of the world. (Ibid.)

There is, in other words, a 'natural' obstacle to any language becoming universal, in what Clark calls the 'strongly developed sense of nationality'. He goes on to assert that English has the best claims of any national language to become the international language. But, he insists, 'the discussion of this question has no more than an academic interest', because it is impossible 'for political reasons' for any national language to assume this role (ibid., pp. 37–8). National identity (as we would now call it) would block the spread of English, despite what Clark considered the compelling need for an international language to serve international commercial and political purposes. There was absolutely no question, for Clark, of such a language replacing any national language in any of its internal functions.

I believe that Clark was basically right. With that early twentieth-century modernist optimism that reason and logic would overcome even the most basic human functions if we just worked at it hard enough, the proponents of an international language – many prominent linguists among them – believed that languages could be cleanly divided, in a centrally planned way, for the very different functions of communication and national identity. Many thought that having a language of 'pure communication' would eliminate the possibility of war. This was idealistic. One of the key realities it failed to take into account is that language is so thoroughly and intricately bound up with human identity, on every level from the personal to the national and beyond, that, outside of trivial contexts, no real separation between them is possible. Moreover, it partakes in a belief widely held in the period from 1870 to the mid-twentieth century that every identity should find 'national' expression. Certainly the events of the early 1990s, when states created in 1919 saw their national identities crumble in favour of a panoply of pre-modern ethnic ones, has made any such faith well-nigh impossible to maintain.

Regarding globalisation, it means so many different things to so many people that it ultimately may not mean anything at all. For young anarchists it seems to mean corporate capitalism. For the French it means the dropping of tariffs and the availability of foreign cheese in French supermarkets, a clear sign of cultural decay. For the British it means being able to holiday somewhere sunny but otherwise behave just like at home. For businesspeople it means being able to invest, produce and sell anywhere in the world. Whatever it is, it ain't new.

A World Bank (2000) briefing paper points out that not only does the current globalisation trend not represent the peak of such activity even in modern times:

> In the modern era, globalization saw an earlier flowering towards the end of the 19th century, mainly among the countries that are today developed or rich. For many of these countries trade and capital market flows relative to GDP were close to or higher than in recent years.

Indeed, in a sense globalisation represents activities that have been going on for as long as trade has been conducted across distant sea and land routes, which is to say beyond recorded human history.

> That earlier peak of globalization was reversed in the first half of the 20th century, a time of growing protectionism, in a context of bitter national and great-power strife, world wars, revolutions, rising authoritarian ideologies, and massive economic and political instability. (Ibid.)

Economists generally are beginning to speak of the world as having recently come out of an exceptional period, and adjusting to a return to what in the longer perspective is normalcy. Yet the wider cultural discourse of 'globalisation' is one of unprecedented change, just like that of the spread of English and the loss of linguistic and cultural diversity. In assessing the 'inevitability' of the current trends running to completion, one needs to bear in mind that, like their historical predecessors, they combine a bit of truth with a lot of illusion, fuelled by hype. There is, after all, not even a single country in which English was once dominant where it is not today *retreating* as a mother tongue, sharing that space either with indigenous languages (as in Canada, New Zealand, Australia, South Africa, Scotland, Wales, Ireland), other ex-colonial languages (Canada, the south-western USA, South Africa) or the languages of major waves of new immigrants (everywhere, but especially England, the USA, Canada, Australia and New Zealand).

With regard to technological developments, in the mid-1990s it looked as though advances in communications technology were leading inevitably to conditions that would favour the spread of English at the expense of national linguistic identities. But subsequent developments have reversed this completely. Then it was common to point to the near worldwide availability of CNN and BBC World as evidence that television news was globalising in English; today those channels are lost in an ever-growing band of news and other channels broadcasting in national and regional languages. Then, the fact that e-mail had to be done in Roman script without accent marks was proof that everyone was going to be writing in English soon; now the number of scripts and character sets for e-mail is into three figures. The ubiquity of the Internet, combined with cellular phones and text messaging, now means that one person from a small village can leave for the capital, or for another continent, and continue to use the village dialect for the bulk of his or her social communication, at an affordable cost. That has probably never been true before. These latest technological developments actually present an unprecedented *obstacle* to linguistic homogenisation.

Richard Harris (1998) again expresses a very widely held view when he writes that 'Globalization at one level requires economic standardization and this increases the demand for a single lingua franca – most likely English.' This may be true, but again, what is true of a lingua franca may not have an impact on mother tongues. Here again recent technological developments are having an impact that disfavours the spread of English, as machine translation programmes, which only a couple of years ago were still in a hopelessly primitive state, have made a quantum leap in sophistication.[7]

Whatever its sources, the perceived emergence of a transnational postmodern culture, grounded in global technological advances and associated first with English, secondly with other transnational languages, has had a significant impact on identity worldwide at the turn of the twenty-first century. For younger people in particular, it has made national identities partly (but only partly) irrelevant. On the Internet, it scarcely matters what country one is from; just the fact of being on the Internet constitutes a greater cultural bond. Their 'home page' is their spiritual home. Ultimately, however, most people want to meet face to face, in the flesh. 'Real' contact and 'virtual' contact continue to be distinguishable. There is no indication that national and ethnic identities will cease to matter; no reported cases of people renouncing their mother tongue in favour of English, other than among third-generation immigrants to English-speaking countries, which has always been the case and occurs in reverse as well.

Ever since Malinowski announced his breakthrough conception of phatic communion, we have taken what is 'meaningful' in linguistic utterances to extend far beyond their propositional content, and to include all those features of utterances beyond the propositional meaning and its expression which hearers use to interpret things about the speaker – geographical and social origin, level of education, gender and sexuality, intelligence, likeability, reliability and trustworthiness, and so on. Indeed, it has been solidly and repeatedly demonstrated that interpretation of the speaker's trustworthiness from the non-propositional content of utterances bears directly upon the hearer's assessment of the 'truth value' of the proposition itself.

So adept are we at judging one another in this way that the amount of linguistic diversity required can be minuscule, if we happen to belong to the same linguistic community. I am able to distinguish on the basis of one or two spoken words whether a person is from Lucas County, Ohio, or Monroe County, Michigan, which border on each other, so early and deep was my socialisation into that particular difference. In the case where two people do not belong to the same linguistic community, however, judgements are made at a higher level of difference, involving wider parameters of diversity. Ultimately, national, ethnic and religious identities themselves will be asserted through linguistic diversity; and if history has taught us anything, it is that individuals, in order to know who they themselves are, want such identities, and will not give up their manifestation in linguistic diversity, whatever the economic or other pressures might be to know a world language for purposes of communication. Knowing who one is belongs to the realm not of communication, but representation.

I am not saying that the spread of English or the loss of small languages (not always replaced by English) is illusory, but that there is an effect of illusion whereby we do not simultaneously perceive the diversity being introduced into English and other world languages by their absorption of these populations that formerly spoke the smaller languages (see also Mufwene, 2001). The reasons for the illusion are, first, that it is hard to keep our attention on communication and representation simultaneously; and second, that we have not recognised the imperative imposed on language shift by that particular form of representation of self and other that is constituted by linguistic identity. Human language has never homogenised because it cannot. The functional necessity is too great of being able to make judgements about the people we encounter and the truth value of what they say, both of which we adjudge largely on the grounds of our interpretation of their linguistic identity.

In sum, two forces operate to keep linguistic homogenisation from taking place: the imperatives of *individual linguistic identity*, which demands variation and prefers comprehension, and those of *national/ethnic/religious linguistic identity*, where the need for establishing and maintaining 'imagined communities', group self-representations based on difference founded in real or supposed history, imposes the need for *Abstand* (see above, Chapter 6, p. 144), structural difference of such an order as probably to impede intercomprehension. What Pennycook (1998, 2001), Canagarajah (1999) and others refer to as 'resistance' to a colonial language is a manifestation of this need for linguistic diversification.

There is a third force: our focus on communication as a function of language makes the existence of multiple languages, and mutually unintelligible dialects of the same language, look like a problem, an obstacle to communication; but it too has a very basic human function. When conducting trade, one needs of course to communicate with the trading partner, but also to confer with one's own side in private, exchanging information kept secret from those one is negotiating with. Human societies would never have developed or survived without this essential tool of incomprehension. Whatever the social or economic pressures for a worldwide lingua franca might be, they will not sweep these obstacles away. Linguistic diversity is something much more unassailable than a 'human right' – it is a tautology.

There is, however, a paradox where 'homogenisation' of language is concerned. Even if I am right that, in absolute terms, homogenisation is impossible, it remains true nonetheless that Standard English is much more different from Scots Gaelic than it is from Scottish English, or that French is much more different from Breton than it is from the regional French of Brittany. The ability of Scottish English or Brittany French to remain distinctive over the long term negates homogenisation in the absolute, while simultaneously weakening speakers' motivation to maintain Gaelic or Breton. As I noted above, the basic reason for the weakening of languages like Gaelic and Breton is the long-term general rural-to-urban population shift, a shift that may ultimately run its course, but probably too late for Gaelic, the native speakers of which are nearly all bilingual and of advancing age.

Attempts to save Gaelic deserve support, through any means that would not deny Gaelic speakers the right to choose education in English for themselves and their children or otherwise inhibit their linguistic freedom. Whether or not this proves possible, we linguists should also recognise that those minority language communities which have moved toward a regionally marked variety of a majority tongue (for economic motives rather than under direct governmental duress) have not entirely forsaken linguistic diversity, even if has been compromised. And it is not the case that their particular version of the language represents a failure to assimilate fully. It is a form of linguistic resistance.

The next chapter will look in depth at the ongoing construction, deconstruction and reconstruction of an intertwined pair of ethnic and religious identities, the 'performers' of which have lived side by side for centuries, sometimes peacefully though with one group dominating the other, sometimes with each trying to kill the other. The identities in question have numerous linguistic and discursive manifestations. One of those that will not be discussed is names, a topic raised in the present chapter; but for two interesting examples of name 'crossing' involving Lebanese Maronite identity, see the dedication page to the present book.

8
Case Study 2: Christian and Muslim Identities in Lebanon

Introduction

This chapter examines the role of language in constructing Lebanese Christian identities, against the backdrop of centuries of Islamic domination in the region and the fact that the ultimate 'standard' of the Arabic language is the Koran. By claiming a Phoenician ancestry, Lebanese Christian communities have constructed a history for themselves that would give them a greater 'authenticity' in the region than their Muslim countrymen, while simultaneously pointing them in the direction of Europe. The construction of a 'North Semitic' identity uniting Phoenician with Aramaic and Syriac,[1] the Maronite liturgical language, both links it to and distinguishes it from 'South Semitic' Arabic. In recent times a no less important factor has been the role of Arabic–French bilingualism as an identity marker for Christians. Since the end of civil war in 1990, however, the implementation of Arabic–English–French trilingualism in the national school curriculum for all Lebanese has undone the ability of the second language to identify the Christian community in this way. Original research is reported concerning the effects of this change on perceptions of 'Arab' and 'Lebanese' identity in the country.

Interwoven with this account is a consideration of the work of Ernest Renan, the great Semiticist, linguist, historian and philosopher of mid-nineteenth century France, who was largely responsible for creating and promulgating modern 'orientalist' views of the Middle East, and who intervened directly at a crucial moment in the history of Lebanon. Renan's well-known views on nationalism (see also above, Chapter 5, pp. 112–15) are contrasted with his statements about Semitic languages and national identity, as well as his actions in Lebanon. There is a particular disjuncture in Renan's thought with regard to 'abstraction', which is a key term for him in both his linguistic–ethnographic and his political analysis. Renan locates a key difference between the Semitic and Indo-European peoples in the lack of abstract terms in the Semitic languages, which he believes affects the way they think. At the same time, intriguingly, he claims that his own way of thinking about nationalism is a step forward because it is moving beyond abstractions. We shall look at how this tension within his work played itself out in some rather significant ways, in both theoretical and political terms.

'What language is spoken in Lebanon?'

On 14 August 2002 I recorded a brief conversation that took place (in English) between a Malaysian Chinese woman who has lived in Scotland for more than 30 years (W1), and a 24-year-old Lebanese woman making her first venture outside her native country (W2). By way of making small talk, W1 asked what (as she later told me) she took to be a rather obvious question:

W1 And what language is spoken in Lebanon?
W2 French.
(*pause*)
W1 Really? Not Arabic?
W2 The Moslem, they speak Arabic all the time. Nothing but Arabic.

The father of W2, a 54-year-old who had accompanied her on the trip (having himself been out of Lebanon only briefly on two previous occasions) and was also taking part in the conversation, nodded assent to his daughter's words but added nothing.

What W1 did not realise was the extent to which her seemingly innocuous and obvious question would be interpreted as a challenge over a very sensitive matter of linguistic and religious–ethnic identity. I am confident that W2 did not misunderstand the question, since her reply, although surprising, was in line with numerous other statements she made to me. These were particularly surprising because, in February and March of 1998, when I visited W2 and her family at their home in

Lebanon, their attitude toward Arabic and French had been markedly different. Then, we spoke to each other mainly in French, for the simple reason that it was our most viable lingua franca. They subjected me to considerable criticism for not speaking better Arabic, since, in their view, as the descendant of two Lebanese grandparents (one of them the uncle of W2's father), I had a filial and cultural duty to know what they described over and over as 'the language of Lebanon'. Over the intervening four years I worked on my Arabic, a language I had in fact grown up with, getting it to a reasonable conversational level – only to discover that now, in a changed religious–political atmosphere, they prefer to speak French.

Historical background

I shall attempt to explain the change in the closing section. First, though, some historical background is needed. The land that constitutes the modern state of Lebanon was part of the Alexandrian, Roman and Byzantine empires. It came under Arab rule in the seventh century after Christ and remained under it until the thirteenth century, minus a few periods of Byzantine reconquest and a few cities held by Crusaders. It was ruled by the Mamluks until 1516, when it became part of the Ottoman Empire, and remained so until the Empire was disbanded in the aftermath of the First World War, in which it had sided with Germany. For most of the Ottoman period, Mount Lebanon was a quasi-autonomous region dominated by the Maronites, a Christian sect who have been uniate with the Vatican since 1182, centuries longer than any of the important Catholic sects in Lebanon (Greeks, Armenians, Syrians and Chaldeans, all of which split off from Orthodox or other non-Catholic sects between the sixteenth and eighteenth centuries). Having the French as their protectors was the main factor in Maronite power within Mount Lebanon. The Lebanese state was established under a French mandate in 1920, and became an independent republic in 1943 after Lebanon was freed from Vichy French rule by British and Free French forces.

Pace my cousin W2, Arabic is the mother tongue of nearly the whole native-born Lebanese population. It serves as the major binding force of national unity, even for those who at the same time locate their identity principally in their differences vis-à-vis other Lebanese, when national unity is what they want to assert. These differences are religious and sectarian first and foremost, but they are mirrored and manifested in other cultural divisions, including differences of who is bilingual in what. These differences are significant enough for W2 to have spontaneously shifted W1's question onto the ground of bilingualism. For what W1's question threateningly implies is that Lebanon has one language only, and more generally, that nations and languages exist in a one-to-one correspondence. If Lebanon has one language only, that language is surely Arabic; and if the 'ownership' of Arabic has to be assigned to one nation, many would maintain that it would have to be the 'nation of Islam', who were after all responsible for spreading Arabic from the southern part of the Semitic-speaking world to northern areas such as Lebanon. Rather than countenance any such implications, W2 simply switched battlegrounds; for when it comes to bilingualism, the Christians of Lebanon, especially Maronites like her, can assert an advantage.

Already during the Ottoman period, various forms of bilingualism set groups of people apart. Speakers bilingual in Arabic and Turkish, the Ottoman administrative language, formed a class of government officials and functionaries that cut across religious divisions. On the other hand, with rare exceptions, only Christians were bilingual in Arabic and the languages of their Western European protectors, especially the French. Arabic–French bilingualism became an important identity marker for certain (not all) Christian sects, notably the Maronites. Their relationship with Arabic is further complicated by the fact that another Semitic tongue, Syriac, is their liturgical language, which means that the role of Arabic in Maronite cultural life is fundamentally different than for the Muslim sects. Still, *Allāh* is the God worshipped by Christians and Moslems alike in the Arabic language, *'Īsā* is the Jesus whom the former consider the Son of God and the latter one of his greatest prophets, and *Maryam* his mother, revered by both Christians and Muslims as the holiest of women.

Distribution of languages by religion

In modern times, the distribution of languages other than Arabic in Lebanon has gone through three stages. In the Ottoman period, up through the First World War, chances were strong that anyone who knew French (or Italian, though it had receded considerably by the end of the nineteenth century) was an educated Christian, and more specifically a Maronite or Roman Catholic. Anyone who knew English was likely to be an educated Muslim (probably Druze) or Orthodox Christian (probably Greek). Knowledge of Turkish was widespread, especially among men.

Table 8.1 Bilingualism by religion, sex and age group (%)

	Arabic–French bilingual	*Arabic–English bilingual*	*Arabic–French–English trilingual*	*Arabic monolingual*	*Illiterate*
Men					
Christian	21	3	5	48	23
Muslim	17	3	2	39	39
Women					
Christian	24	1	2	28	45
Muslim	7	2	0	22	69
Boys					
Christian	37	3	6	32	22
Muslim	32	5	1	34	28
Girls					
Christian	39	1	2	29	29
Muslim	28	2	0	37	33

From Abou (1962, p. 111).

Under the French mandate and its aftermath, knowledge of French spread across religions and sects. It was still statistically more probable that someone who knew French was Christian rather than Muslim, but not by a wide margin. Similarly with the Druze and Greek Orthodox majority for English. In 1962 Abou found the distribution shown in Table 8.1. Abou's use of 'illiterate' as a separate category suggests how strongly multilingualism in Lebanon has been above all an *educational* fact. The spread of education through the population over time can be seen by comparing the figures for men and women on the one hand and boys and girls on the other. Knowledge of French has nearly doubled among the youngest generation; in the case of Muslim girls, it has quadrupled. Illiteracy has dropped sharply for every group except the Christian males, three-quarters of whom were already literate in the adult generation. The coming of English, although slow, is visible, again by comparing the generations. (For further information on bilingualism in Lebanon, see Abou, 1978; Guenier, 1994; Pecheur, 1993; Srage, 1988; and for an early study on bilingualism in the 'Arab world' generally, Nakhla, 1935).

The co-construction of religious and ethnic identity: Maronites and Phoenicians

A later section of this chapter will present some more recent data for the distribution of languages by religion in Lebanon. Before that, I want to look in detail at one facet of the Christian cultural context and one facet of the Muslim cultural context, each of which has contributed to the construction of ethnic, linguistic and religious difference where, by all obvious appearances, there is unity.[2]

For centuries the Christian populations of Lebanon, Syria, Palestine, Jordan and Iraq have been nearly an island in the vast sea of Islam. Actually they have been a sort of peninsula, with Lebanon as the primary link to the Christian world to the west. In these circumstances it is perhaps not surprising that a significant cultural effort has gone toward creating a cultural authenticity rooted in the belief that, if they are an island, they did not emerge from the sea, but were there long before the sea existed. An interesting contribution to this effort is the 1984 book *History of the Maronites* by Father Boutros Dau. Part One is called 'The Phœnician Ancestors of the MARONITES', and its first chapter is entitled 'Origin of the Phœnicians – a People three million years old'. It divides the 3 million year history of the Maronites into seven periods, the first being:

> 1 – The prehistoric extending from three million years to the sixth millenium [*sic*] B.C. From this period were found:
> a – Fish fossils about 75,000,000 years old found at Sahil 'Alma and in Haqil Byblos,
> b – Implements from the Stone Age found at al-'Aqbiyah [and eight other locations],
> c – [...] a human skeleton embedded in a rock shelter at Kasr 'Aqil above Antilyas six miles north of Beirut [...] of a boy about eight years old who may have lived 25,000 to 30,000 years ago [...]. (Dau, 1984, pp. 11–12)

Quite how this evidence establishes that the Maronites are 'a People three million years old' – 10 to 20 times older than the current estimated age of the species *Homo sapiens* – is not explained. The next paragraph gives more information about the skeleton in (c), though, oddly, without noting that it has already been mentioned:

> A fairly typical early Lebanese child skeleton with strong mediterranean appearance dating back 30,000 years ago was discovered at Antelias. This discovery proves that since at least 30,000 years, Lebanese people have been of a proper mediterranean type, independent and wholly different from that of an Arab type. It is therefore contrary to all beliefs to maintain that Lebanese people are Arabs. (Ibid., p. 12)

An interesting slip there: 'contrary to all *beliefs*' when one would have expected 'all evidence'. The historical periods continue up to Period 8, the 'Phœnicio Greco-Roman period (332 B.C.–400 A.D.)', during which

> [...] Christ is born, the cities of Phœnician coast gradually embraced christianity. The mountain [Mt Lebanon] persisted in paganism until it was converted by the disciples of St. Maron during the fifth through the seventh century. (Ibid., p. 16)

And that brings us finally to:

> 9 – The Phœnicio-Maronite period (400 A.D.–present time): The population remained ethnically and nationally the same as before, but the religion changed, and with religion the name Maronite replaced that of Phœnician; politically, the mountain became the center of gravity instead of the coastal cities, and the name Lebanon replaced politically that of Phœnicia. (Ibid.)

In other words, *Lebanon* equals *Maronite* equals *Phoenician.* It now starts to become clear why it is important to stretch the Phoenicians further and further back into prehistory. If Maronite Christianity predates Islam by only some two centuries, that does not give it much in the way of historical priority. If, on the other hand, the Maronites were already in Lebanon over 3 million years before the birth of the Prophet Muhammad, their claims to be the *true* Lebanese people are beyond refute.

The cultural fictions concerning the Phoenicians are clearly cultural first and 'ethnic' second. For despite Father Dau's remark about the 'child skeleton with strong mediterranean appearance', there is no credible physical anthropological distinction to be drawn such that Lebanese people, or even just Maronites, fall clearly into a 'Mediterranean' rather than an 'Arab' category. As for the Phoenicians, all the archaeological evidence suggests that they were a Semitic people, in other words of exactly the same ethnic and cultural origins as the Arabs.

Constructing Islamic Arabic uniqueness

Father Dau stands in a long and venerable line of people devoted to scholarly disproof of apparent ethnic and cultural unity. Much classical Islamic scholarship was aimed at furthering the belief that Arabia in the time of Muhammad was isolated from the rest of the Semitic world, which plainly was not the case. Jeffery's 1938 study of *The Foreign Vocabulary of the Qur'ān* spends a great deal of time sorting through the ideologically motivated etymologies put forward to claim that *no word in the Koran is of non-Arabic origin*. Even when the source of the borrowing was a very close Hebrew congener, so long as it was charged with Jewish or Christian religious significance, scholars held it to be unrelated.

In the following examples I have transliterated foreign scripts and omitted the details as to which scholars maintained which views (the full information can be found by following up the citations). First, some cases of words borrowed into Arabic from Greek, a language associated exclusively with Christianity:

- *Iblīs* 'the Devil': 'The tendency among the Muslim authorities is to derive the name from *bls* "to despair", he being so called because God caused him to despair of all good [...]. The more acute philologers, however, recognized the impossibility of this [...]. That the word is a corruption of the Gk. *diábolos* has been recognized by the majority of Western scholars' (Jeffery, 1938, p. 47).
- *burūj* 'Towers': 'The philologers took the word to be from *baraja* "to appear" ([...]), but there can be little doubt that *burūj* represents the Gk. *púrgos* (Lat. *burgus*), used of the towers on a city wall [...]' (ibid., p. 79).
- *qalam* 'pen': 'The native authorities take the word from *qalama* "to cut" ([...]), but this is only folk-etymology, for the word is the Gk. *kálamos* "a reed" and then "a pen", though coming through some Semitic form' (ibid., p. 243).

Indeed, the name for the Byzantine Greeks themselves, *ar-Rūm*, was subjected to this same interpretational process:

> 'A considerable number of the early authorities took it as an Arabic word derived from *rām* 'to desire eagerly', the people so called because of their eagerness to capture Constantinople ([...]). Some even gave them a Semitic genealogy [...]. The ultimate origin, of course, is Lat. *Roma*, which in Gk. is *'Rṓmē*, which came into common use when *hē Neà 'Rṓmē* [...] became the name of Constantinople after it had become the capital of the Empire. (Ibid., pp. 146–7)

Turning to the Semitic languages, the scholars subjected the name of *Isrā'īl* 'Israel' – the patriarch and the nation of his descendants – to no less extraordinary etymological acrobatics: 'Some of the exegetes endeavoured to derive it from *srī* "to travel by night", because when Jacob fled from Esau he travelled by night ([. . .]). It was very generally recognized as a foreign name, however' (ibid., p. 61). Jeffery goes on to note that the absence of an initial glottal stop means that the word was probably not borrowed directly from the Hebrew, but came instead from a Christian origin, since the Greek, Syriac and Ethiopic forms of the name all lack the stop.

Other Hebrew borrowings for which Koranic commentators went into denial include:

- *aḥbār*, plural of *ḥibr* or *ḥabr* 'a Jewish Doctor of the Law': 'The Commentators knew that it was a technical Jewish title and quote as an example of its use Ka'b al-Aḥbār, the well-known convert from Judaism. It was generally taken, however, as a genuine Arabic word derived from *ḥabira* "to leave a scar" (as of a wound), the Divines being so called because of the deep impression their teaching makes on the lives of their students' (ibid., pp. 49–50).
- *asbāṭ* 'the Tribes' (i.e. the Twelve Tribes of Israel): 'The philologers derive it from *sbṭ* "a thistle", their explanation thereof being interesting if not convincing ([. . .]). Some, however, felt the difficulty, and Abū'l-Laith was constrained to admit that it was a Hebrew loan-word' (ibid., p. 57). Jeffery goes on to note that it may have been borrowed via the Syriac.
- *Taurāh* 'the Torah' 'was recognized by some of the early authories to be a Hebrew word [. . .]. Some, however, desired to make it an Arabic word derived from *warā* ["to conceal, keep secret"]' (ibid., p. 96).

Finally, I have reserved for last what are undoubtedly the two most significant cases, since they consist of nothing less than the names of God and the prophet whom Christians believe to be the Son of God. Concerning *Allāh* Jeffery writes,

> One gathers [. . .] that certain early Muslim authorities held that the word was of Syriac or Hebrew origin. The majority, however, claimed that it was pure Arabic, though they set forth various theories as to its derivation. Some held that it has no derivation, [. . .] while the Baṣrans derived it from *al lāh*, taking *lāh* as a verbal noun from *lyh* 'to be high' or 'to be veiled'. The suggested origins [. . .] were even more

> varied, some taking it from *alaha* 'to worship', some from *aliha* 'to be perplexed', some from *aliha 'ilya* 'to turn to for protection', and others from *waliha* 'to be perplexed'. Western scholars are fairly unanimous that the source of the word must be found in one of the older religions. (Ibid., p. 66)

But most problematic of all was *'Īsā* 'Jesus', a form which does not occur in Arabic earlier than the Koran (ibid., p. 220) and is difficult to derive from its Hebrew original following normal sound correspondences. Jeffery writes: 'Many Muslim authorities take the word as Arabic and derive it from *'is* "to be a dingy white", whence *'ayasu* "a reddish whiteness" ([...]), or from *'aisu* meaning "a stallion's urine" (ibid., p. 219). Stallion's urine is not the most obvious source from which to derive the name of a revered prophet, even if he is another religion's Messiah. But I doubt that the Muslim authorities were, as we say, taking the piss, since Arabic culture has always revered the awesome power and majesty of the stallion, and it is easy to imagine that its urine would be perceived as a magical substance with connections to the animal's near-mythical generative capacities. Still, the very impulse to prove a pure Arabic origin for the name of everyone who figures in the Koran, even when their name in their own language was known to be reasonably close to the Arabic form, is a testament to the power of ideology over empirical observation, if any such testament were needed.

Recent shifts in Lebanese language/identity patterns

After the start of civil war in the mid-1970s, the position of French, which had been strong and growing in 1962 (see Table 8.1) began to decline sharply. Something like the old Ottoman-era distribution re-established itself, so that now, as Table 8.2 shows, approximately half the Francophones of Lebanon are Maronites. The decline of French has been paralleled by the rise of English. Recent data are not available on knowledge of English across Lebanon, but quite a bit can be surmised from the survey Abou et al. (1996) have done of the Francophone community. When asked what languages besides Arabic would be most useful for the future of Lebanon, 61.5 per cent of the Francophones answered that English would be most useful. Only 31.8 per cent said that French would be most useful, and a mere 3.1 per cent said both English and French (Abou et al., 1996, p. 99). Even more startlingly, the Maronite Francophones were more inclined than the Muslim Francophones to answer English rather than French. Two out of three Maronite

Table 8.2 Distribution of Francophones by religion

Religious community	*Francophones*
Sunni	10.5%
Shi'ite	12.1%
Druze	2.9%
Maronite	49.3%
Greek Orthodox	12.7%
Greek Catholic	9.6%
Others	2.9%
Total	100.0%
Number in sample	6,703

Source: From Abou et al. (1996, p. 68).

Francophones named English as the most important language for the country's future (ibid., p. 100). It seems clear from these data that another major linguistic realignment is in progress.

A research study which I initiated in 1998, the results of which have been published in Ghaleb & Joseph (2000), targeted adult residents (over 17 years of age) of the Greater Beirut area. A university student was trained to solicit and administer the instrument. Diverse areas of the capital were pinpointed for data collection. The student would randomly select an adult passing by her location and request their participation in the study. The amount of time needed to complete the form was estimated at 15 minutes each. Our research was based on a combination of questionnaire and interview. The major independent variables we examined were: age, sex, religious affiliation, type of schools and university attended, level of education attained, profession/occupation, place of origin, and area of residence within Beirut. Moderator variables included time spent abroad (and where spent), contact with persons abroad, and so on.

A total of 281 participants in the Greater Beirut area completed the forms. The participants were subdivided as shown in Table 8.3. In breaking down the first foreign language by religion, as shown in Table 8.4, we found no significant differences between Muslims and Christians.

When it comes to attitudes, however, differences begin to emerge. Although English figured as the foremost world language by the respondents, when considering Lebanon's needs, a less overwhelming response was found. In answer to the query, 'Do you think English or French is currently more important as a second language for Lebanon?', the responses showed that both English and French figured as being

Table 8.3 Participants by gender and religion

Religion	*Male*	*Female*	*Total*
Muslims	55	101	156
Christians	38	72	110
No response	6	9	15
Total	99	182	281

Source: Ghaleb & Joseph (2000).

Table 8.4 Participants' first foreign language by religion

Respondents' first foreign language	*Muslims*	*Christians*	*Total*
English	91 [58.3%]	60 [54.5%]	151 [53.7%]
French	59 [37.8%]	43 [39.1%]	102 [36.3%]
English and French	2 [1.3%]	3 [2.7%]	5 [1.8%]
Other	4 [2.6%]	4 [3.6%]	8 [2.8%]
No response			15 [5.3%]
Total	156	110	281

Source: Ghaleb & Joseph (2000).

Table 8.5 Most important foreign language for Lebanon by religion

Participants' religion	*English*	*French*	*Both*	*Neither*	*Total*
Muslims	77 (49.7%)	14 (9.0%)	58 (37.4%)	6 (3.9%)	155
Christians	37 (33.6%)	10 (9.0%)	61 (55.5%)	2 (1.8%)	110
No response					16
Total	114	24	119	8	281
Per cent (/265)	43.0	9.1	44.9	3.0	100

Source: Ghaleb & Joseph (2000).

important. However, for those that selected just one language for their response, English was considered to be the more important of the two, as Table 8.5 shows. These figures show a difference from those cited in Abou et al. (1996, p. 99). Table 8.6 displays the contrast. My interpretation of the difference is that, for whatever reason, Abou's subjects did not perceive 'both' as a valid choice. Interesting results were found from the query, 'Do you associate English and French with particular

Table 8.6 Comparison of figures for most important foreign language for Lebanon (%)

	English	*French*	*Both*
Abou et al.	61.5	31.8	3.1
Ghaleb–Joseph	43.0	9.1	44.9

Table 8.7 Which religion English is associated with

	Religion of respondent		
Associate English with:	*Muslim (/155)*	*Christian (/110)*	
Christians	2 (1.3%)	7 (6.4%)	
Muslims	18 (11.6%)	7 (6.4%)	
Both	25 (16.1%)	9 (8.2%)	
Neither	107 (69.0%)	85 (77.3%)	
No response			21

Source: Ghaleb & Joseph (2000).

Table 8.8 Which religion French is associated with

	Religion of respondent		
Associate French with:	*Muslim (/155)*	*Christian (/110)*	
Christians	73 (47.1%)	43 (39.1%)	
Muslims	1 (0.6%)	–	
Both	1 (0.6%)	–	
Neither	81 (52.3%)	63 (57.3%)	
No response			19

Source: Ghaleb & Joseph (2000).

religious groups in Lebanon? If so, which ones?' The responses showed that, of 281 responses, a little less than 50 per cent associated French with Christians while the overwhelming majority did not associate English with either religion (see Tables 8.7 and 8.8). So a tendency persists whereby French is associated with Christians, and, what is surprising, it appears to be stronger among Muslims than among Christians themselves. This despite the fact that the two groups report French as their first language in roughly equal proportions.

What this suggests is that old cultural patterns die hard. Since 1997 all Lebanese education from primary up has been trilingual, in line with educational policy developed specifically to close up the linguistic divide. But there is no guarantee that it will work, unless Christians and Muslims want their communities to draw closer together. Otherwise, discursive means can always be rediscovered for reconstituting their supposed uniquenesses.

Still more recent developments

As noted on p. 196 above, I observed a marked change in attitudes toward bilingualism among my own relations in Lebanon between 1998 and 2002.[3] It took a considerable amount of observation and conversational interaction to determine what had changed such that W2 and her father, who four years earlier had felt that Arabic was their language, now instead made strong assertions of their Arabic–French bilingualism. In 1998 Lebanon was, in retrospect, at the peak of its modern stability. Open hostilities between Christians and Muslims had ceased, the economy was approaching something like normality and major rebuilding projects were under way. Admittedly, there were two open wounds to national pride: the Israeli occupation of southern Lebanon, and the fact that Syria was openly running the rest of Lebanon, with its troops stationed throughout the country and the government unable to take any action without Syrian consent. Yet in the minds of most Lebanese these twin occupations effectively balanced each other out.

Muslims, although the more furious over the Israeli occupation, were recompensed by the presence of de facto Muslim national control. Indeed, the presence of Israeli troops in the south of Lebanon had been the rationale (or pretext) for Syria's entry into Lebanon. Christians were by no means content with the Israeli occupation, but it did not pose the same level of threat to them; and as for the hand of Syria, they exhibited an amazing capacity to deny that their country had in fact lost its sovereignty. This capacity was no doubt fed by the welcome fact of the economic upturn. Whatever the situation of the government might be, one is less likely to resent it when times are peaceful and prosperous.

What upset the balance for the Christians was the fact that, when Israel withdrew from southern Lebanon in May 2000, Syria did not then withdraw its own troops from the rest of the country, as it had always promised to do. In the absence of any significant international objection, the occupation of Lebanon by Syria became an apparently permanent arrangement. Then, the following year, as the long international economic boom of the 1990s came to a halt, the Lebanese economy ceased to grow. Times were no longer good, and any Christians who had been in denial that their country was now effectively a vassal state of its Muslim neighbour and traditional rival shed their illusions.

And that is how, in the summer of 2002, the answer to the question 'What language is spoken in Lebanon?' came to be 'French'. A different answer, one that would amalgamate Lebanon to the rest of the Middle East and the Arab world, has become unacceptable to W2, however obvious that answer may be. An answer that asserts the uniqueness of Lebanon within the Middle East and the Arab world – however counter-intuitive it may appear – becomes the immediate reply.

Renan and the 'heritage of memories'

Common memories plus a common will equals the common soul that makes the nation. This is Renan's astute insight into the general classical Western European idea of the nation, founded in the context of wars against external enemies. But when this idea was taken over in situations where the memories were of great battles against *internal* enemies – where what Christians remembered was mainly battles against Muslims and vice versa – then the common memories themselves became a textual battleground.

The conception of the language itself became a major front in the battle, partly for its own symbolic sake, partly because the language is understood to be the vehicle in which the text of memory will be constructed and transmitted. In the classical situation of the founding of a modern European nationalism, the 'language war' takes the form of a *questione della lingua*, the Italian term having been generalised because it was in Italy that the first really significant struggle of this kind took place, starting already in the early fourteenth century (see Joseph, 1987, and Chapter 5 above). Similar debates about which particular dialect would be the basis of the national language raged during the Renaissance in France, the Iberian peninsula, Germany, Scandinavia and the British Isles, and later in the Balkans, Poland, Turkey and India, to name just a few of the most important cases. Their ferocity would defy belief were it not that the location of the common soul was at stake.

But in Lebanon there never was a *questione della lingua* in the classical sense, only a *questione della seconda lingua*, a second-language question. Certainly the raw material for a language debate of the classical sort was there, in the wide-ranging differences from Koranic Arabic to colloquial Lebanese Arabic. If a concept of 'Lebanese Arabic' as a separate language had ever developed indigenously, then different forms of it based on the dialects of Christian and Muslim villages and towns could certainly have been developed and argued for. No doubt even slight differences would have been seized upon and exaggerated, as happened in the modern history of the standard Romanian language: when pro-Soviet forces were in power, Slavic variants in the language were made the standard forms, and when more westward-looking forces were in power, Romance variants were instead favoured. Hence the spelling of the name of the language itself has switched back and forth between *Român* and *Romîn*, with *â* and *î* designating the same high back unrounded vowel sound, but with the spelling *Român* seen as highlighting the Romance affinities of the language and therefore the Western rather than Eastern 'soul' of the nation.

What the Arabic 'language' is has, rather amazingly, remained uncontroversial in Lebanon. This is a different matter from the 'speech' of given individuals, which is easily interpreted by others so as to place the speaker in a particular village or quarter, religion and sect, level of education and so on. A key linguistic variable in this respect – not just in Lebanon, but in much of the Arabic-speaking world – is the pronunciation or omission of the sound /q/, spelled as the letter *qaf* (see e.g. Al-Wer, 1999; Benrabah, 1994; Sawaie, 1987). Yet no one would consider the leaving out of the letter *qaf* in writing to be anything other than an error, certainly not a distinctive feature of a distinctive form of Standard Arabic. So the Lebanese linguistic battleground is essentially restricted to spoken languages, ancient languages and foreign languages, none of which has quite the power of 'the language' – the current written standard – for embodying the soul of the nation.

Things become more complicated if the language has the name of a people closely associated with the religion of one of the two major sides in the war. *Arabic* obviously suggests *Arabs*, a predominantly (but by no means exclusively) Muslim people. This begs the question of how exactly the Christians of Lebanon, who claim an older historical–cultural presence than their Muslim countrymen, came to be speakers of Arabic. It would seem perfectly natural to the modern observer if they had continued to speak Aramaic to one another, and not just to God. Aramaic in fact continues to be spoken among a handful of small, isolated communities, including in Syria, though not in Lebanon. The likeliest scenario is that they lost the colloquial use of Aramaic over a period of at least four generations (the minimal length of time it takes for 'language death' – a hyperbolic metaphor – to occur) in which peaceful intercourse with Arabic-speaking countrymen was not only possible but profitable, not just in a mercenary sense but in the broadest and best sense that the sharing of the language was part of the building of a unified society. The fact that for 1000 years, from the seventh to the sixteenth century, Arabic was the most prestigious and cultivated language of science and learning, could only have added to its appeal to the Levantine Christians, and helps explain why they acquired the language. It does not however explain why they lost the Aramaic–Arabic bilingualism they must have maintained over a transitional period of some generations.

The Lebanese Christian answer to the quandary posed by the associative chain *Arabic–Arabs–Islam* has consisted of a somewhat contradictory twofold strategy. On the one hand, they deny that the Arabic language and Arab identity belong more to Islam than to them. On the other hand, they deny that they are Arabs. They claim to descend from ancestors who predated the arrival of the Arabs – which may be true, but logically makes no difference to the argument unless it were the case that the later, Muslim Arab interlopers did not intermarry with the earlier, Christian pre-Arab population. There is ample historical documentation from many periods to show that such intermarriages occurred. Not only that, but many Christian individuals, families and clans became converts to Islam – 'renegades', to use the Spanish Christian term (see Bennassar & Bennassar, 1989). The unspeakable historical fact in Lebanon is that, chances are, any given Lebanese Christian and Muslim are blood relations if one goes back a few centuries, not even millennia. Of course, the arrival of large numbers of Palestinians after the founding of the modern state of Israel helped to camouflage this fact, since, not having been part of this long history of conversion and intermarriage, they were visibly more foreign. But it is hardly necessary to point out that Semitic kinship has counted for less than nothing in the internecine religious wars of the modern Levant.

Lebanon is a case where Renan's 'rich heritage of memories' is as much an obstacle to nationhood as a positive force, and temporary 'forgetting' is impossible. But denial is not impossible, hence the denial that Lebanese Christians are 'Arabs'; nor is creative remembering impossible, hence the elaboration of myths of Phoenician ancestry. As for Renan's 'present-day agreement', it too is far from straightforward. It too is a text. How, after all, does one determine the 'common will'? In modern Lebanon, there is little 'desire to live together' between Christians and Muslims, yet little practical possibility of living apart, as two separate nations. In the 1990s, it seemed that the redistribution of power had reduced the tensions that made living together quite as difficult as it had been for the previous two decades; though in mid-2000 the abrupt

Israeli withdrawal from southern Lebanon made clear, to anyone who may have doubted it, how fragile that reduction of tensions always was.

Virtually every existing nation determines the 'common will' primarily through a constitution written (or sometimes unwritten, as in the UK) by a select few, promulgated from above, and, in democratic nations, executed (to a certain degree) by plebiscite or the action of elected officials. In Lebanon, the text of the 'common will', the 1926 constitution, was 'customarily interpreted in such a way that the Maronites should always have the principal power. Then, to keep the common will from changing, no census was taken for decade after decade, until finally the gap between the textual 'common will' and the manifest will of those not in power became too wide. The 'fiction' that is the constitution is in this sense ultimately bound by how the world is; it must be a semi-realistic fiction, not a fantasy. But not even Renan (1882, p. 27) is so idealistic as to believe that 'The existence of a nation is – pardon my metaphor – a daily plebiscite [. . .]',[4] or he would not have inserted that apology. He does not however apologise for the following assertion: 'We have rid politics of metaphysical and theological abstractions. What remains after that? There remains man, his desires, his needs' (Renan, 1882, p. 28).[5]

It is always intriguing to look back on an earlier period and see what people thought did and did not count as 'metaphysical' and 'abstract'. That Renan could have called the nation 'a soul, a spiritual principle', and then claim to have got rid of the metaphysical, is astounding to today's reader. When he claims to deal not with abstractions, but with *l'homme* 'man', it is again surprising that he does realise that 'man' is already an abstraction. 'A man' is not abstract, if a specific man is intended ('a man I know'), but if generic it too is the abstraction of a category ('A man's home is his castle'). The 'needs of man' are the abstract needs of an abstract category, and likewise for the desires, which moreover are metaphysical, since it is presumably not physical desire that Renan has in mind.

The nation can never be rid of the abstract or the metaphysical, by definition. This is the thrust of Anderson's characterisation of it as an 'imagined community'. The same is true of 'the language'. It is never the way in which 'a man' speaks, but the way 'man' speaks in a particular community. Like 'man' himself, it is abstracted – not from the way all people speak, but from a combination of the powerful and the ideal. The extent to which the ideal is independent of the powerful has long been a matter of debate, particularly in Marxism and after, down through Althusser to Foucault and Habermas. The case of Lebanon suggests that, where language is concerned, the alignment of the ideal and the powerful is not accidental, certainly, but subject to every imaginable permutation and some that are frankly unimaginable.

There is a further resonance to the last quote from Renan. In his early work on the origin of language, he referred to the Semitic tongues as 'these totally physical languages, in which abstraction is unknown and metaphysics impossible' (Renan, 1858, p. 190).[6] This is the ideal condition he claims (unconvincingly) to have achieved in his analysis of nationalism. It is possible that he was using the terms abstraction and metaphysics consistently, but in a special sense that we are already at too great a historical remove to understand. It is also possible that they meant one thing for him when discussing the Semitic, and another when discussing himself.

Linking marginal ethnic identities: Celts and Phoenicians

Another place where linguistic fictions are quite powerful is the British Isles. In Scotland, where I reside, the 'real' languages of this place are held to be Gaelic, first and foremost, and then Scots, despite its relation to English. The political motivation for this belief is obvious. If Scotland is an essentially Celtic place, just as Lebanon is an essentially Phoenician one, it is clear who the authentic and inauthentic Scots are, and hence who are the rightful rulers. The oldest attested language of Scotland survives in a small number of inscriptions in a script known as Pictish. Nothing is known about the people who wrote the inscriptions. Indeed there have long been arguments about the language itself, since some of the inscriptions cannot be deciphered but are clearly not in an Indo-European language, while others are in a dialect of the Celtic branch of the Indo-European family. One possibility is that Pictish writing was already in use when the Celts arrived, and was then adapted for use with their language. The Celts I am talking about are the ones who populated the whole of Britain and the Isle of Man before the arrival of the Romans, and who spoke a language of the p-Celtic branch which is referred to as British, or by the Welsh word for British, Brythonic. Their language was already by this time distinctively split from the q-Celtic branch as spoken in Ireland. The p-Celtic 'British' language was the only form of Celtic to be spoken throughout the whole of Scotland, lowlands as well as highlands, and indeed through the whole of Britain. It survives today as Welsh, and as a result of a later migration, as Breton in north-west France.

Around the time St Maron began converting the Lebanese to Christianity, Irish speakers of q-Celtic began moving into the north-west of Scotland. This influx continued over the next centuries, even as the Germanic tribes began moving into England and upward into the south-east of Scotland, bringing with them the dialects that would develop into English and Scots. It was their Germanic dialects that replaced the p-Celtic British language from the lowlands of Scotland. The q-Celtic Irish language never came that far south. That language did however become well established in the highlands, where it continued to be known as Erse, or Irish, with the literate in the language looking to Ireland as their linguistic standard.

Only in the seventeenth century did a movement begin to identify the Irish language of the highlands as something other than Irish, namely Gaelic, and to establish a spelling system different from the Irish one. Indeed, as the notion of Gaelic linguistic independence took hold over the succeeding centuries, spellings were changed for no other reason than to differentiate them from the Irish norm. Two cultural forces were in play here. First, Scottish 'nationalism' became an issue for the first time with the Union of the Crowns in 1603. Of course Scottish independence had been an issue for centuries, but these first steps toward the modern conception of the 'nation' as an authentic, self-contained indigenous group having a natural right to self-government were something new, and in Scotland as elsewhere in Europe, new linguistic fictions were developing as an integral part of the new conception. As Scots identity was to be defined principally as not English, the language known as Erse offered a more powerful symbol than the language known as Scots, just because Scots was recognisably close to English. But the name Erse, together with the Irish literary norms, connoted distinctiveness without authenticity to Scotland. Hence the attractiveness of the new name Gaelic, which established the necessary fiction of an authentically Scottish language even before people set about deliberately representing it following norms distinct from the Irish. The second cultural force in play was religion. Compared with England, Scotland was extreme in both its Catholicism and its Protestantism, and of course Irish was almost uniquely associated with Catholic. With the Protestant Church of Scotland as the established church, and other dissenting sects entrenched among the crofters and other representatives of the most 'authentic' Scottish Celticness, the appeal of distinguishing Gaelic from Irish was considerable. The Scottish Catholics who might have been expected to resist it were in many cases torn between the religious and nationalistic agenda.

The Romantics of the late eighteenth and early nineteenth centuries went still further in essentialising the cultural and ethnic differences between the Celtic and Germanic 'races'. Here again the positive content of the Celtic fictions was always less important than their negative character of being counter to whatever was English. Thus was it possible to ignore the fact that Celts and Germanics, like Christians and Muslims in the Middle East, were never sealed off from each other culturally, not in the British Isles nor even in their respective original homelands around Belgium and the north of Germany, which overlapped. Yet anything which suggested Celtic uniqueness was seized upon.

Crowley (1996a) relates part of what was in fact a very large cultural movement in the late eighteenth and early nineteenth century to establish the belief that Celtic was the language of Adam, and that Hebrew and the other Semitic languages are descended from it. William Shaw (1749–1831), a Scot, wrote that 'Galic', as he spelled it, 'is the language of Japhet, spoken before the deluge, and probably the speech of paradise' (Shaw, 1780, p. ii). Charles Vallancey (1721–1812) was reluctant to go quite so far, but believed that the ancient Irish 'must have been a colony from Asia, because nine words in ten are pure Chaldic and Arabic' (Vallancey, 1802, p. 14). This is not total fantasy, as there were Celtic outposts as far east as central Turkey. But far more was extrapolated from this, and from the fact that neither Arabic nor q-Celtic has the consonant *p*, than modern scholarship is ready to accept as valid. Lest anyone should think that these beliefs are long dead, the 1999 Summer Course booklet from the University of Edinburgh's Centre for Continuing Education begins its listing for Scottish Gaelic with the following paragraph:

> Here is a very special opportunity to study this modern Celtic language sometimes referred to as *the language of the Garden of Eden*. Spoken for nearly 2,000 years, Gaelic is now enjoying an energetic revival. [Italics in original.]

At the bottom of the page is a poem in Gaelic calling it the language of Adam.

In an earlier work Vallancey (1772, p. vii) had classified Irish with the 'Punic language of the Carthaginians' (see also Vallencey, 1787). 'Punic' is the Roman form of 'Phoenician'. Celtic–Phoenician racial and cultural unity became a common notion which one encounters still today in Ireland and Lebanon, as well as in the north-west Spanish province of Galicia, by Galicians who have their own Celtic cultural fictions bound up with their anti-Spanish nationalism. The great utility of both the Celts and the Phoenicians in constructing texts of national identity is that they left so little in the way of records that would allow modern historians to pin them down. They are peoples constructed first and foremost out of common styles discovered among artefacts dug up over vast stretches of the world, and then, secondly, out of the desire of marginalised peoples in the modern world to establish an ancestral priority for themselves that cannot be disproved.

Language, abstraction and the identity of Renan

I have suggested that, at least as viewed from today's perspective, there is a disjuncture in the thought of Renan with regard to 'abstraction', which is a key term for him in both his linguistic–ethnographic and his political analysis. On the one hand, the difference of the Semitic peoples from the Indo-European is the supposed lack of abstract terms in their languages, which Renan believes makes them incapable of abstract thinking. Although this is not presented as an entirely negative trait in the Romantic framework inherited by Renan from Herder, it is central to the dehumanisation of Semitic peoples that many have detected in his work. On the other hand, Renan claims that the virtue of his own analysis of nationalism is its doing away with abstractions, its rehumanising of nationalism by restoring it to the dimension of human will and desire. Yet by any present-day understanding of what abstraction means, he remains so far from attaining this goal that his very conception of 'man' is a dehumanised abstraction.

The texts cited above constructing Maronite and Islamic identities are part of the creation and maintenance of cultural fictions, which are abstractions made in part from generalised observation, in part from an ideal of desire that defies observation. This ideal of desire can even force an interpretation onto the observable facts that it would be difficult to sustain objectively, as in the case of Father Dau's child skeleton. The process of abstraction, when applied to people, is always dehumanising, by definition. In the context of peoples of irreconcilable beliefs and vastly unequal sharing of economic resources and political authority, there is a constant danger of dehumanising the enemy into an animal or a thing, a danger fuelled by linguistic and cultural abstraction of this sort. It reduces war as a moral problem from the level of murder to that of slaughtering beasts or removing rubbish.

Among the many interesting attributes of discourses of marginality is their ability to empower people who are not necessarily marginal. This has certainly been the case in post-1997 Britain, where the most powerful figures in the 'English' Blair government have been Scots, yet where the justification for the devolution of central power to Scotland is conducted in the discourse of Scottish, and indeed Celtic, marginality. There are similarities here with the Maronites of Lebanon, who have traditionally held the lion's share of power. However, the Maronites' perception of themselves as a marginal people under siege is not fantasy when viewed in the larger Middle Eastern context and the spread of Islam over previously Christian lands from the seventh century to the present. The Scots have the disadvantage that their national identity is underpinned by two living languages whose partisans' respective claims largely cancel each other out. The Maronites are lucky to have built their identity on one barely living language – even Gaelic is healthy in comparison with modern Aramaic – and a classical one, Syriac. Both peoples have the additional advantage of a prehistoric language, Pictish and Phoenician, the evidence concerning which is scant enough to allow unlimited flexibility in creating and manipulating cultural fictions.

Some people have made marginality the cornerstone of their personal identity. One such was Ernest Renan, who, along with his biographers and commentators in the later nineteenth century, made much of his Breton origins and 'Celtic soul':

> Ernest Renan was born at Tréguier, in the Côtes du Nord, on the 28th of February 1823. For the third time in sixty years Brittany gave birth to a man-child who should transform and renew the religious temper of his times.
>
> Chateaubriand and Lamennais were scarcely past their prime when the young Renan first went to school in Tréguier. In him, as in them, the racial element is strong [...] stubborn as Breton granite under its careless grace of flowers.
>
> [...] Celtic magicians, they see the world through a haze of their own, at once dim and dazzling, full of uncertain glimpses and brilliant mists, like the variable weather of their moors. (Darmesteter, 1898, pp. 3–4)

> The extraordinary strength of idealism, the infinite delicacy of sentiment, which form the inmost quintessence of the Celt, impose on him [the Breton] an image of seemliness, a pure decorum, to which he incessantly conforms the old Adam rebellious in his heart. (Ibid., p. 7)

The reference to 'Adam rebellious' in the last paragraph invokes the idea of the Garden of Eden as a Celtic paradise, and the rebelliousness is not only that of Adam and Eve, but of Renan in his lifelong struggles with Christianity and the French Catholic establishment. A priest who became the apostle of anticlericalism, he was denied the Chair of Hebrew and Syro-Chaldaic Languages in the Collège de France for which he was the obvious candidate, from 1857, when it fell vacant, until 1862, when the government could no longer delay his appointment. Then, five months after he was named to the chair, he was officially dismissed from it. But with the stubbornness of Breton granite, he refused to accept the dismissal.

In 1860, Napoleon III, in a bid to assuage Renan, who at 37 was one of the most highly respected scholars in France as well as a force in liberal political thought, offered to send him on an archaeological mission to the Levant – specifically, to 'Phoenicia'. Renan readily accepted to go, accompanied by his devoted elder sister Henriette.

> The arrangements for their departure were not yet completed when the Druses fell on the Christians of Mount Lebanon, and massacred them in a Holy War [...] Napoleon immediately decided to protect the unfortunate Maronites. The vessel which carried M. Renan and his sister to Beyrouth was one of those which transported a French division to Syria. Renan, in his candid absorption in the ends of Science, appears to have accepted the whole affair – massacres, Turkish incapacity, French army *partant pour la Syrie,* &c., – as providentially combined in the interests of archæology: 'The presence of our soldiers on the spot was a most favourable element in my design. Thereby my excavations were singularly simplified – they were made by the soldiers. Thus my mission to Phœnicia took that place in the Syrian Expedition, which the French army, in its noble preoccupation with the things of the mind, has ever loved to accord to Science in her more distant ventures' [*Mission de Phénicie,* Ière Livraison, p. 2]. (Darmesteter, 1898, p. 132)

Oblivious to the complex struggle of nationhood taking place around him, the future theoretician of nationalism devoted himself to the unearthing of Phoenician tombs and the loading of them onto ships bound for France.

Renan could not have had much sympathy for the Maronites, who had brought 1300 years of misery onto themselves by their granite-like stubbornness (perhaps they are Celtic after all) to let go of Christianity – precisely what Renan, in his major life crisis, had *not* refused to do. During his stay in Lebanon, he wrote what would become his most widely read work, *Vie de Jésus* (*Life of Jesus*), by no means a profane book, but seen in its time as scandalous for its denial of the miracles reported to have been performed by Jesus in the New Testament. The ironies abound. French soldiers sent to Lebanon to protect Maronites from persecution for their Christian faith are commandeered by Renan to unearth the tombs of ancient Phoenicians, the ancestors in whom Maronite identity is rooted, and to remove those tombs to Europe. This is how Renan spends his days; his evenings are devoted to writing a work that will strike a heavy blow against traditional Christianity in Europe herself, while helping propel Renan to ever wider personal fame, and pre-eminence as a liberal thinker and would-be politician.

But the humiliations awaiting Renan were at once so bruising and so banal that he might have wondered whether they were not a revenge of Jesus' own miraculous making. Before they had left 'Phoenicia', malaria attacked Renan and his beloved sister and soulmate Henriette.[7] The malaria spared Renan, barely, but Henriette died. He did not even bother to ship her body back with the Phoenician tombs he was sending to France – she whom a more grateful brother might have named as co-author of the *Vie de Jésus*, in the writing of which

> Henriette was his perpetual confidant, as soon as the page was written she copied it fair. [...]
>
> 'This book,' she would say, 'I shall love. Because we have done it together. [...]'. (Darmesteter, 1898, p. 140)

He left her body with the wealthy Maronites in whose house she died, to bury in their family vault. In later years, Renan's attempts to convert his fame into political power were repeatedly rebuffed by the electorate. Nowadays, he is principally remembered as one of Edward Said's three 'inaugural heroes' of orientalism, along with Silvestre de Sacy and Edward William Lane (Said, 1978, p. 122).

In the light of his still influential speech on nationalism of 1882, we might ask what were the memories, desires and forgettings that constituted the identity, or to use his word, the 'soul', of Ernest Renan. The memory of Breton-Celtic difference allowed him to deny (i.e. forget) that he was French, and of a devout Catholic heritage. Not so very far back in prehistory the Celts were pagans, after all. Yet the notion of Celtic–Semitic unity was not one embraced by Renan, the foremost Celtic Semiticist of his time. It was a convenient one to dismiss (i.e. forget), since to do otherwise might cast doubt on the supposed scientific objectivity he so prided himself on in his Semitic researches. On the one occasion when he actually travelled to a land of Semitic population, it was convenient to ignore (i.e. forget) their existence and instead dig up the tombs of their ancestors. To forget that these ancestors might perhaps belong to the place where they had been buried, and where they would be deeply woven into the text of common memory that is the foundation of nationhood, rather than in France – though in fairness, he did leave his sister's body in their place. To forget the Maronites as he was trying to forget his own Christianity. In 1882, the very year in which he was elected to the presidency of the Société Asiatique, to forget in his speech on nationalism that the nations of Western Europe were not the only nations, and that nationalisms were not universally the most important loci of identity, as the struggles he had witnessed with his own eyes in Lebanon must have taught him. *They have all forgotten many things*.

Whatever else one may say about Ernest Renan, when he talked about the importance of forgetting in forging an identity, he knew whereof he spoke. Yet his was a complex personality that deserves better than the vilification of Said or the piecemeal resuscitations of Anderson. The fatal flaw of the orientalist framework within which Renan worked was not so much that it imagined the Oriental as the 'Other', the reverse image of the European self – that is perhaps an inevitable process, as recent studies of 'occidentalism' have implied. Rather, it is that the Other is dehumanised in the process. Perhaps that too is inevitable. As evidence, consider the treatment of Renan himself, by Said for example. There is no attempt to measure the man; 'Renan' is dehumanised into a set of ideas, or more precisely texts, some of which are not even things Renan wrote, but Said's interpretations of what he wrote.

It could be argued that, after the man's death, all that can be known about him are surviving texts, those he has written and those written about him, including ones 'written' in living memory. We can go further, and ask whether we can know anything about even a living person beyond the texts they present to us for interpretation, including the very language they use and the way they use it, from which we construct the identity we attribute to them.

If that is so, then understanding other people, a necessity for living in peace with them, is a matter of textual manipulation and interpretation, and so is war. *Pace* Said, I submit that his treatment of Renan reproduces the very textual processes that are behind orientalism itself, and behind texts establishing warring identities such as the one by Father Dau. There is enough evidence that Renan's writings contributed to the development of European racism in the second half of the nineteenth century (on which see Joseph, forthcoming a) for him to deserve a full assessment, taking account of the contexts in which he wrote, his influence on liberal politics generally and policy toward the Middle East in particular, and his actual scientific contributions to Semitic linguistics (which I do not believe have ever been independently judged). The outcome is unlikely to be a Saint Renan. It might still be an evil Renan, but if it is at the same time a human Renan, we will have gained a fuller understanding of what made him into someone we hate. In doing so, we will have put into practice that humanisation the absence of which causes language to get abstracted into dehumanised forms.

Maalouf's utopian anti-identity

Amin Maalouf was born in Lebanon in 1949 into a Melchite (Greek Catholic) family, but was baptised as a Protestant because that was the influence prevailing in his father's family at the time. To counterbalance this his mother insisted that he be educated in the Jesuit-run French school, and when he left Lebanon in 1976, after the outbreak of civil war, it was to Paris that he emigrated and where he lives to this day, writing his novels and historical and other non-fictional work in French rather than his mother tongue.

Maalouf recognises the powerful, universal need for identity, and sees it as one that increases in the face of perceived 'globalisation'. He argues that, although religion has become the primary refuge of identity in the Arab world following the collapse of Arab nationalism (after Nasser) and the Marxist alternative, there is no inevitability in this remaining the case. On the contrary, it would be hugely desirable for it not to do so, because combining the spiritual dimension of religion, which fulfils a basic human need and should be universalist, with the no less basic need for identity which, though shared by everyone, is by definition particularist, produces an overly powerful cocktail in which it is too easy for reason to give way to murderous, even genocidal emotion.

Unlike Renan, Maalouf does not see himself as an 'outsider' to French culture. He is well aware that many of his countrymen do see him as such relative to themselves; but also that, were he to chance upon an ethnic Frenchman and a Muslim North African fighting each other at knifepoint, and the Frenchman understood his origins, he would certainly appeal to him for help on the grounds of shared religion, citizenship, language and other cultural common ground. The Muslim would argue that the Arabic he shares with Maalouf, together with their mutual Semitic outsiderness in France, represents a deeper bond. Maalouf would admit that both of them are right, and, if he could not convince both of them to lay down their weapons, would no doubt take the side of whichever appeared to be the weaker in this particular battle.

In Maalouf's view, it is by combining particularist identities in the same individuals that one defuses them. This is the case with some of his most memorable characters, particularly Léon l'Africain (Leo Africanus), based on an actual sixteenth-century personage. Hassan al-Wazzan was born in Granada, fled to the Maghreb upon Granada's reconquest, became an ambassador, and was captured by Sicilian pirates on his return from a pilgrimage to Mecca. The pirates gave him as a gift to Pope Leo X, who adopted him. As Jean-Léon de Médicis he wrote a monumental *Description of Africa* that became the standard guide to the continent until modern times. He converted to Christianity, but late in life resumed his adherence to Islam. In Maalouf's novel, an aged Léon tells his son:

> In Rome, you were 'the son of the African'; in Africa, you will be 'the son of the *Roumi*'. Wherever you are, certain people will want to pry into your skin and your prayers. Take care not to assuage their instincts, my son, take care not to give way under their multitude! Muslim, Jew or Christian, they will have to take you as you are, or lose you. When the human spirit appears narrow to you, tell yourself that God's earth is vast, and vast His hands and His heart. Never hesitate to take your distance, beyond every sea, every border, every homeland, every belief. (Maalouf, 1986, p. 349, my translation)[8]

This readiness to distance himself from any form of national or religious identity is essential to Leo's character. One's beliefs and belongings should be answerable only to oneself and to God. Identity, in that sense, is deep and unchanging, but it is unknowable to anyone else. For our fellow human beings we construct identities; they are what cause the trouble, and we must be prepared to shed them.

Maalouf dwells on the fact that this is the natural state of mind for a person of mixed descent:

> A man with a Serbian mother and a Croatian father, and who manages to accept this dual affiliation, will never take part in any form of ethnic 'cleansing'. A man with a Hutu mother and a Tutsi father, if he can accept the two 'tributaries' that brought him into the world, will never be a party to butchery or genocide. And neither the Franco-Algerian lad, nor the young man of mixed German and

> Turkish origins whom I mentioned earlier, will ever be on the side of the fanatics if they succeed in living peacefully in the context of their own complex identity.
>
> [...] We are not dealing with a handful of marginal people. There are thousands, millions of such men and women, and there will be more and more of them. (Maalouf, 2000 [1998], pp. 30–1)

This is a very appealing vision, at least superficially, because of its neutrality and its political correctness. But so much rides on the individual's acceptance of the dual heritage, and Maalouf himself acknowledges the danger it poses:

> On the other hand, those who cannot accept their own diversity may be among the most virulent of those who embody that part of themselves which they would like to see forgotten. History contains many examples of such self-hatred. (Ibid., p. 31)

Yet at the end of his book he imagines all these differences vanished:

> I dream of the day when I can call all the Middle East my homeland, as I now do Lebanon and France and Europe; the day when I can call all its sons, Muslim, Jewish and Christian, of all denominations and all origins, my compatriots. In my own mind, which is always speculating and trying to anticipate the future, it has already come to pass. But I want it to happen one day on the solid ground of reality, and for everyone. (Ibid., p. 132)

Again, a glorious vision; but in the words of Spivak (2000 [1993], p. 397), 'Making sense of ourselves is what produces identity.' Identity is what gives meaning, a plot, to our lives; and plots, as the tradition from Propp to Greimas has it, always involve a gift and a quest. Quests imply the existence of inimical forces in the way of achieving one's goal, gifts the existence of a protector, a protector the existence, again, of inimical forces from which one needs protection. For someone like Maalouf or me, far removed from the fray, it is easy to take the high ground and proclaim the real quest to be that for peace and brotherhood. No one can argue against that without condemning himself as a fanatic. Maalouf's vision is not entirely utopian – except that the only real prospect for it coming to pass is if the Christians, Jews and Muslims of the Middle East were all to line up against one common enemy that they resented more than they do each other. That is, actually, how the

Ottoman Empire worked; and for all its flaws, particularly in its later history, we should not forget that all those current hot spots from Bosnia and Kosovo to Palestine and Israel to Iraq and Libya were all within the Sultan's rule, with essentially the same internal forces at war against each other as now, except without a force comparable to modern Israel. As the American-led invasion of Iraq in 2003 has shown, if a Western power or conglomerate of powers were to intervene to 'sort things out', with every intention of doing so fairly, not favouring any ethnic group over the others (assuming for the moment that this is possible), they would draw upon themselves all the region's wrath, uniting people across identity boundaries, and in so doing go some ways toward bringing Maalouf's vision to pass. In Renan's terms, Middle Easterners forget their enmities toward one another only to forge a unity directed at the common enemy, which, alas, might then be perceived as including Maalouf and me.

In my view, what is really dangerous is the hope for 'ultimate solutions', including Maalouf's. As terrible as it is to say, his utopian vision of peace has something essential in common with the dystopian vision of those Israeli hardliners who would create 'compatriotism' through *force majeure*, and those Palestinian radicals who await the day when the Israelis will be pushed into the sea. Where they are driven by religious belief, Maalouf is driven by a belief in the infinite perfectibility of man that likely came to him through his French education. It is the same rationalist heritage that drove Renan to reject religious orthodoxy, though, as it happens, he located that rejection in his own un-Frenchness, his Celtic streak with its supposed Semitic connections.

Afterword: Identity and the Study of Language

This book has attempted to give an overview of how national, ethnic and religious identities are constructed through language, and how languages are constructed through them. It has tried to show how such an understanding of language has come to be a part of modern linguistics, and to make the case for the importance of linguistic identity within a scientific understanding of language. One does not need to look far to find the contrary position. Many linguists, especially those who believe in the 'autonomy' of the linguistic mind, would question whether language as it connects to identity has anything to do with language in the sense that they study it, as a formal system of representation and communication. But any study of language needs to take consideration of identity if it is to be full and rich and meaningful, because identity is itself at the very heart of what language is about, how it operates, why and how it came into existence and evolved as it did, how it is learned and how it is used, every day, by every user, every time it is used.

It is because speakers and writers inherently know this that both the form and content of linguistic production are shaped, and frequently driven, by the imperatives of identity. Comprehension and interpretation too are shaped and frequently driven by the perception of identity. The very identities of the languages we use have been shaped in this way. The historical identification of 'a language', such as Chinese, English or Quechua, has always been closely connected with the establishment of a national, ethnic or religious identity. Anderson (1991) has popularised the idea that the language is the bedrock on which the fiction of the nation is built. While his work is to be commended for drawing so much attention to the language–nation link, study of the history of languages themselves suggests that neither is bedrock to the edifice of the other, but that they are instead like twin edifices built in such a way that each sustains the weight of the other (a metaphor whose engineering viability I cannot vouch for). But Anderson can hardly be blamed, when linguists themselves, unable to come conceptually to terms with 'a language' in this everyday sense, have preferred to deny its existence entirely, or else to relegate it to a limbo of epiphenomena that are insufficiently real to merit or sustain scientific inquiry.

'Language' in the sense of what a particular person says or writes, considered from the point of view of both form and content, is central to individual identity. It inscribes the person within national and other corporate identities, including establishing the person's 'rank' within the identity. It constitutes a text, not just of what the person says, but *of the person*, from which others will read and interpret the person's identity in the richest and most complex ways. Indeed, the over-readings they produce will be richer than the text itself can sustain.

The term 'standard language' connects to all of these roles, though most obviously to national identity, since 'a language' construed nationalistically always overlays a great amount of dialectal variation. In some cases, like that of 'the Chinese language', the dialects subsumed within it are as different from one another as are English and Swedish. To realise the fiction of the standard language and to maintain it therefore requires establishing institutions – on the grand scale, schools, editorships, dictionaries and grammars, authoritative texts, systems of examination and hiring; on the smaller scale, prizes, corrections, snubs and scoffs, rewards and punishments. Some of these institutions also have part of the charge of establishing nationhood – in particular, schools, and the authoritative texts of national history, civics, literature, even rhetoric and grammar, that they employ – in both explicit and 'banal' ways. Behind the grand-scale institutions the motivating forces usually include duty to the nation, religious duty, or both, and while these same forces can be behind the small-scale institutions, they are joined there with strong elements of personal motivation. One of the key social roles of the standard language is to establish a hierarchy for measuring individuals; another is to attempt to *control* what elements of individual identity are available for (over)interpretation in language.

As discussed in earlier chapters, in so far as identity involves categorisation, it is a type of representation, and in so far as it involves linguistic interaction among people, it is a type of communication. It would no doubt be possible to break identity down into components each of which is classifiable as communication or (self-) representation. At the very least, however, we have to say that, as your interpretation of who you are, your identity has an extraordinarily privileged place among your linguistic representations of the world to yourself; and other people's interpretation of your identity has a highly privileged place *for you* within their representations of the world to themselves. Indeed, the assertion would be uncontroversial that one's self-representation of identity is the organising and shaping centre of one's representations of the world. Similarly, in communication, our interpretation of what is said and written to us is shaped by and organised around our interpretation of the identity of those with whom we are communicating.

Whether we say that identity is fundamental to the two traditional purposes of language, or itself constitutes a third purpose that underlies the other two, makes little difference. What matters is to understand that, if people's use of language is reduced analytically to how meaning is formed and represented in sound, or communicated from one person to another, or even the conjunction of the two, something vital has been abstracted away: the people themselves, who, prior to such abstraction, are always present in what they say, through the identity recoverable in (or at least interpretable from) their voice, spoken, written or signed. A full account of linguistic meaning would have to include how the identity of the speakers is manifested and interpreted; it would have to recognise that the speakers themselves are part of the meaning, represented within the representation. A full account of linguistic communication would have to start with, not a message, but again the speakers themselves, and their interpretation of each other that determines, interactively, their interpretation of what is said.

In this sense, the broader significance of research into language and identity is that it contributes to the *rehumanising* of linguistics. This rehumanising project has been under way, in fits and starts, since the first third of the nineteenth century, not all that long after the study of language and languages came to be detached both from the study of actual texts, and from any consideration of the role of the will (see Joseph, 2002b, p. 47). Through the nineteenth and twentieth centuries, attempts to reinscribe human beings into language as linguists study it have consistently been overwhelmed by the impulse to abstract them out again, on the grounds that they complicate things so much as to make scientific results impossible to get at. It would be a strange view of science that took the only valid way to study diet, for example, to be to abstract away both food and eaters in order to determine abstract dietary principles and parameters. This might be an interesting intellectual exercise, but no one would seriously consider that it alone could be scientific, and that no study of what actual people actually eat, and its impact upon their lives, could possibly be so. Sadly, for some time now linguists have been lamenting the shrinking of the discipline, and finding various outside forces to blame, failing to consider to what extent the problem might lie with an ideologically driven insistence that only a dehumanised linguistics could be scientific. Real science demands, and has always demanded, not just methodological rigour, but broad vision. Neither is sufficient on its own. The future of linguistics depends upon our ability to reinvent rigour in a way that will allow the full range of the field's potential scientific applications to be realised.

Notes

1 Introduction

1 This passage became a key impetus for Hodson (1939), the article which contains the first known occurrence of the word 'socio-linguistics' (see Hymes, 1979; Joseph, 2002a, p. 108).

2 Linguistic Identity and the Functions and Evolution of Language

1 For a fuller history of these developments see Nerlich & Clarke (1996).
2 Even Taylor's argument is limited to communication; any consideration of representation in animal language he would reject as a form of anthropomorphism. The basic obstacle is again the insistence on the unjustly important status of the agentive languaging subject.
3 Remarkably similar views were put forward by Thomas Reid (1710–96), founder of the Scottish 'Common Sense' school of philosophy, who referred to these 'subtle clues' as 'natural signs' (see Reid, 1764, 1785).

3 Approaching Identity in Traditional Linguistic Analysis

1 For fuller accounts of Saussure's system see Joseph (1999) and (forthcoming b), and for its structuralist aftermath, Joseph (2001). A more complete account of language and politics in the twentieth century may be found in Joseph (2004).
2 It is noteworthy that the population of Copenhagen in 1925 was greater than it is today, mainly because of suburbanisation since the 1950s. Actually, though, Jespersen's views on urbanisation and its linguistic effects were already developed in his writings of the 1890s.
3 Other writings by Sapir on the subject of language and personality include Sapir (1927) and (1994).
4 Historians of linguistics often put the phrase 'Sapir–Whorf Hypothesis' in 'scare quotes' because neither Sapir nor Whorf ever articulated it as a hypothesis, and for each of them it represented a rather more complex set of ideas than either the normally encountered 'strong' view or its 'weak' counterpart comprises (see further Joseph, 2002b, pp. 71–2). Having made this disclaimer I shall omit the scare quotes henceforth.
5 See Whorf (1956); Joseph et al. (2001, Ch. 4); and for a full investigation of Whorf's thought and critiques that have been launched against both his analysis of Hopi and the conclusions he drew from it, Lee (1995).

6 Nevertheless, Firth's complex systemic analyses of language share certain features with contemporary structuralisms (see Firth, 1950, 1951; Joseph, 2002b, p. 58).
7 Still, even now some Marxists, Holborow (1999) for example, insist that (post-) structuralism is the direct opposite of their own doctrine because it situates reality in language rather than uniquely in the class struggle.

4 Integrating Perspectives from Adjacent Disciplines

1 Bernstein's earliest works make clear who he takes to be his predecessors: 'It is very clear to any student of the sociology of language the debt that is owed to Edward Sapir and his followers who pointed the way to the scientific study of the social institution of language' (Bernstein, 1959, p. 322). In his very first publication in this vein (Bernstein, 1958), Whorf is the key 'follower' of Sapir from whom Bernstein takes inspiration.
2 For further critical reflections on Lambert's early work see Edwards (1999).
3 On the complex relationship between French structuralism and Marxism, see Joseph (2001).
4 This is an aspect of Marx's Romantic heritage – cf. the remarks on the Romantic view on 'genius' on p. 44 above.
5 Habitus is in fact an extremely venerable term, much used in medieval philosophy in a sense quite close to the one it has in Bourdieu's revival of it.

5 Language in National Identities

1 While actual conditions on the ground may have approached it in certain places at certain times, it is hard to believe that any nation could have closed itself completely to all outsiders for very long. The spread of religions and other cultural constructs and artefacts suggests that if any community was ever immune from outside contact and influence, it could only have been for relatively brief periods of intense reaction against a mounting threat of invasion or infiltration; and in the end, if the threat was strong enough to provoke such an extreme reaction, it probably came to pass at least in part.
2 '[V]ulgarem locutionem appellamus eam quam infantes adsuefiunt ab adsistentibus, cum primitus distinguere voces incipiunt; vel quod brevius dici potest, vulgarem locutionem asserimus, quam sine omni regula, nutricem imitantes, accipimus.'
3 'Est et inde alia locutio secundaria nobis, quam Romani gramaticam vocaverunt. Hanc quidem secundariam Greci habent et alii, sed non omnes. Ad habitum vero huius pauci perveniunt, quia non nisi per spatium temporis et studii assiduitatem regulamur et doctrinamur in illa.'
4 'Harum quoque duarum nobilior est vulgaris: tum quia prima fuit humano generi usitata; tum quia totus orbis ipsa perfruitur, licet in diversas prolationes et vocabula sit divisa; tum qui naturalis est nobis, cum illa potius artificialis existat.'
5 'Postquam venati saltus et pascua sumus Ytalie nec panteram quam sequimur adinvenimus, ut ipsam reperire possimus, rationabilius investigemus de illa,

ut solerti studio redolentem ubique et necubi apparentem nostris penitus irretiamus tenticulis.'

6 '[U]numquodque mensurabile fit secundum quod in genere est, illo quod simplicissimum est in ipso genere. Quapropter in actionibus nostris, quantumcunque dividantur in species, hoc signum inveniri oportet quo et ipse mensurentur.'

7 'Que quidem nobilissima sunt earum que Latinorum sunt actiones, hec nullius civitatis Ytalie propria sunt et in omnibus comunia sunt: inter que nunc potest illud discerni vulgare quod superius venabamur, quod in qualibet redolet civitate nec cubat in ulla [...].'

8 '[S]iempre la lengua fue compañera del imperio, i de tal manera lo siguio que junta mente començaron, crecieron i florecieron, i despues junta fue la caida de entrambos.'

9 'I, por que mi pensamiento i gana siempre fue engrandecer las cosas de nuestra nacion i dar alos ombres de mi lengua obras en que mejor puedan emplear su ocio, que agora lo gastan leiendo novelas o istorias embueltas en mil mentiras i errores, acorde ante todas las otras cosas reduir en artificio este nuestro lenguaje castellano, para que lo que agora i de aqui adelante en el se escriviere pueda quedar en un tenor, i estenderse en toda la duracion delos tiempos que estan por venir, como vemos que se a hecho enla lengua griega i latina, las cuales, por aver estado debaxo de arte, aunque sobre ellas an passado muchos siglos, toda via quedan en una uniformidad.'

10 '[D]espues que Vuestra Alteza metiesse debaxo de su iugo muchos pueblos barbaros i naciones de peregrinas lenguas, i conel vencimiento aquellos ternian necessidad de recebir las leies quel vencedor pone al vencido i con ellas nuestra lengua, entonces por esta mi *Arte* podrian venir enel conocimiento della, como agora nos otros deprendemos el arte dela gramatica latina para deprender el latin.'

11 '*Marcio* [P]ues tenemos ya que el fundamento de la lengua castellana es la latina, resta que nos digáis de dónde vino y tuvo principio que en España se hablassen las otras quatro maneras de lenguas que oy se hablan, como son la catalana, la valenciana, la portuguesa y la vizcaína.

'*Valdés* [D]os cosas suelen principalmente causar en una provincia diversidales de lenguas. La una es no estar debaxo de un príncipe, rey o señor, de donde proçede que tantas diferencias ay de lenguas quanta diversidad de señores; la otra es que, como siempre se pegan algo una[s] provinçias comarcanas a otras, aconteçe que cada parte de una provinçia, tomando algo de sus comarcanas, su poco a poco se va diferençiando de las otras, y esto no solamente en el hablar, pero aun también en el conversar y en las costumbres. España, como sabéis, ha estado debaxo de muchos señores [...]. La qual diversidad de señoríos, pienso yo que en alguna manera aya causado la diferencia de las lenguas, bien que cualquiera dellas se conforma más con la lengua castellana que con ninguna otra, porque, aunque cada una dellas ha tomado de sus comarcanos, como Cataluña ha tomado de Francia y de Italia, y Valencia que ha tomado de Cataluña, todavía veréis que principalmente tiran al latín que es, como tengo dicho, el fundamento de la lengua castellana [...].'

12 Castilian and Portuguese were in fact much more alike in Valdés' time than today, especially in their written forms. Nevertheless, Valdés greatly exaggerates their similarity.

13 'Le temps viendra peut-être, et je l'espère moyennant la bonne destinée française, que ce noble et puissant Royaume obtiendra à son tour les rênes de la monarchie et que notre langue (si avec François n'est du tout ensevelie la langue française) qui commence encore à jeter ses racines, sortira de terre et s'élèvra en telle hauteur et grosseur qu'elle se pourra égaler aux mêmes Grecs et Romains [...].'

14 '[N]otre langue française n'est si pauvre qu'elle ne puisse rendre fidèlement ce qu'elle emprunte des autres, si infertile qu'elle ne puisse produire de soi quelque fruit de bonne invention au moyen de l'industrie et diligence des cultivateurs d'icelle si quelques-uns se trouvent tant amis de leur pays et d'eux-mêmes qu'ils s'y veuillent employer.'

15 '[N]e les [traducteurs] doit retarder s'ils rencontrent quelquefois des mots qui ne peuvent être reçus en la famille française, vu que les Latins ne se sont point efforcés de traduire tous les vocables grecs, comme *rhétorique, musique, arithmétique, géométrie, philosophie* [...] et généralement la plus grande part des termes usités aux sciences naturelles et mathématiques. Ces mots-là donc seront en notre langue comme étrangers en une cité [...]. Donc la philosophie semée par Aristote et Platon au fertile champ attique était replantée en notre plaine française, ce ne serait la jeter entre les ronces et épines où elle devînt stérile, mais ce serait la faire de lointaine prochaine, et d'étrangère citadine de notre république.'

16 Du Bellay obviously uses 'republic' in its general sense of 'polity' rather than the more specific sense that contrasts it with a monarchy or oligarchy.

17 'Une nation est une âme, un principe spirituel. Deux choses qui, à vrai dire, n'en font qu'une, constituent cette âme, ce principe spirituel. L'une est dans le passé, l'autre dans le présent. L'une est la possession en commun d'un riche legs de souvenirs; l'autre est le consentement actuel, le désir de vivre ensemble, la volonté de continuer à faire valoir l'héritage qu'on a reçu indivis.'

18 Gellner (1964, Ch. 7) argued that nationalism was best understood as the result of the uneven way in which modernisation had spread, causing massive economic and social changes, disrupting traditional lifestyles and motivating people to move from the countryside into cities. Traditional village and tribal structures upon which social organisation had been based no longer functional and had to be replaced, and what was available to replace them in the urban context was language and language-based culture, especially print culture. Modern education, funded by the state, grew up around the printed word, and functioned as an institution for creating new social hierarches based upon literacy and standards of language. But the new hierarchies engendered new tensions, as people struggled to retain old privileges under the new regime. Ethnic alliances took on a new importance in this struggle, and from the new ethnic awareness nationalist movements developed, 'inventing' nations where, in reality, they did not exist.

In later work, Gellner (1973, 1983) reformulated this theory to take account of certain facts it could not explain. One of these had to do with the central role he had assigned to language: it would lead one to predict that nationalisms would not arise in the absence of a recognised national language, yet there were plenty of examples of that happening, for instance in the Arabic-speaking world and Hispanophone Latin America (as well as the

English-speaking world, where separate American, Canadian, etc. sub-varieties are recognised, but not as distinct languages). Moreover, relatively stable nations had formed around a multiplicity of languages, as in the case of Switzerland. Gellner therefore shifted the focus away from language, and ever more onto the institutional structure of the public education system and its role in defining and maintaining a culture within which nationalism as a political principle is embedded and enacted in a wide range of ways.

19 'L'existence d'une nation est (pardonnez-moi cette métaphore) un plébiscite de tous les jours.'
20 'L'esprit de chaque peuple et sa langue sont dans la plus étroite connexité [...].'
21 The quotations are from Renan (1882, p. 9) and Gellner (1964, p. 169). The Renan quote may be translated: 'The essence of a nation is that all the individuals have many things in common, and also that they have all forgotten many things.'
22 Anthony Smith in particular has emphasised how much of the effort of nationalism construction is aimed at reaching back to the past in the interest of 'ethno-symbolism' (see e.g. Smith, 1998, Ch. 8).

6 Case Study 1: the New Quasi-Nation of Hong Kong

1 Only relatively, however, because different systems for writing Chinese are in use. The PRC has adopted 'simplified' characters, where Hong Kong uses traditional ones, for example. Moreover, Chinese readers can often tell from a text (whether printed or handwritten) what is the regional provenance of its author.
2 Hong Kong was invaded and taken over by Japanese forces in December 1941. At the end of the Second World War, authority over it should, by international law, have been handed over to the geographcially nearest allied power, in this case the Kuomintang government of China. In fact, however, it was returned to British sovereignty.
3 It should be added that the related notion of 'progress' in language change survived longer, for example in Jespersen (1894). See also Aitchison (1981).
4 The data raise certain problems, starting with how to reconcile them with government statistics indicating that Filipinos, most of them employed as domestic helpers, formed more than 1 per cent of the 1993 population, and presumably all spoke and understood home languages that would have to be classed as 'other' in the table. Nevertheless, the figures follow the same patterns reported by Tsou (1996). Secondly, what appears to be a 7 per cent drop in the percentage of Cantonese speakers from 1983 to 1993 is not really one. The difference is accounted for by the fact that in the second survey, 'Chinese' was offered as an option, and was selected by some 7 per cent of respondents, whose 1983 counterparts presumably selected 'Cantonese'. Finally, the fact that the data are from self-reporting rather than 'objective' observation is potentially a problem, but that is the only way in which comparison could be made across the six-decade time span, since all the pre-1983 data are from self-reporting to census takers. Moreover, for the issues of language and

identity that are currently bound up with language use in Hong Kong, people's subjective impressions of their own language abilities matter at least as much as any external assessment.

5 Of course, spoken Hong Kong English also displays numerous phonological features that distinguish it from Standard English, and they have not been discussed here. A very full survey of them can be found in Gibbons (1979, pp. 8–18).

6 Cantonese is a 'tone language', which is to say that the pitch contour of a word contributes to distinguishing meaning. In the following pages the tones are indicated as follows: à (high falling), á (high rising), ā (high level), àh (low falling), áh (low rising), ah (low level). Doubling of the vowel indicates that it is long.

7 For Standard English in (a) and (b) I am following the notation of Baker (1995), which is useful for this kind of work because it does not commit one to any particular theory of syntax.

7 Language in Ethnic/Racial and Religious/Sectarian Identities

1 Ever since Homer, accounts of war have functioned as powerful narrative loci of national identity.

2 Although younger readers may not feel at all close to the period in which these events took place, one of my own first publications was a review (Joseph, 1980) of the 1978 book by Heinz Kloss (1904–87), whose role as a Nazi linguist is documented by an entire chapter of Hutton (1999). Kloss's conceptual distinctions, one of which is discussed in the first section of this chapter, continue to have wide appeal, and ought not to be banished on account of the context in which they were formulated. Quite the contrary: they are useful for illustrating Hutton's discomfiting central conclusion, namely that Nazi-era linguistics was not anomalous or 'un-scientific' by present-day standards, but quite continuous with the work linguists have done since the nineteenth century and continue to do.

3 The rise of militant Islamic identity put an end to the last attempts at 'pan-Arabism', mentioned in an earlier section, a movement that sought to unite Arabs regardless of their religious affiliations.

4 In what follows I have removed all references to subjects' family names. Only their given names are discussed.

5 In fact it has been taking place since the end of the Middle Ages, with a marked acceleration in the period of the Industrial Revolution.

6 As an example, Harris, in the quote on p. 182 above, is so caught up in the 'presumption [...] that English is the de facto lingua franca of the global economy' that he appears quite oblivious to the presence of a Latin phrase and an Italian phrase in this very sentence. Their presence does not of course make it un-English, but does allow Harris's own voice to be interpreted as that of an academic writer – and therefore someone who obviously knows what he is talking about.

7 I personally do not believe that human translators will ever be replaced, but their job is made more specific and efficient by the computerised draft translation, which has cut significantly the cost of doing business in multiple languages.

8 Case Study 2: Christian and Muslim Identities in Lebanon

1 Syriac, an eastern dialect of Aramaic, became an important literary language as early as the third century after Christ. With the coming of Islam it ceded most functions to Arabic, other than Christian liturgical ones.

2 For an overview of language and ethnic identity in the Arabic-speaking world see Holt (1996).

3 I should point out that I had not met them prior to 1998; my grandfather had emigrated in 1898, and the two sides of the family had lost touch after his death in 1963.

4 See above, p. 231, n. 19.

5 'Nous avons chassé de la politique les abstractions métaphysiques et théologiques. Que reste-t-il, après cela? Il reste l'homme, ses désirs, ses besoins.'

6 ' [. . .] ces langues toutes physiques, auxquelles l'abstraction est inconnue et la métaphysique impossible'.

7 Just before he fell unconscious, Renan 'had time to remark the Maronite peasants passing his window on their way to church, and in this foreign half-savage country, the familiar sight filled him with a feeling of utter desolation and helplessness which he has since recorded' (Darmesteter, 1898, p. 142). To give some perspective on how little time has elapsed between Renan's voyage and the present day, my great-grandfather Yusuf (1848–1941) could easily have been one of the peasant boys passing by Renan's window that 19th of September 1861, and he survives in the living memory of family members aged only in their sixties. In fact they mainly remember watching him on his daily walks to and from church.

8 'à Rome, tu étais « le fils de l'Africain »; en Afrique, tu seras « le fils du *Roumi* ». Où que tu sois, certains voudront fouiller ta peau et tes prières. Garde-toi de flatter leurs instincts, mon fils, garde-toi de ployer sous la multitude! Musulman, juif ou chrétien, ils devront te prendre comme tu es, ou te perdre. Lorsque l'esprit des hommes te paraîtra étroit, dis-toi que la terre de Dieu est vaste, et vastes Ses mains et Son cœur. N'hésite jamais à t'éloigner, au-delà de toutes les mers, au-delà de toutes les frontières, de toutes les patries, de toutes les croyances.'

Bibliography

Abou, Sélim. *Le bilinguisme arabe–français au Liban: Essai d'anthropologie culturelle* (Paris: Presses Universitaires de France, 1962).
Abou, Sélim. 'Le français au Liban et en Syrie'. In Albert Valdman (ed.) *Le français hors de France* (Paris: Champion, 1978), 287–309.
Abou, Sélim, Choghig Kasparian & Katia Hadded. *Anatomie de la francophonie libanaise* (Beirut: Université St-Joseph; Montreal: AUPELF-UREF, 1996).
Adekunle, Mobolaji. 'English in Nigeria: Attitudes, Policy and Communicative Realities'. In Ayo Bamgbose, Ayo Banjo & Andrew Thomas (eds) *New Englishes: a West African Perspective* (Trenton, NJ: Africa World Press, 1997), 57–86.
Aitchison, Jean. *Language Change: Progress or Decay?* (Cambridge: Cambridge University Press, 1981).
Alexander, Neville. 'Language Politics in South Africa'. In Simon Bekker, Martine Dodds & Meshack M. Khosa (eds) *Shifting African Identities* (Cape Town: Human Sciences Research Council Publishers, 2001) 141–52.
Alici, Didem Mersin. 'The Role of Culture, History and Language in Turkish National Identity Building: an Overemphasis on Central Asian Roots'. *Central Asian Survey*, 15 (1996) 217–31.
Alvarez-Caccamo, Celso. 'The Pigeon House, the Octopus and the People: the Ideologization of Linguistic Practices in Galiza'. *Plurilinguismes*, 6 (1993) 1–26.
Al-Wer, Eman. 'Why Do Different Variables Behave Differently? Data from Arabic'. In Yasir Suleiman (ed.) *Language and Society in the Middle East and North Africa: Studies in Variation and Identity* (Richmond, Surrey: Carzon, 1999) 38–57.
Anderson, Benedict. *Imagined Communities: Reflections on the Origin and Spread of Nationalism*, 2nd edn (London and New York: Verso, 1991). [1st edn 1983.]
Archilés, Ferran & Manuel Martí. 'Ethnicity, Region and Nation: Valencian Identity and the Spanish Nation-State'. *Ethnic and Racial Studies*, 24 (2001) 779–97.
Asher, R. E. & T. C. Kumari. *Malayalam* (London and New York: Routledge, 1997).
Ashley, Leonard R. N. 'Language and Identity in Cuba Today'. *Geolinguistics*, 28 (2002) 22–33.
Austin, J. L. *How to Do Things with Words* (Oxford: Clarendon Press, 1962).
Bacon-Shone, John & Kingsley Bolton. 'Charting Multilingualism: Language Censuses and Language Surveys in Hong Kong'. In M. C. Pennington (ed.) *Language in Hong Kong at Century's End* (Hong Kong: Hong Kong University Press, 1998), 43–90.
Baggioni, Daniel. *Langues et nations en Europe* (Paris: Payot, 1997).
Bailey, Cyril (ed. and transl.). *Epicurus: the Extant Remains* (Oxford: Clarendon Press, 1926).
Baker, C. L. *English Syntax*, 2nd edn (Cambridge, Mass.: MIT Press, 1995).
Bakhtin, Mikhail. 'Discourse in the Novel'. In Michael Holquist (ed.), *The Dialogic Imagination: Four Essays by M. Bakhtin*, transl. by Caryl Emerson & Michael Holquist (Austin: University of Texas Press, 1981. Original work written 1934–35, first published 1975).

Baldwin, J. R. & Michael L. Hecht. 'The Layered Perspective on Cultural (In)tolerance(s): the Roots of a Multi-disciplinary Approach to (In)tolerance'. In R. L. Wiseman (ed.) *Intercultural Communication Theory* (Thousand Oaks, Calif.: Sage, 1995), 59–91.

Barbour, Stephen. 'Language and National Identity in Europe'. In Charlotte Hoffmann (ed.) *Language, Culture and Communication in Contemporary Europe* (Clevedon: Multilingual Matters, 1996) 28–46.

Barnes, J. A. 'Class and Communities in a Norwegian Island Parish', *Human Relations*, 7 (1954) no. 1.

Barros, Maria Candida D. M., Luiz C. Borges & Marcio Meira. 'A lingua geral como identidade construida'. *Revista de Antropologia*, 39 (1996) 191–219.

Bechhofer, Frank, David McCrone, Richard Kiely & Robert Stewart. 'Constructing National Identity: Arts and Landed Elites in Scotland'. *Sociology*, 22 (1999) 515–34.

Bekker, Simon, Martine Dodds & Meshack M. Khosa (eds). *Shifting African Identities* (Cape Town: Human Sciences Research Council Publishers, 2001).

Belaj, Vitomir. 'Der Mythos von den Urkroaten und ihren Eigenschaften'. In Dittmar Dahlmann & Wilfried Potthoff (eds) *Mythen, Symbole and Rituale: Die Geschichtsmächtigkeit der Zeichen in Südosteuropa in 19. and 20. Jahrhundert* (Frankfurt: PeterLong, 2000) 37–49.

Bell, Allan. 'Language Style as Audience Design'. *Language in Society*, 13 (1984) 145–204.

Bell, Allan. 'The Phonetics of Fish and Chips in New Zealand: Making National and Ethnic Identities'. *English World-Wide*, 18 (1997) 243–70.

Bell, Allan. 'Styling the Other to Define the Self: a Study in New Zealand Identity Making'. *Journal of Sociolinguistics*, 3 (1999) 523–41.

Bellier, Irene. 'European Identity, Institutions and Languages in the Context of the Enlargement'. *Journal of Language and Politics*, 1 (2002) 85–114.

Bennassar, Bartolomé & Lucile Bennassar. *Les Chrétiens d'Allah: L'histoire extraordinaire des renégats, XVIe–XVIIe siècles* (Paris: Perrin, 1989).

Benrabah, Mohamed. 'Attitudinal Reactions to Language Change in an Urban Setting'. In Yasir Suleiman (ed.) *Arabic Sociolinguistics: Issues and Perspectives* (London: Carzon, 1994) 213–25.

Ben-Rafael, Eliezer. *Language, Identity, and Social Division: the Case of Israel* (Oxford: Clarendon Press, 1994).

Berger, Ruth. 'Die Neuentwicklung einer Nationalsprache: Israel und die Türkei'. In Karl E. Grözinger (ed.) *Sprache und Identität im Judentum* (Wiesbaden: Harrassowitz, 1998), 199–229.

Bernstein, Basil. 'Some Sociological Determinants of Perception: an Enquiry into Sub-cultural Differences'. *British Journal of Sociology*, 9 (1958) 159–74.

Bernstein, Basil. 'A Public Language: Some Sociological Implications of a Linguistic Form'. *British Journal of Sociology*, 10 (1959) 311–26.

Bernstein, Basil. 'Social Class, Speech Systems and Psycho-Therapy'. *British Journal of Sociology*, 15 (1964) 54–64.

Bernstein, Basil. *Class, Codes and Control*, vol. 5: *Pedagogy, Symbolic Control, and Identity: Theory, Research, Critique* (London: Taylor & Francis, 1996).

Berré, Michel. 'Le Français à l'école primaire en Flandre vers 1880–1890: Identités nationales et techniques d'enseignement'. In Marie-Christine Kok Escalle & Francine Melka (eds) *Changements politiques et statut des langues: Histoire et épistémologie 1780–1945* (Amsterdom: Rodopi, 2001), 235–52.

Besnier, Niko. 'Literacy and the Notion of Person on Nukulaelae Atoll'. *American Anthropologist*, 93 (1991) 570–87.

Besnier, Niko. *Literacy, Emotion and Authority: Reading and Writing on a Polynesian Atoll* (Cambridge: Cambridge University Press, 1995).

Billig, Michael. *Banal Nationalism* (London: Sage, 1995).

Bivona, Rosalia. ' "L'Italie est faite, il faut faire les Italiens": La Construction de l'identité nationale dans les manuels scolaires'. In Marie-Christine Kok Escalle & Francine Melka (eds) *Changements politiques et statut des langues: Histoire et épistémologie 1780–1945* (Amsterdom: Rodopi, 2001), 215–33.

Blake, Renee. 'Barbadian Creole English: Insights into Linguistic and Social Identity'. *Journal of Commonwealth and Postcolonial Studies*, 4 (1996) 37–54.

Blanchet, Philippe. 'Regard sur la dynamique actuelle de la langue et de la culture provençales, ou, le regain d'identité fait-il reculer la diglossie?' *La France Latine*, 120 (1995) 201–30.

Blanke, Richard. ' "Polish-Speaking Germans?": Language and National Identity among the Masurians'. *Nationalities Papers*, 27 (1999) 429–53.

Blommaert, Jan. *State Ideology and Language in Tanzania* (Cologne: Rüdiger Köppe, 1999a).

Blommaert, Jan (ed.). *Language Ideological Debates* (Berlin: Mouton de Gruyter, 1999b).

Boissevain, Jeremy. *Friends of Friends: Networks, Manipulators and Coalitions* (Oxford: Blackwell, 1974).

Boissevain, Jeremy & J. Clyde Mitchell (eds). *Network Analysis: Studies in Human Interaction* (The Hague: Mouton, 1973).

Bolton, Kingsley. *Chinese Englishes: a Sociolinguistic History* (Cambridge: Cambridge University Press, 2003a).

Bolton, Kingsley, (ed.). *Hong Kong English: Autonomy and Creativity* (Hong Kong: Hong Kong University Press, 2003b).

Bolton, Kingsley & Helen Kwok. 'The Dynamics of the Hong Kong Accent: Social Identity and Sociolinguistic Description'. *Journal of Asian Pacific Communication*, 1 (1990) 147–72.

Bonner, Donna M. 'Garifuna Children's Language Shame: Ethnic Stereotypes, National Affiliation, and Transnational Immigration as Factors in Language Choice in Southern Belize'. *Language in Society*, 30 (2001) 81–96.

Bourdieu, Pierre. *Ce que parler veut dire: l'économie des échanges linguistiques* (Paris: Fayard, 1982). English version (with additional material), *Language and Symbolic Power: the Economy of Linguistic Exchanges*, ed. by John B. Thompson, transl. by Gino Raymond & Matthew Adamson (Cambridge: Polity, in association with Basil Blackwell, 1991).

Boves, T., R. van Hout, W. H. Vieregge & U. Knops. 'Een formalisering van de concepten convergentie en divergentie uit de taalaccommodatie theorie'. *Gramma*, 14 (1990) 65–80.

Bradac, James J., Aaron Castelan Cargile & Jennifer S. Hallett. 'Language Attitudes: Retrospect, Conspect, and Prospect'. In W. Peter Robinson & Howard Giles (eds) *The New Handbook of Language and Social Psychology* (Chichester and New York: John Wiley & Sons, 2001), 137–55.

Breitborde, Lawrence. *Speaking and Social Identity: English in the Lives of Urban Africans* (Berlin and New York: Mouton de Gruyter, 1998).

Brown, Adam. *Singapore English in a Nutshell: an Alphabetical Description of its Features* (Singapore: Federal Publications, 1999).

Brown, Penelope & Stephen C. Levinson. *Politeness: Some Universals in Language Usage* (Cambridge: Cambridge University Press, 1987).

Brown, Roger & Albert C. Gilman. 'The Pronouns of Power and Solidarity'. In Thomas A. Sebeok (ed.) *Style in Language* (Cambridge, Mass.: MIT Press, 1960), 253–76.

Bruner, Jerome S., with the assistance of Rita Watson. *Child's Talk: Learning to Use Language* (Oxford: Oxford University Press, 1983).

Bruner, Jerome S. *Acts of Meaning* (Cambridge, Mass.: Harvard University Press, 1990).

Brutt-Griffler, Janina. *World English: a Study of its Development* (Clevedon: Multilingual Matters, 2002).

Bucken-Knapp, Gregg. *Elites, Language, and the Politics of Identity: the Norwegian Case in Comparative Perspective* (Albany: State University of New York Press, 2003).

Cameron, Deborah. *Feminism and Linguistic Theory*, 2nd edn (Basingstoke: Macmillan, 1992).

Cameron, Deborah. *Verbal Hygiene* (London and New York: Routledge, 1995).

Canagarajah, A. Suresh. *Resisting Linguistic Imperialism in English Teaching* (Oxford: Oxford University Press, 1999).

Canut, Cécile. 'Le nom des langues au Mali: Identité(s) en question'. In Andrée Tabouret-Keller (ed.) *Le nom des langues*, Vol. I: *Les enjeux de la nomination des langues* (Leuven: Peeters, 1997), 225–39.

Carey, Stephen. 'Language Management, Official Bilingualism, and Multiculturalism in Canada'. *Annual Review of Applied Linguistics*, 17 (1997) 204–23.

Centeno Añeses, Carmen. 'Lengua, identidad nacional, postmodernidad'. *Revista de Estudios Hispánicos*, 26 (1999) 217–37.

Chennells, Anthony. 'African Cultural Nationalism and Fictional Resistances: Examples from Zimbabwe'. In Jochen Achilles & Carmen Birkle (eds) *(Trans) Formations of Cultural Identity in the English-Speaking World* (Heidelberg: Carl Winter, 1998).

Cherry, Roger D. '*Ethos* versus Persona: Self-Representation in Written Discourse'. *Written Communication*, 5 (1998) 251–76.

Chew, Phyllis Ghim-Lian. 'Islands and National Identity: the Metaphors of Singapore'. *International Journal of the Sociology of Language*, 143 (2000) 121–37.

Choi, Po-King. 'A Search for Cultural Identity: the Students' Movement of the Early Seventies'. In Anthony Sweeting (ed.) *Differences and Identities: Educational Arguments in Late Twentieth Century Hong Kong* (Hong Kong: Faculty of Education, University of Hong Kong, 1990), 81–107.

Cifuentes, Barbara. 'Las lenguas amerindias y la conformacion de la lengua nacional en Mexico en el siglo XIX'. *Language Problems and Language Planning*, 18 (1994) 208–22.

Cillia, Rudolf de. ' "Alles bleibt, wie es isst": Osterreichs EU-Beitritt und die Frage des Osterreichischen Deutsch'. *Jahrbuch Deutsch als Fremdsprache: Intercultural German Studies*, 23 (1997) 239–58.

Clampitt-Dunlap, Sharon. 'Nationalism and Native-Language Maintenance in Puerto Rico'. *International Journal of the Sociology of Language*, 142 (2000) 25–34.

Clark, W. J. *International Language: Past, Present and Future, with Specimens of Esperanto and Grammar* (London: J. M. Dent & Co., 1907).

Clyne, Michael. 'Pluricentric Languages and National Identity: an Antipodean View'. In Edgar W. Schneider (ed.) *Englishes around the World: Studies in Honour of Manfred Görlach*. Vol. II: *Caribbean, Africa, Asia, Australasia* (Amsterdam and Philadelphia: John Benjamins, 1997), 287–300.

Conversi, Daniele. *The Basques, the Catalans and Spain: Alternative Routes to Nationalist Mobilisation* (London: Hurst & Co., 1997).

Cooper, Thomas. *Lectures on the Elements of Political Economy* (Columbia, SC: Doyle E. Sweeny, 1826).

Covino, Sandra. 'Lingua e identità nazionale: un binomio problematico. La questione dell'italiano a Malta in alcuni studi recenti'. *Rivista Italiana di Dialettologia*, 23 (1999) 265–92.

Crowley, Terry. 'The Language Situation in Vanuatu'. *Current Issues in Language Planning*, 1 (2000) 47–132.

Crowley, Tony. *Language in History: Theories and Texts* (London and New York: Routledge, 1996a).

Crowley, Tony. 'Signs of Belonging: Languages, Nations, and Culture in the Old and New Europe'. In Charlotte Hoffmann (ed.) *Language, Culture and Communication in Contemporary Europe* (Clevedon: Multilingual Matters, 1996b), 47–60.

Crystal, David. *English as a Global Language* (Cambridge: Cambridge University Press, 1997).

Dagher, Joseph. 'Parémiologie et village libanais: Étude socio-linguistique de quelques matériaux'. *Arabica*, 41 (1994) 1–29.

Dahlmann, Dittmar & Wilfried Potthoff (eds). *Mythen, Symbole und Rituale: Die Geschichtsmächtigkeit der Zeichen in Südosteuropa im 19. und 20. Jahrhundert* (Frankfurt: Peter Lang, 2000).

Danilevsky, Nikolai Jakovlevich. *Rossiya i Evropa: Vzglyad na kul'turnyya i politicheskiya otnosheniya Slavyanskago mira k Germano-Romanskomy*, 3rd edn (St Petersburg: Strakhov, 1888). [1st edn 1869.]

Darmesteter, Madame James (A. Mary F. Robinson). *The Life of Ernest Renan* (London: Methuen, 1898).

Dau, Rev. Butros. *Religious, Cultural and Political History of the Maronites* (Lebanon [no city]: Rev. Butros Dau, 1984).

Davies, Alan. 'Ironising the Myth of Linguicism'. *Journal of Multilingual and Multicultural Development*, 17 (1996) 485–96.

Delbridge, Arthur. 'Lexicography and National Identity: the Australian Experience'. In David Blair & Peter Collins (eds) *English in Australia* (Amsterdam and Philadelphia: John Benjamins, 2001), 303–16.

Der-Karabetian, Aghop & Armine Proudian-Der-Karabetian. 'Ethnicity and Civil War: the Lebanese–Armenian Case'. Research report distributed by ERIC, 1984.

Dessalles, Jean-Louis. *Aux origines du langage: Une histoire naturelle de la parole* (Paris: Éditions Hermès, 2000).

Deutsch, Karl W. *Nationalism and Social Communication: an Inquiry into the Foundations of Nationality* (joint publ.: Cambridge, Mass.: Technology Press of the Massachusetts Institute of Technology; New York: Wiley, 1953).

Dollerup, Cay. 'The Uzbek Language Scene'. *Language International*, 7 (1995) 3, 29–32.

Dunbar, Robin. *Grooming, Gossip and the Evolution of Language* (London and Boston: Faber & Faber, 1996).

Duranti, Alessandro. *From Grammar to Politics: Linguistic Anthropology in a Western Samoan Village* (Berkeley: University of California Press, 1994).

Eckert, Penelope & Sally McConnell-Ginet. 'Think Practically and Look Locally: Language and Gender as Community-Based Practice'. *Annual Review of Anthropology*, 21 (1992) 461–90.

Edwards, John. *Language, Society and Identity* (Oxford and New York: Basil Blackwell, in association with London: André Deutsch, 1985).

Edwards, John R. 'Refining our Understanding of Language Attitudes'. *Journal of Language and Social Psychology*, 18 (1999) 101–10.

Ehret, Rebekka. 'Language Attitude and the Linguistic Construction of Ethnic Identity: the Case of Krio in Sierra Leone'. In Martin Putz (ed.) *Language Choices: Conditions, Constraints, and Consequences* (Amsterdam and Philadelphia: John Benjamins, 1997), 327–37.

Ennaji, Moha. 'The Arab World (Maghreb and Near East)'. In Joshua Fishman (ed.) *Handbook of Language and Ethnic Identity* (Oxford: Oxford University Press, 1999), 382–95.

Erfurt, Jurgen. 'Sprachkonflikte und sprachliche Identitat in der frankophonen Diaspora Kanadas'. In James R. Dow & Michele Wolff (eds) *Languages and Lives: Essays in Honor of Werner Enninger* (New York: Peter Lang, 1997), 155–69.

Errington, J. Joseph. *Shifting Languages: Interaction and Identity in Javanese Indonesia* (Cambridge: Cambridge University Press, 1998).

Escalle, Marie-Christine Kok & Francine Melka (eds) *Changements politiques et statut des langues: Histoire et épistémologie 1780–1945* (Amsterdam: Rodopi, 2001).

Fairclough, Norman. *Language and Power* (London: Longman, 1989).

Fairclough, Norman. *Discourse and Social Change* (London: Polity, 1992).

Fichte, Johann Gottlieb. *Reden an die deutsche Nation* (Berlin: Realschulbuchhandlung, 1808). English version, *Addresses to the German Nation*, transl. by R. F. Jones and G. H. Turnbull, ed. by George A. Kelly (New York: Harper Torch Books, 1968).

Firth, J. R. 'Personality and Language in Society'. *Sociological Review*, 42 (1950) 37–52. Repr. in J. R. Firth, *Papers in Linguistics, 1934–51* (London: Oxford University Press, 1957), 177–89.

Firth, J. R. 'Modes of Meaning'. *Essays and Studies* (The English Association), n.s. 4 (1951) 118–49. Repr. in J. R. Firth *Papers in Linguistics, 1934–1951* (London: Oxford University Press, 1957), 190–215.

Firth, J. R. *Papers in Linguistics, 1934–1951* (London: Oxford University Press, 1957).

Fish, Stanley. *Is There a Text in This Class?* (Cambridge, Mass.: Harvard University Press, 1980).

Fishman, Joshua (ed.). *Handbook of Language and Ethnic Identity* (Oxford: Oxford University Press, 1999).

Foucault, Michel. *Surveiller et punir: Naissance de la prison* (Paris: Gallimard, 1975). Engl. transl., *Discipline and Punish: the Birth of the Prison*, by Alan Sheridan (Harmondsworth: Penguin, 1977).

Fowler, Roger. 'Notes on Critical Linguistics'. In Ross Steele & Terry Threadgold (eds) *Language Topics: Essays in Honour of Michael Halliday*, Vol. 2 (Amsterdam and Philadelphia: John Benjamins, 1987).

Fowler, Roger, Robert Hodge, Gunther Kress & Tony Trew. *Language and Control* (London: Routledge and Kegan Paul, 1979).

Francard, Michel. 'La légitimité linguistique passe-t-elle par la reconnaissance du statut de variété "nationale"? Le cas de la communauté française Wallonie-Bruxelles'. *Revue québécoise de linguistique*, 26 (1998) 2, 13–23.

Frangoudaki, Anna. 'The Metalinguistic Prophecy on the Decline of the Greek Language: Its Social Function as the Expression of a Crisis in Greek National Identity'. *International Journal of the Sociology of Language*, 126 (1997) 63–82.

Frantzen, Allen J. & John D. Niles (eds). *Anglo-Saxonism and the Construction of Social Identity* (Gainesville: University Press of Florida, 1997).

Frawley, William J. & James P. Lantolf. 'Second Language Discourse: a Vygotskyan Perspective'. *Applied Linguistics*, 6 (1985) 19–43.

Friedman, Edward. 'A Failed Chinese Modernity'. *Daedalus*, 122 (1993) 2 (Spring), 1–17.

Friedman, Victor A. 'Macedonian Historiography, Language, and Identity, in the Context of the Yugoslav Wars of Succession'. *Indiana Slavic Studies*, 10 (1999) 71–86.

Friggieri, Oliver. 'La question linguistique à Malte: Éveil d'une identité nationale'. *AWAL: Cahiers d'Études Berberes*, 17 (1998) 123–6.

Furfey, Paul Hanly. 'Men's and Women's Languages'. *American Catholic Sociological Review*, 5 (1944) 218–23.

Garde, Paul. 'Langue et nation: le cas serbe, croate et bosniaque'. *Cahiers de l'ILSL*, 8 (1996) 123–47.

Gardt, Andreas (ed.). *Nation und Sprache: Die Diskussion ihres Verhältnisses in Geschichte und Gegenwart* (Berlin: Walter de Gruyter, 2000).

Garuba, Harry. 'Language and Identity in Nigeria'. In Simon Bekker, Martine Dodds & Meshack M. Khosa (eds) *Shifting African Identities* (Cape Town: Humen Sciences Research Council Publishers, 2001), 7–20.

Garvin, Paul L. (ed. and trans.). *A Prague School Reader in Esthetics, Literary Structure, and Style*, rev. edn (Washington, DC: Georgetown University Press, 1959).

Gellner, Ernest. *Thought and Change* (London: Weidenfeld & Nicolson, 1964).

Gellner, Ernest. 'Scale and Nation'. *Philosophy of the Social Sciences*, 3 (1973) 1–17.

Gellner, Ernest. *Nations and Nationalism* (Ithaca, NY: Cornell University Press, 1983).

Gellner, Ernest. *Nationalism* (London: Weidenfeld & Nicolson, 1997).

Ghaleb, Mary L. & John E. Joseph. 'Factors Affecting Students' Perceptions of the Status and Use of Languages in Lebanon' (in Arabic with English and French abstracts). Ch. 9 of Kassim Shaaban (ed.) *Language and Education / Al-Lugga wa Al-Taaleem* (Beirut: Lebanese Association for Educational Studies, 2000).

Gibbons, John. 'U-Gay-Wa: a Linguistic Study of the Campus Language of Students at the University of Hong Kong'. In Robert Lord (ed.) *Hong Kong Language Papers* (Hong Kong: Hong Kong University Press, 1979), 3–43.

Goffman, Erving. *The Presentation of Self in Everyday Life* (Edinburgh: University of Edinburgh Social Sciences Research Centre, 1956).

Gordon, David C. 'The Arabic Language and National Identity: the Cases of Algeria and of Lebanon'. In William R. Beer and James E. Jacob (eds) *Language Policy and National Unity* (Totowa, NJ: Rowman & Allanheld, 1985), 134–50.

Gorham, Michael S. 'Natsiia ili snikerizatsiia? Identity and Perversion in the Language Debates of Late- and Post-Soviet Russia'. *Russian Review*, 59 (2000) 614–29.
Görlach, Manfred. 'Language and Nation: the Concept of Linguistic Identity in the History of English'. *English World-Wide: a Journal of Varieties of English*, 18 (1997) 1–34.
Graddol, David & Ulrike H. Meinhof (eds) *English in a Changing World*. AILA Review 13 (1999).
Grossenbacher-Schmid, Ruth. 'Zur Sprachsituation in der Schweiz'. *Sprachspiegel*, 54 (1998) 206–10.
Guenier, Nicole. ' "Je suis un Libanais typique": Sécurité et insécurité linguistiques chez les Libanais francophones'. *Cahiers de l'Institut de Linguistique de Louvain*, 20 (1994) 35–44.
Gumperz, John J. (ed.) *Language and Social Identity* (Cambridge: Cambridge University Press, 1982).
Gumperz, John J. & Jenny Cook-Gumperz. 'Introduction: Language and the Communication of Social Identity'. In John. J. Gumperz (ed.) *Language and Social Identity* (Cambridge: Cambridge University Press, 1982), 1–21.
Guneratne, Arjun. 'Modernization, the State, and the Construction of a Tharu Identity in Nepal'. *Journal of Asian Studies*, 57 (1998) 749–73.
Gutschmidt, Karl & Claudia Hopf. 'Nationalsprachen und Sprachnationalismus in Südosteuropa'. In Uwe Hinrichs & Uwe Büttner (eds) *Handbuch der Südosteuropa-Linguistik* (Wiesbaden: Harrassowitz, 1999), 803–27.
Haarmann, Harald. 'Europeanness, European Identity and the Role of Language: Giving Profile to an Anthropological Infrastructure'. *Sociolinguistica*, 9 (1995) 1–55.
Haas, Mary R. 'Men's and Women's Speech in Koasati'. *Language*, 20 (1944) 142–9.
Halliday, M. A. K. *Language as Social Semiotic: the Social Interpretation of Language and Meaning* (London: Edward Arnold, 1978).
Hannan, Kevin. *Borders of Language and Identity in Teschen Silesia* (New York: Peter Lang, 1996).
Hardie, Kim. 'Lowland Scots: Issues in Nationalism and Identity'. In Charlotte Hoffmann (ed.) *Language, Culture and Communication in Contemporary Europe* (Clevedon: Multilingual Matters, 1996), 61–74.
Harris, Richard G. 'The Economics of Language in a Virtually Integrated Global Economy'. In Albert Breton (ed.) *Economic Approaches to Language and Bilingualism* (Ottawa: Department of Public Works and Government Services Canada, 1998).
Harris, Roy. 'The Worst English in the World?'. Inaugural Lecture from the Chair of English, The University of Hong Kong. *Supplement to the Gazette*, University of Hong Kong, 36, 1 (April 1989), 37–46.
Havlíček, Karel. 'Slovan a Čech'. *Pražské noviny*, vol. 1 (1846), 15 Feb.–12 Mar.
Havránek, B. 'Úkoly spisovného jazyka a jeho kultura'. In B. Havránek & M. Weingart (eds) *Spisovná čeština a jazyková kultura* (Prague: Melantrich, 1932), 32–84. (Engl. trans., 'The Functional Differentiation of the Standard Language', in Paul L. Garvin (ed. and trans.) *A Prague School Reader in Esthetics, Literary Structure and Style*, rev. edn (Washington, DC: Georgetown University Press, 1959), 3–16).

Havránek, B. 'Zum Problem der Norm in der heutigen Sprachwissenschaft und Sprachkultur'. *Actes du 4e Congrès International de Linguistes* (Copenhagen, 1938), 151–6.

Havránek, B. & M. Weingart (eds). *Spisovná čeština a jazková kultura* (Prague: Melantrich, 1932).

Haynes, Lilith M. 'One People, One Nation, One Destiny: Race, Ethnicity and Guyanese Sociolinguistic Identity'. In Edgar W. Schneider (ed.) *Studies in Honour of Manfred Görlach* (Amsterdam and Philadelphia: John Benjamins, 1997), 25–39.

Hecht, Michael L. '2002: a Research Odyssey toward the Development of a Communication Theory of Identity'. *Communication Monographs*, 60 (1993) 76–82.

Hecht, Michael L., Ronald L. Jackson II, Sheryl Lindsley, Susan Strauss & Karen E. Johnson. 'A Layered Approach to Communication: Language and Communication'. In W. Peter Robinson & Howard Giles (eds) *The New Handbook of Language and Social Psychology* (Chichester and New York: John Wiley & Sons, 2001), 429–49.

Hobsbawm, E. J. *Nations and Nationalism since 1780: Programmes, Myth, Reality* (Cambridge: Cambridge University Press, 1990).

Hodson, T. C. 'Socio-linguistics in India'. *Man in India*, 19 (1939) 94–8.

Hoffmann, Charlotte (ed.). *Language, Culture, and Communication in Contemporary Europe* (Clevedon: Multilingual Matters, 1996).

Holborow, Marnie. *The Politics of English: a Marxist View of Language* (London: Sage, 1999).

Holman, Eugene. 'Multilingualism and National Identity in Post-Soviet Estonia'. *Sociolinguistica*, 9 (1995) 136–40.

Holt, Mike. 'Divided Loyalties: Language and Ethnic Identity in the Arab World'. In Yasir Suleiman (ed.) *Language and Ethnic Identity in the Middle East and North Africa* (London: Curzon, 1996), 11–24.

Homans, George. 'Social Behaviour as Exchange'. *American Journal of Sociology*, 62 (1958) 597–606.

Huang, Shuanfan. 'Language, Identity and Conflict: a Taiwanese Study'. *International Journal of the Sociology of Language*, 143 (2000) 139–49.

Huss, Leena & Anna-Riitta Lindgren. 'Scandinavia'. In Joshua Fishman (ed.) *Handbook of Language and Ethnic Identity* (Oxford: Oxford University Press, 1999), 300–18.

Hutton, Christopher M. *Linguistics and the Third Reich: Mother-tongue Fascism, Race and the Science of Language* (London and New York: Routledge, 1999).

Hvitfeldt, Christina & Gloria Poedjosoedarmo. 'Language Use and Identity across Generations in Singapore'. In Shobhana L. Chellian & Willem J. de Reuse (eds) *Papers from the Fifth Annual Meeting of the Southeast Asian Linguistics Society, 1995* (Tempe: Program for Southeast Asian Studies, Arizona State University, 1998), 183–200.

Hylland Erisken, T. 'Linguistic Diversity and the Quest for National Identity: the Case of Mauritius'. *Ethnic and Racial Studies*, 13 (1990) 1–24.

Hymes, Dell. 'The Origin of "Sociolinguistics" '. *Language in Society*, 8 (1979) 141.

Iglesias Álvarez, Ana. 'Consecuencias sociolingüísticas dos movementos migratorios internos en Galicia: o caso de Vigo'. *Cadernos de Lingua*, 22 (2000) 39–70.

Ivanič, Roz. *Writing and Identity: the Discoursal Construction of Identity in Academic Writing* (Amsterdam and Philadelphia: John Benjamins, 1998).

Jaffe, Alexandra. *Ideologies in Action: Language Politics on Corsica* (Berlin: Mouton de Gruyter, 1999).

Jahn, Jens-Eberhard. 'Il gruppo nazionale italiano (GNI) nel contesto etnolinguistico istriano'. *Rivista Italiana di Dialettologia*, 22 (1998) 91–114.

Jahn, Jens-Eberhard. 'The Political, Ethnic and Linguistic Borders of the Upper Adriatic after the Dissolution of Yugoslavia'. *Poznan Studies in Contemporary Linguistics*, 35 (1999) 73–81.

Jeffery, Arthur. *The Foreign Vocabulary of the Qur'ān* (Baroda, Gujarat, India: Oriental Institute, 1938).

Jenkins, Richard. *Pierre Bourdieu* (London and New York: Routledge, 1992).

Jensen, Janne Bleeg. 'Politics of Language and Language of Politics: Corsican Language Activism and Conflicts between Internal and External Representations of National Identity'. *Folk: Journal of the Danish Ethnographic Society*, 41 (1999) 77–98.

Jespersen, Otto. *Progress in Language, with Special Reference to English* (London: Swan Sonnenschein & Co., 1894).

Jespersen, Otto. *Mankind, Nation, and Individual from a Linguistic Point of View* (Cambridge, Mass.: Harvard University Press, 1925).

Johnstone, Barbara. *The Linguistic Individual: Self-Expression in Language and Linguistics* (New York and Oxford: Oxford University Press, 1996).

Jones, Mari C. 'Death of a Language, Birth of an Identity: Brittany and the Bretons'. *Language Problems and Language Planning*, 22 (1998) 129–42.

Jónsson, Einar Már. 'Orð, orð, orð . . .'. *Skírnir: Tímarit Hins Íslenska Bókmentafélags*, 174 (2000) 385–407.

Joseph, John E. Rev. of Heinz Kloss, *Die Entwicklung neuer germanischer Kultursprachen seit 1800*, 2nd edn (Düsseldorf: Schwann, 1978). *Language Problems and Language Planning*, 4 (1980) 160–2.

Joseph, John E. *Eloquence and Power: the Rise of Language Standards and Standard Languages* (London: Frances Pinter; New York: Blackwell, 1987).

Joseph, John E. 'English in Hong Kong: Emergence and Decline'. *Current Issues in Language and Society*, 3 (1996) 60–79. Repr. in Sue Wright & Helen Kelly-Holmes (eds) *One Country Two Systems, Three Languages: Changing Language Use in Hong Kong* (Clevedon: Multilingual Matters, 1997), 60–79.

Joseph, John E. 'Why Isn't Translation Impossible?'. In Susan Hunston (ed.) *Language At Work: Selected Papers from the Annual Meeting of the British Association for Applied Linguistics held at the University of Birmingham, September 1997* (Clevedon: Multilingual Matters, 1998), 86–97.

Joseph, John E. 'Structuralist Linguistics: Saussure'. In Simon Glendinning (ed.) *The Edinburgh Encyclopedia of Continental Philosophy* (Edinburgh: Edinburgh University Press, 1999), 515–27.

Joseph, John E. *Limiting the Arbitrary: Linguistic Naturalism and its Opposites in Plato's* Cratylus *and Modern Theories of Language* (Amsterdam and Philadelphia: John Benjamins, 2000a).

Joseph, John E. 'Language as Fiction: Writing the Text of Linguistic Identity in Scotland'. In Heinz Antor & Klaus Stierstorfer (eds) *English Literatures in International Contexts* (Heidelberg: C. Winter, 2000b), 77–84.

Joseph, John E. 'The Tao of Identity in Heteroglossic Hong Kong'. *International Journal of the Sociology of Language*, 143 (2000c) 15–30.

Joseph, John E. 'The Exportation of Structuralist Ideas from Linguistics to Other Fields: an Overview'. In Sylvain Auroux et al. (eds) *History of the Language Sciences: an International Handbook on the Evolution of the Study of Language from the Beginnings to the Present*, Vol. 2 (Berlin and New York: Walter de Gruyter, 2001), 1880–908.

Joseph, John E. 'Is Language a Verb? Conceptual Change in Linguistics and Language Teaching'. In Hugh Trappes-Lomax & Gibson Ferguson (eds) *Language in Language Teacher Education* (Amsterdam and Philadelphia: John Benjamins, 2002a), 29–48.

Joseph, John E. *From Whitney to Chomsky: Essays in the History of American Linguistics* (Amsterdam and Philadelphia: John Benjamins, 2002b).

Joseph, John E. 'Rethinking Linguistic Creativity'. In Hayley Davis & Talbot J. Taylor (eds) *Rethinking Linguistics* (London and New York: RoutledgeCurzon, 2003), 121–50.

Joseph, John E. 'Language and Politics'. In Alan Davies & Catherine Elder (eds) *The Handbook of Applied Linguistics* (Oxford and New York: Blackwell, 2004), 347–66.

Joseph, John E. 'Body, Passions and Race in Classical Theories of Language and Emotion'. In Edda Weigand (ed.) *Emotion in Dialogic Interaction: Advances in the Complex* (Amsterdam and Philadelphia: John Benjamins, forthcoming a).

Joseph, John E. 'The Linguistic Sign'. *The Cambridge Companion to Saussure*, ed. by Carol Sanders (Cambridge: Cambridge University Press, forthcoming b).

Joseph, John E. 'The Shifting Role of Languages in Lebanese Christian and Moslem Identities'. In Joshua A. Fishman & Babatunde Omoniyi (eds) *Sociology of Language and Religion* (forthcoming c).

Joseph, John E. 'Linguistic Identity and the Limits of Global English'. In Anna Duszak & Urszula Okulska (eds) *Speaking from the Margin: Global English from a European Perspective* (Berne and Oxford: Peter Lang, forthcoming d).

Joseph, John E., Nigel Love & Talbot J. Taylor. *Landmarks in Linguistic Thought* Vol. II: *The Western Tradition in the Twentieth Century* (London and New York: Routledge, 2001).

Joseph, John E. & Talbot J. Taylor (eds). *Ideologies of Language* (London and New York: Routledge, 1990).

Kachru, Braj B. 'South Asian English: Toward an Identity in Diaspora'. In Robert J. Baumgardner (ed.) *South Asian English: Structure, Use, and Users* (Urbana: University of Illinois Press, 1996), 9–28.

Kamusella, T. D. I. 'Language as an Instrument of Nationalism in Central Europe'. *Nations and Nationalism*, 7 (2001) 235–51.

Kasper, Gabriele. 'Politeness'. In R. E. Asher (ed.) *Encyclopedia of Language and Linguistics* (Oxford: Pergamon, 1994) Vol. 6, 3206–11.

Kaye, Jacqueline & Abdelhamid Zoubir. *The Ambiguous Compromise: Language, Literature and National Identity in Algeria and Morocco* (London and New York: Routledge, 1990).

Keane, W. 'Knowing One's Place: National Language and the Idea of the Local in Eastern Indonesia'. *Cultural Anthropology*, 12 (1997) 37–63.

Kedourie, Elie. *Nationalism* (London: Hutchinson, 1960). [4th edn, Oxford and Cambridge, Mass.: Blackwell, 1993.]

King, Linda. *Roots of Identity: Language and Literacy in Mexico* (Cambridge: Cambridge University Press, 1994).

Kirk, John M. & Donall Ó Baoill (eds). *Linguistic Politics: Language Policies for Northern Ireland, the Republic of Ireland, and Scotland* (Belfast: Queen's University, 2001).

Kloss, Heinz. *Der Entwicklung neuer germanischer Kultursprachen seit 1800*, 2nd edn (Düsseldorf: Schwann, 1978). [1st edn 1952.]

Kohn, Hans. *The Idea of Nationalism: a Study in its Origins and Background* (New York: Macmillan, 1944).

Kohn, Hans. *Nationalism: Its Meaning and History*, 2nd edn (Princeton, NJ and London: D. Van Nostrand, 1965).

Koller, Werner. 'Nation und Sprache in der Schweiz'. In Andreas Gardt (ed.) *Nation und Sprache: Die Diskussion ihres Verhältnisses in Geschichte und Gegenwart* (Berlin: Walter de Gruyter, 2000), 563–609.

Kreindler, Isabelle. 'Multilingualism in the Successor States of the Soviet Union'. *Annual Review of Applied Linguistics*, 17 (1997) 91–112.

Kristinsson, Sigurður. 'AlÞjóðleg fræði á íslensku?' *Skírnir: Tímarit Hins Íslenska Bókmenntafélags*, 175 (2001) 180–94.

Kroskrity, Paul V. (ed.). *Regimes of Language: Ideologies, Polities, and Identities* (Santa Fe, NM: School of American Research Press, 2000).

Kuipers, Joel C. *Language, Identity and Marginality in Indonesia: the Changing Nature of Ritual Speech on the Island of Sumba* (Cambridge: Cambridge University Press, 1998).

Kuter, Lois. 'Breton vs. French: Language and the Opposition of Political, Economic, Social, and Cultural Values'. In Nancy C. Dorian (ed.) *Investigating Obsolescence: Studies in Language Contraction and Death* (Cambridge: Cambridge University Press, 1992), 75–89.

Kuter, Lois. 'Breton Identity and Language: Three Surveys'. *Bro Nevez*, 50 (1994) 11–13.

Labov, William. 'The Social Motivation of a Sound Change'. *Word*, 19 (1963) 273–309.

Labov, William. *The Social Stratification of English in New York City* (Washington, DC: Center for Applied Linguistics, 1966).

Laitin, David D. *Identity in Formation: the Russian-Speaking Population in the Near Abroad* (Ithaca: Cornell University Press, 1998).

Lakoff, Robin. 'Language and Woman's Place'. *Language in Society*, 2 (1973) 45–80.

Lakoff, Robin. *Language and Woman's Place* (New York: Harper & Row, 1975).

Lantolf, James P. (ed.). *Sociocultural Theory and Second Language Learning* (Oxford: Oxford University Press, 2000).

Lau, Chi Kuen. *Hong Kong's Colonial Legacy* (Hong Kong: Chinese University Press, 1997).

Lecercle, Jean-Jacques. *Interpretation as Pragmatics* (Houndmills, Basingstoke: Macmillan, 1999).

Lee, Penny. *The Whorf Theory Complex: a Critical Reconstruction* (Amsterdam and Philadelphia: John Benjamins, 1995).

Le Page, R. B. 'Processes of Pidginization and Creolization'. In Albert Valdman (ed.) *Pidgin and Creole Linguistics* (Bloomington: Indiana University Press, 1977), 227–55.

Le Page, R. B. & Andrée Tabouret-Keller. *Acts of Identity: Creole-Based Approaches to Language and Ethnicity* (Cambridge: Cambridge University Press, 1985).

Lestel, Dominique. *Les origines animales de la culture* (Paris: Flammarion, 2001).

Levinger, Jasna. 'Language and Identity in Bosnia-Herzegovina'. In Paul A. Chilton, Mikhail V. Ilyin & Jacob L. Mey (eds) *Political Discourse in Transition in Europe, 1989–1991* (Amsterdam and Philadelphia: John Benjamins, 1998), 251–64.

Lin, A. M. Y. 'Analysing the "Language Problem" Discourses in Hong Kong: How Official, Academic and Media Discourses Construct and Perpetuate Dominant Models of Language, Learning and Education'. *Journal of Pragmatics*, 28 (1997) 427–40.

Lo Bianco, Joseph. 'The Language of Policy: What Sort of Policy Making is the Officialization of English in the United States?' In Thom Huebner & Kathryn A. Davis (eds) *Sociopolitical Perspectives on Language Policy and Planning in the USA* (Amsterdam and Philadelphia: John Benjamins, 1999), 39–65.

Longmire, B. Jean. 'Projecting a Cambodian Social Identity'. In Martha Ratliff & Eric Schiller (eds) *Papers from the First Annual Meeting of the Southeast Asian Linguistics Society, 1991* (Tempe: Program for Southeast Asian Studies, Arizona State University, 1992), 243–9.

Lord, Christopher & Olga Strietska-Ilina (eds). *Parallel Cultures: Majority/Minority Relations in the Countries of the Former Eastern Bloc* (Aldershot: Ashgate, 2001).

Lord, Robert. 'Language Policy and Planning in Hong Kong: Past, Present, and (Especially) Future'. In Robert Lord & Helen N. L. Cheung (eds) *Language Education in Hong Kong* (Hong Kong: Chinese University Press, 1987), 3–24.

Lord, Robert & Helen N. L. Cheung (eds). *Language Education in Hong Kong* (Hong Kong: Chinese University Press, 1987).

Lotherington, Heather. 'The Pacific'. In Joshua Fishman (ed.) *Handbook of Language and Ethnic Identity* (Oxford: Oxford University Press, 1999), 414–30.

Luke Kang Kwong (ed.). *Into the Twenty First* [sic] *Century: Issues of Language in Education in Hong Kong* (Hong Kong: Linguistic Society of Hong Kong, 1992).

Maalouf, Amin. *Léon l'Africain* (Paris: J.-C. Lattès, 1986).

Maalouf, Amin. *Les identités meurtrières* (Paris: Bernard Grasset, 1998). English transl., *On Identity*, by Barbara Bray (London: Harvill, 2000).

McGarty, C., S. A. Haslam, K. J. Hutchinson & J. C. Turner. 'The Effects of Salient Group Membership on Persuasion'. *Small Group Research*, 25 (1994) 267–93.

McLaughlin, Fiona. 'Haalpulaar Identity as a Response to Wolofization'. *African Languages and Cultures*, 8 (1995) 153–68.

Maley, Willy. 'Spenser's Irish English: Language and Identity in Early Modern Ireland'. *Studies in Philology*, 91 (1994) 417–31.

Malinowski, Bronislaw. 'The Problem of Meaning in Primitive Languages'. Supplement to C. K. Ogden & I. A. Richards *The Meaning of Meaning: a Study of the Influence of Language upon Thought and of the Science of Symbolism* (London: Kegan Paul, Trench, Trubner & Co.; New York: Harcourt, Brace & Co., 1923), 451–510.

Marx, Karl. *Misère de la philosophie: Réponse à* La philosophie de la misère *de M. Proudhon* (Paris: A. Frank; Brussels: C. G. Vogler, 1847. Anon. Engl. transl., *The Poverty of Philosophy*, Moscow: Foreign Languages Publishing House, 1955).

Mawkanuli, Talant. 'The Jungar Tuvas: Language and National Identity in the PRC'. *Central Asian Survey*, 20 (2001) 497–517.

Menke, Hubertus. 'Sprache als Mittel der Selbstbehauptung: Zum Sprachkonflikt in der "(Duits-)Nederlandse Gereformeerde Kerke" zu Altona/Hamburg'. In Jorg Hennig & Jurgen Meier (eds) *Varietäten der deutschen Sprache: Festschrift für Dieter Mohn* (Frankfurt: Peter Lang, 1996), 93–106.

Meyerhoff, Miriam. 'Communities of Practice'. In J. K. Chambers, Peter Trudgill & Natalie Schilling-Estes (eds) *The Handbook of Language Variation and Change* (Oxford and New York: Blackwell, 2002), 526–48.

Millán-Varela, Carmen. 'Translation, Normalisation and Identity in Galicia(n)'. *Target: International Journal of Translation Studies*, 12 (2000) 267–82.

Milroy, Lesley. *Language and Social Networks* (Oxford and New York: Blackwell, 1980).

Mitchell, J. Clyde (ed.). *Social Networks in Urban Situations* (Manchester: Manchester University Press, 1969).

Morris, Nancy. 'Language and Identity in Twentieth Century Puerto Rico'. *Journal of Multilingual and Multicultural Development*, 17 (1996) 17–32.

Mufwene, Salikoko S. *The Ecology of Language Evolution* (Cambridge: Cambridge University Press, 2001).

Mukařovský, J. 'Jazyk spisovný a jazyk básniký'. In B. Havránek & M. Weingart (eds) *Spisouná čeština a jazková kultura* (Prague: Melantrich, 1932), 32–84. (Engl. trans., 'Standard Language and Poetic Language', in Paul L. Garvin (ed. and trans.) *A Prague School Reader in Esthetics, Literary Structure and Style*, rev. edn (Washington, DC: Georgetown University Press, 1959), 123–49.)

Müller, Max. *Lectures on the Science of Language, delivered at the Royal Institution of Great Britain in April, May, and June, 1861* (London: Longman, Green, Longman & Roberts, 1861).

Müller, Max. 'Lectures on Mr Darwin's Philosophy of Language: Third Lecture'. *Littell's Living Age*, 5th series, vol. 3, no. 1523 (1873) 410–28.

Nakhla, Raphael. 'Le bilinguisme dans les pays de langue arabe'. *Lettres de Fourvière* (Lyon), 3e série, no. 8 (1935), 180–257. Lyon.

Nauerby, Tom. *No Nation is an Island: Language, Culture and National Identity in the Faroe Islands* (Aarhus, Denmark: SNAI-North Atlantic Publications and Aarhus University Press, 1996).

Nebrija, Antonio de. *Gramática castellana: Texto establecido sobre la ed. «princeps» de 1492*, ed. by Pascual Galindo Romeo & Luis Ortiz Muñoz, 2 vols (Madrid: Edición de la Junta del Centenario, 1946). [Orig. publ. 1492.]

Nerlich, Brigitte & David C. Clarke. *Language, Action and Context. The Early History of Pragmatics in Europe and America* (Amsterdam and Philadelphia: John Benjamins, 1996).

Newton, Gerald. 'Letzebuergesch and the Establishment of National Identity'. In Gerald Newton (ed.) *Luxembourg and Letzebuergesch: Language and Communication at the Crossroads of Europe* (Oxford: Oxford University Press, 1996), 181–215.

Ngonyani, Deo. 'Language Shift and National Identity in Tanzania'. *Ufahamu: Journal of the African Activist Association* (Los Angeles, Calif.), 23 (1995) no. 2, 69–72.

Nihtinen, Atina. 'Language, Cultural Identity and Politics in the Cases of Macedonian and Scots'. *Slavonica*, 5 (1999) 46–58.

Nkweto Simmonds, Felly. 'Naming and Identity'. In Delia Jarrett-Macauley (ed.) *Reconstructing Womanhood, Reconstructing Feminism* (London and New York: Routledge, 1996), 109–15.

Norton, Bonny. *Identity and Language Learning: Gender, Ethnicity and Educational Change* (Harlow: Longman, 2000).

Oakes, Leigh. *Language and National Identity: Comparing France and Sweden* (Amsterdam and Philadelphia: John Benjamins, 2001).

O'Barr, William M. *Linguistic Evidence: Language, Power, and Strategy in the Courtroom* (San Diego: Academic Press, 1982).

Ogden, C. K. & I. A. Richards. *The Meaning of Meaning: a Study of the Influence of Language upon Thought and of the Science of Symbolism* (London: Kegan Paul, Trench, Trubner & Co.; New York: Harcourt, Brace & Co., 1923).

Omar, Asmah Haji. 'Language Planning and Image Building: the Case of Malay in Malaysia'. *International Journal of the Sociology of Language*, 130 (1998) 49–65.

Omoniyi, Tope. 'Afro-Asian Rural Border Areas'. In Joshua Fishman (ed.) *Handbook of Language and Ethnic Identity* (Oxford: Oxford University Press, 1999), 369–81.

O'Reilly, Camille. *The Irish Language in Northern Ireland: the Politics of Culture and Identity* (Houndmills, Basingstoke: Macmillan, 1999).

Orlandi, Eni Puccinelli & Eduardo Guimaraes. 'La formation d'un espace de production linguistique: La grammaire au Brésil'. *Langages*, 32 (1998) 130, 8–27.

Pandian, Jacob. 'Re-Ethnogenesis: the Quest for a Dravidian Identity among Tamils of India'. *Anthropos: International Review of Anthropology and Linguistics*, 93 (1997) 545–52.

Parakrama, Arjuna. *De-Hegemonizing Language Standards: Learning from (Post)Colonial Englishes about 'English'* (Basingstoke, Hampshire: Macmillan; New York: St. Martin's Press, 1995).

Parry, M. Mair, Winifred V. Davies & Rosalind A. M. Temple (eds). *The Changing Voices of Europe: Social and Political Changes and Their Linguistic Repercussions, Past, Present and Future* (Cardiff: University of Wales Press, with the Modern Humanities Research Association, 1994).

Payton, Philip. 'Identity, Ideology and Language in Modern Cornwall'. In Hildegard Tristram (ed.) *The Celtic Englishes* (Heidelberg: Carl Winter, 1997), 100–22.

Pêcheur, Jacques. 'Bienvenu au Liban: Sous le signe de la francophonie'. *Le français dans le monde*, no. 259 (août-sep. 1993) 29–30.

Pennycook, Alastair. *English and the Discourses of Colonialism* (London: Routledge, 1998).

Pennycook, Alastair. *Critical Applied Linguistics: a Critical Introduction* (Mawah NJ and London: Lawrence Erlbaum, 2001).

Perta, Carmela. 'Language Obsolescence: the Case of Arbëresh in Italy'. Paper presented at the Annual Postgraduate Conference, Theoretical and Applied Linguistics, The University of Edinburgh, 26 May 2003.

Phillipson, Robert. *Linguistic Imperialism* (Oxford: Oxford University Press, 1992).

Piaget, Jean. *The Language and Thought of the Child*. Trans. by Marjorie & Ruth Dabain, 3rd edn (London and New York: Routledge & Kegan Paul, 1929; repr. Humanities Press, 1959).

Pinker, Stephen. *The Language Instinct* (New York: William Morrow, 1994).

Platt, John & Heidi Weber. *English in Singapore and Malaysia: Status, Features, Functions* (Oxford: Oxford University Press, 1980).

Platt, John, Heidi Weber & Ho Mian Lian. *The New Englishes* (London: Routledge, 1984).

Press, J. Ian. 'Breton Speakers in Brittany, France and Europe: Constraints on the Search for an Identity'. In M. Parry et al. (eds) *The Changing Voices of Europe: Social and Political Changes and Their Linguistic Repercussions, Past, Present and Future* (Cardiff: University of Wales Press, with the Modern Humanities Research Association, 1994), 213–26.

Ramaswamy, Sumathi. *Passions of the Tongue: Language Devotion in Tamil India, 1891–1970* (Berkeley: University of California Press, 1997).

Rampton, Ben. *Crossing: Language and Ethnicity among Adolescents* (London: Longman, 1995).

Rastorfer, Jean-Marc. *On the Development of Kayah and Kayan National Identity: a Study and a Bibliography* (Bangkok: Southeast Asian Publ. House, 1994).

Redouane, Rabia. 'From Duality to Complementarity: the Case of Bilingualism in Morocco'. *Language Problems and Language Planning*, 22 (1998) 1–18.

Reid, Thomas. *An Inquiry into the Human Mind on the Principles of Common Sense* (Edinburgh: Printed for A. Millar, London, and A. Kincaid & J. Bell, Edinburgh, 1764). Critical edn by Derek R. Brookes (Edinburgh: Edinburgh University Press, 1997).

Reid, Thomas. *Essays on the Intellectual Powers of Man* (Edinburgh: Printed for John Bell, and G. G. J. & J. Robinson, London, 1785).

Renan, Ernest. *De l'origine du langage*, 2nd edn (Paris: Michel Lévy, Frères, 1858). [1st edn 1848.]

Renan, Ernest. *Qu'est-ce qu'une nation? Conférence faite en Sorbonne, le 11 mars 1882* (Paris: Calmann Lévy, 1882).

Robinson, W. Peter & Howard Giles (eds). *The New Handbook of Language and Social Psychology* (Chichester and New York: John Wiley & Sons, 2001).

Rohfleisch, Irene. 'Das Dilemma der nationalen Identität in Oberschlesien'. In Szilvia Deminger, Thorsten Fögen, Joachim Scharloth & Simone Zwickl (eds) *Einstellungsforschung in der Soziolinguistik und Nachbardisziplinen / Studies in Language Attitudes* (Frankfurt: Peter Lang, 2000), 99–108.

Rowley, G. G. 'Literary Canon and National Identity: *The Tale of Genji* in Meiji Japan'. *Japan Forum*, 9 (1997) 1–15.

Sacks, Harvey. *Lectures on Conversation*. Ed. by Gail Jefferson. 2 vols (Oxford and Cambridge, Mass.: Blackwell, 1992).

Sacks, Harvey, Emanuel A. Schegloff & Gail Jefferson. 'A Simplest Systematics for the Organization of Turn-taking for Conversation'. *Language*, 50 (1974) 696–735.

Safran, William. 'Politics and Language in Contemporary France: Facing Supranational and Infranational Challenges'. *International Journal of the Sociology of Language*, 137 (1999) 39–66.

Said, Edward. *Orientalism* (New York: Pantheon, 1978).

Said, Edward. *The World, the Text and the Critic* (Cambridge, Mass.: Harvard University Press, 1983).

Samara, Mico. 'Le problème de la langue et de la nation albanaise: 19ème–20ème siècle'. In Patrick Seriot et al. (eds) *Langue et nation en Europe centrale et orientale du XVIIIème siède à nos jours* (Lausanne: Université de Lausanne, 1996), 261–76.

Sapir, Edward. *Abnormal Types of Speech in Nootka* (Canada Department of Mines, Geological Survey, Memoir 62, Anthropological Series, no. 5, 1915). (Repr. in Sapir, 1949, pp. 179–96.)

Sapir, Edward. 'Speech as a Personality Trait'. *American Journal of Sociology*, 32 (1927) 892–905. (Repr. in Sapir, 1949, pp. 533–43.)

Sapir, Edward. 'Language'. *Encyclopaedia of the Social Sciences*, Vol. 9 (1933), 155–69. (Repr. in Sapir, 1949, pp. 7–32.)

Sapir, Edward. *Selected Writings in Language, Culture, and Personality*. Ed. by David G. Mandelbaum (Berkeley and Los Angeles: University of California Press, 1949).

Sapir, Edward. *The Psychology of Culture: a Course of Lectures*. Ed. by Judith T. Irvine (Berlin and New York: Mouton de Gruyter, 1994).

Saussure, Ferdinand de. *Cours de linguistique générale*. Publié par Charles Bally & Albert Sechehaye avec la collaboration d'Albert Riedlinger (Paris and Lausanne:

Payot, 1916. Engl. transl., *Course in General Linguistics*, by Wade Baskin, New York: Philosophical Library, 1959; another by Roy Harris, London: Duckworth; La Salle, Ill.: Open Court, 1983).

Sawaie, M. 'Speakers' Attitudes toward Linguistic Variation: a Case Study of Some Arabic Dialects'. *Linguistische Berichte*, 107 (1987) 3–22.

Sayer, Derek. 'The Language of Nationality and the Nationality of Language: Prague 1780–1920'. *Past and Present*, 153 (Nov. 1996) 164–210.

Scacchi, Anna. 'La lingua del Nuovo Mondo: L'American English tra utopia e mito'. In Alessandro Portelli (ed.) *La formazione di una cultura nazionale: La letteratura degli Stati Uniti dall'indipendenza all'età di Jackson, 1776–1850* (Rome: Carocci, 1999), 93–109.

Schieffelin, Bambi B., Kathryn A. Woolard & Paul V. Kroskrity (eds). *Language Ideologies: Practice and Theory* (New York and Oxford: Oxford University Press, 1998).

Schneider, Edgar W. (ed.) *Englishes around the World: Studies in Honour of Manfred Görlach*, Vol. II: *Caribbean, Africa, Asia, Australasia* (Amsterdam and Philadelphia: John Benjamins, 1997).

Sciriha, Lydia. 'The Interplay of Language and Identity in Cyprus'. *The Cyprus Review*, 7 (1995) 2, 7–34.

Seraphim, Peter Heinz. *Das Judentum im osteuropäischen Raum* (Essen: Essner Verlagsanstalt, 1938).

Sercombe, Peter G. 'Adjacent Cross-Border Iban Communities: a Comparision with Reference to Language'. *Bijdragen tot de Taal-, Land- en Volkenkunde*, 155 (1999) 596–616.

Sériot, Patrick (ed.). *Langue et nation en Europe centrale et orientale du XVIII*[ème] *siècle à nos jours* (Lausanne: Université de Lausanne, 1996).

Seton-Watson, Hugh. *Nations and States: an Enquiry into the Origins of Nations and the Politics of Nationalism* (London: Methuen, 1977).

Shafer, Boyd C. *Nationalism: Myth and Reality* (London: Gollancz, 1955).

Shaw, William. *A Galic and English Dictionary* (London: Printed for the author, by W. & A. Strahan, 1780).

Shepard, Carolyn A., Howard Giles & Beth A. LePoire. 'Communication Accommodation Theory'. In W. Peter Robinson & Howard Giles (eds) *The New Handbook of Language and Social Psychology* (Chichester and New York: John Wiley & Sons, 2001), 33–56.

Siebenmann, Gustav. 'Sprache als Faktor der kulturellen Identitat: Der Fall Kataloniens'. In Hugo Dyserinck & Karl Ulrich Syndram (eds), *Komparatistik und Europaforschung: Perspektiven vergleichender Literatur- und Kulturwissenschaft* (Bonn: Bouvier, 1992), 231–51.

Silverstein, Michael. 'Whorfianism and the Linguistic Imagination of Nationality'. In Paul V. Kroskrity (ed.) Regimes of Language: Ideologies, Polities, and Identities (Santa Fe, NM: School of American Research Press, 2000), 85–138.

Siu, Helen F. 'Cultural Identity and the Politics of Difference in South China'. *Daedalus*, 122, no. 2 (Spring 1993) 19–43.

Skutnabb-Kangas, Tove. *Linguistic Genocide in Education – Or Worldwide Diversity and Human Rights?* (Mahwah, NJ: Lawrence Erlbaum, 2000).

Smith, Anthony D. *Nationalism and Modernism: a Critical Survey of Recent Theories of Nations and Nationalism* (London and New York: Routledge, 1998).

Smuts, General, the Right Hon. J. C. *Holism and Evolution*, 2nd edn (London: Macmillan, 1927. 1st edn 1926).

So, Daniel W. C. 'Searching for a Bilingual Exit'. In Robert Lord & Helen N. L. Cheung (eds) *Language Education in Hong Kong* (Hong Kong: Chinese University Press, 1987), 249–68.

So, Daniel W. C. 'Language-Based Bifurcation of Secondary Schools in Hong Kong: Past, Present and Future'. In K. K. Luke (ed.) *Into the Twenty First Century: Issues of Language in Education in Hong Kong* (Hong Kong: Linguistic Society of Hong Kong, 1992), 69–95.

Solé, Yolanda Russinovich. 'Language, Affect and Nationalism in Paraguay'. In Ana Roca & John B. Jensen (eds) *Spanish in Contact: Issues in Bilingualism* (Somerville, Mass.: Cascadilla, 1996), 93–111.

Spender, Dale. *Man Made Language* (London: Routledge & Kegan Paul, 1980).

Spires, Scott. 'Lithuanian Linguistic Nationalism and the Cult of Antiquity'. *Nations and Nationalism*, 5 (1999) 485–500.

Spivak, Gayatri Chakravorty. 'The Politics of Translation', excerpt from *Outside in the Teaching Machine* (London and New York: Routledge, 1993), repr. in Lawrence Venuti (ed.) *The Translation Studies Reader* (London and New York: Routledge, 2000), 397–416.

Srage, Mohamed Nader. 'La diglossie et le bilinguisme scolaire à Beyrouth'. *Cahiers de l'Institut de Linguistique de Louvain*, 14 (1988) 71–3.

Stefanink, Bernd. 'Une politique linguistique au service de l'identité nationale: le rôle joué par les linguistes dans la constitution de l'État national roumain, de 1821 à 1859'. *Revue Roumaine de Linguistique*, 39 (1994) 479–91.

Steinke, Klaus. 'Bulgarische Wiedergeburt und Scoala ardeleana: Zur Typologie der Erweckungsbewegungen in Südosteuropa'. In Dittmar Dahlmann & Wilfried Potthoff (eds) *Mythen, Symbole and Rituale: Die Geschichtsmächtigkeit der Zeichen in Südosteuropa in 19. und 20. Jahrhundert* (Frankfart: Peter Lang, 2000), 185–99.

Stephens, Thomas M. *Dictionary of Latin American Racial and Ethnic Terminology*, 2nd edn (Gainesville: University Press of Florida, 1999).

Stevenson, Patrick. 'The German Language and the Construction of National Identities'. In John L. Flood, Paul Salmon, Olive Sayce & Christopher Wells (eds) *'Das unsichtbare Band der Sprache': Studies in German Language and Linguistic History in Memory of Leslie Seiffert* (Stuttgart: Heinz Akademischer, 1993), 333–56.

Strassoldo, Raimondo. *Lingua, identità, autonomia: Ricerche e riflessioni sociologiche sulla questione friulana* (Udine: Ribis, 1996).

Street, Brian. 'The New Literacy Studies: Implications for Education and Pedagogy'. *Changing English*, 1 (1993) 113–26.

Stroud, Christopher. 'Portuguese as Ideology and Politics in Mozambique: Semiotic (Re)Constructions of a Postcolony'. In Jan Blommaert (ed.) *Language Ideological Debates* (Berlin: Mouton de Gruyter, 1999), 343–80.

Stubkjaer, Flemming Talbo. 'Die Standardaussprache des osterreichischen Deutsch im Konzept "Deutsch als plurizentrische Sprache"'. *Jahrbuch Deutsch als Fremdsprache: Intercultural German Studies*, 23 (1997) 187–207.

Suleiman, Yasir. 'Nationalism and the Arabic Language: a Historical Overview'. In Yasir Suleiman (ed.) *Arabic Sociolinguistics: Issues and Perspectives* (London: Curzon, 1994a), 3–24.

Suleiman, Yasir (ed.). *Arabic Sociolinguistics: Issues and Perspectives* (London: Curzon, 1994b).

Suleiman, Yasir (ed.). *Language and Ethnic Identity in the Middle East and North Africa* (London: Curzon, 1996).

Suleiman, Yasir (ed.). *Language and Society in the Middle East and North Africa: Studies in Variation and Identity* (Richmond, Surrey: Curzon, 1999).

Suleiman, Yasir. *The Arabic Language and National Identity: a Study in Ideology* (Edinburgh: Edinburgh University Press, 2003).

Tabouret-Keller, Andrée. 'Western Europe'. In Joshua Fishman (ed.) *Handbook of Language and Ethnic Identity* (Oxford: Oxford University Press, 1999), 334–49.

Tajfel, Henri. 'Social Categorization, Social Identity and Social Comparison'. In H. Tajfel (ed.) *Differentiation between Social Groups: Studies in the Social Psychology of Intergroup Relations* (London: Academic Press, 1978), 61–76.

Tajfel, Henri. 'Social Stereotypes and Social Groups'. In J. Turner & H. Giles (eds) *Intergroup Behavior* (Oxford: Blackwell, 1981), 144–65.

Tajfel, Henri & J. C. Turner. 'An Integrative Theory of Inter-group Conflict'. In W. G. Austin & S. Worchel (eds) *The Social Psychology of Intergroup Relations* (Monterey, Calif.: Brookes/Cole, 1979), 33–47.

Tannen, Deborah. *You Just Don't Understand: Women and Men in Conversation* (New York: Morrow, 1990).

Tannen, Deborah (ed.). *Gender and Conversational Interaction* (New York: Oxford University Press, 1993).

Tannen, Deborah. *Gender and Discourse* (New York: Oxford University Press, 1994).

Taylor, Talbot J. *Linguistic Theory and Structural Stylistics* (Oxford: Pergamon, 1981).

Taylor, Talbot J. *Theorizing Language: Analysis, Normativity, Rhetoric, History* (Amsterdam and Oxford: Pergamon, 1997).

Thakerer, J., Howard Giles & Jenny Cheshire. 'Psychological and Linguistic Parameters of Speech Accommodation Theory'. In C. Fraser & K. R. Scherer (eds), *Advances in the Social Psychology of Language* (Cambridge: Cambridge University Press, 1982), 205–55.

Thorne, B. & N. Henley, N. (eds). *Language and Sex: Difference and Dominance* (Rowley: Newbury House, 1975).

Todorov, Tzvetan. *Mikhail Bakhtin: the Dialogical Principle.* Trans. by Wlad Godzich (Minneapolis: University of Minnesota Press, 1984. Original work published 1981).

Toribio, Almeida Jacqueline. 'Language Variation and the Linguistic Enactment of Identity among Dominicans'. *Linguistics*, 38 (2000) 1133–59.

Tristram, Hildegard L. C. (ed.). *The Celtic Englishes* (Heidelberg: Carl Winter, 1997).

Tse, John Kwock-Ping. 'Language and a Rising New Identity in Taiwan'. *International Journal of the Sociology of Language*, 143 (2000) 151–64.

Tsou, Benjamin K. 'Aspects of the Two Language System and Three Language Problem in the Changing Society of Hong Kong'. *Current Issues in Language and Society*, 3 (1996) 22–33. Repr. in Sue Wright & Helen Kelly-Holmes (eds) *One Country, Two Systems, Three Languages: Changing Language Use in Hong Kong* (Clevedon: Multilingual Matters, 1997), 22–33.

Tu Wei-ming. 'Cultural China: the Periphery as the Center'. *Daedalus*, 120 (1991) 2 (Spring), 1–32.

Turner, George W. 'Australian English as a National Language'. In Edgar W. Schneider (ed.) *Englishes around the World: Studies in Honour of Manfred Görlach* Vol. II: *Caribbean, Africa, Asia, Australasia* (Amsterdam and Philadelphia: John Benjamins, 1997), 335–48.

Turner, J. C. *Social Influences* (Buckingham: Open University Press, 1991).

Turner, J. C., M. A. Hogg, P. J. Oakes, S. D. Reicher & M. J. Wetherell. *Rediscovering the Social Group: a Self-Categorization Theory* (Oxford: Blackwell, 1987).

Turville-Petre, Thorlac. *England the Nation: Language, Literature, and National Identity, 1290–1340* (Oxford: Clarendon Press; New York: Oxford University Press, 1996).

Valdés, Juan de. *Diálogo de la lengua*. Ed. by Rafael Lapesa, 5th edn (Zaragoza: Ebro, 1965). [Written 1535–36, orig. publ. 1737.]

Vallancey, Charles. *An Essay on the Antiquity of the Irish Language, being a collation of the Irish with the Punic language . . .* (Dublin: S. Powell, 1772).

Vallancey, Charles. *Comparaison de la langue punique et de la langue irlandoise au moyen de la scène punique de la comédie de Plaute intitulée: Le Carthaginois*. Transl. from the English, with a preface by A. L. Millin de Grandmaison. (No city, 1787.)

Vallancey, Charles. *Prospectus of a Dictionary of the Language of the Aire Coti, or, Ancient Irish, compared with the language of the Cuti, or Ancient Persians, with the Hindoostanee, the Arabic, and Chaldean languages* (Dublin: Printed by Graisberry and Campbell, 1802).

Van Bijlert, Victor A. 'Sanskrit and Hindu National Identity in Nineteenth Century Bengal'. In Jan E. M. Houben (ed.) *Ideology and Status of Sanskrit: Contributions to the History of the Sanskrit Language* (Leiden: E. J. Brill, 1996), 347–66.

Van den Bersselaar, Dmitir. 'The Language of Igbo Ethnic Nationalism'. *Language Problems and Language Planning*, 24 (2000) 123–47.

Verschueren, Jef (ed.). *Language and Ideology: Selected Papers from the 6th International Pragmatics Conference* (Antwerp: International Pragmatics Association, 1999).

Voloshinov, V. N. *Marxism and the Philosophy of Language*. Trans. by Ladislav Matejka & I. R. Titunik (Cambridge, Mass. and London: Harvard University Press, 1973). (Original work published 1929.)

Vygotsky, Lev S. *Thought and Language*. Ed. & trans. by Eugenia Hanfmann & Gertrude Vakar (Cambridge, Mass.: MIT Press, 1962).

Wang Gungwu. 'To Reform a Revolution: Under the Righteous Mandate'. *Daedalus*, 122 (1993) 2 (Spring), 71–94.

Wenger, Étienne. *Communities of Practice: Learning, Meaning and Identity* (Cambridge: Cambridge University Press, 1998).

Whorf, Benjamin Lee. *Language, Thought, and Reality: Selected Writings of Benjamin Lee Whorf*. Ed. by John B. Carroll (Cambridge, Mass.: MIT Press, 1956).

Wiesinger, Peter. 'Nation und Sprache in Österreich'. In Andreas Gardt (ed.) *Nation and Sprache: Die Diskussion ihres Verhältnisses in Geschichte und Gegenwart* (Berlin: Walter de Gruyter, 2000), 525–62.

Williams, Colin H. 'The Celtic World'. In Joshua Fishman (ed.) *Handbook of Language and Ethnic Identity* (Oxford: Oxford University Press, 1999), 267–85.

Winichakul, Thonchai. *Siam Mapped: a History of the Geo-Body of a Nation* (Honolulu: University of Hawaii Press, 1994).

Wodak, Ruth (ed.). *Language, Power and Ideology* (Amsterdam and Philadelphia: John Benjamins, 1989).

Wodak, Ruth, Rudolf de Cillia, Martin Reisigl & Karin Liebhart. *The Discursive Construction of National Identity*. Trans. by Angelika Irsch & Richard Mitten (Edinburgh: Edinburgh University Press, 1999).

Woods, David R. 'Attitudes toward French, National Languages, and Mother Tongues across Age and Sex in Congo'. In Akinbiyi Akinlabi (ed.) *Theoretical Approaches to African Linguistics* (Trenton, NJ: Africa World Press, 1995).

World Bank. 'What Is Globalization?' World Bank Briefing Papers: Assessing Globalization, Part One (2000). <http://www.worldbank.org/html/extdr/pb/globalization/paper1.htm>

Wright, Roger. *Late Latin and Early Romance* (Liverpool: Francis Cairns, 1982).

Wright, Sue. *Community and Communication: the Role of Language in Nation State Building and European Integration* (Clevedon: Multilingual Matters, 2000).

Wright, Sue. *Language Policy and Planning* (Houndmills: Palgrave Macmillan, 2004).

Wright, Sue & Helen Kelly-Holmes (eds). *One Country, Two Systems, Three Languages: Changing Language Use in Hong Kong* (Clevedon: Multilingual Matters, 1997).

Yau Shun Chiu. 'Language Policies in Post-1997 Hong Kong'. In K. K. Luke (ed.) *Into the Twenty First Century: Issues of Language in Education in Hong Kong* (Hong Kong: Linguistic Society of Hong Kong, 1992), 15–29.

Young, Robert J. C. *Colonial Desire: Hybridity in Theory, Culture and Race* (London and New York: Routledge, 1995).

Index

Abou, S. 203–6
abstract objectivism 49
abstraction 195, 211–12, 215
accent 13
accommodation, perceptual/ subjective 72
  see also Communication Accommodation Theory
acting 35
Adekunle, M. 130
advertising 17
aesthetics 16
agency 23, 39–40, 58, 73–5, 78, 85
Aitchison, J. 232
Albania 128, 164–5
Alexander, N. 130
Algeria 130
Alici, D. M. 129
Alsace(-Lorraine) 98, 112
Althusser, L. 9, 57, 211
Alvarez-Caccamo, C. 127
al-Wazzan, H. 221
Al-Wer, E. 209
American Indian languages 45, 53–5
American Revolution 96, 108
Amish 17
Andalucia 165–6
Anderson, B. 13, 65, 112–17, 120, 123–5, 211, 219, 224–5
animal communication 16, 25–9, 228
anomia 1
Arab identity 194, 199–200, 210, 220
Arabic 129, 167, 173–4, 180, 183, 194–8, 201–3, 207–10, 214, 220, 231, 233
  Lebanese 208–9
  qaf variation 209
Aramaic 194, 209–10, 216, 233
Arbëresh (Italian Albanians) 164–5
arbitrariness of linguistic signs 47
Archilés, F. 127
Aristotle 25, 42–4
artificial 96, 103, 115
Asher, R. E. 175
Ashley, L. R. N. 131
audience design 50, 72–3
Austin, J. L. 19–20
Australasia 131
Australia 131, 148, 189
Austria 111, 128
authenticity 64, 115, 151, 194, 213
authorial intent 83

Babel, Tower of 95
Bacon-Shone, J. 136–7
Baggioni, D. 126
Bailey, C. 43
Baker, C. L. 232
Bakhtin, M. M. 49–50
Balkans 128, 208
banal nationalism 117–18, 121, 162
Barbados 131
Barbour, S. 126
Barnes, J. A. 63
Barros, M. C. D. M. 131
Basque 104–5, 127, 165
Bechhofer, F. 118
behaviourism 29, 36, 87
Belaj, V. 128
Belgium 127, 214
Belize 131
Bell, A. 72, 131
Bellier, I. 126
Bengal 129
Bennassar, B. & L. 210
Benrabah, M. 209
Ben-Rafael, E. 129
Berber 186
Berger, R. 129
Bernstein, B. 68–70, 229
Berré, M. 127
Besnier, N. 9
Bible 95, 98, 174, 178
Billig, M. 77, 117–18, 121

bi-/multilingualism 26, 70, 77, 123, 128, 130–1, 134–5, 142–3, 158–9, 183–4, 194, 197–8, 207, 210
Bismarck, O. von 111
Bivona, R. 127
Black English and class 170
Blair, T. 216
Blake, R. 131
Blanchet, P. 127
Blanke, R. 128
Blommaert, J. 65, 130
Bloomfield, L. 87
Boccaccio, G. 102
body vs mind 16, 43–4, 115
Boissevain, J. 63
Bolton, K. 129, 136–7
Bonner, D. M. 131
Borneo 130
Borovský *see* Havlíček Borovský
Bosnia-Hercegovina 128, 223
Bourdieu, P. 10, 13, 20, 58, 74–6, 78, 90, 117–18, 229
Boves, T. R. 72
Bradac, J. J. 71
Brazil 131, 149
Breitborde, L. 130
Breton 127, 192, 212
Breton identity 216–18
Britain *see* UK
British (Brythonic, p-Celtic) 212–13
Brown, A. 161
Brown, P. 59
Brown, R. 59
Brunei 130
Bruner, J. S. 87–9
Brussels 127
Brutt-Griffler, J. 149
Bucken-Knapp, G. 127–8
Buddhism 176
Bulgaria 128
bureaucracy, effect on communication 78
Burma *see* Myanmar

Cambodia 129, 180–1
Cameron, D. 62
campanilismo 163
Canada 70, 106, 130–1, 148, 189
Canadian raising 60
Canagarajah, A. S. 192
Cantonese 132–9, 144–7, 150–1, 153, 158–60, 184, 232
Canut, C. 130
capital, social/cultural 75
Carey, S. 131
caste 64
Castilian *see* Spanish
Catalan 104–5, 127, 165–6
categorisation 55–6
Celtic origin myths 127, 166, 212–18
Centeno Añeses, C. 131
centre and periphery 104–5
Chaldean 173, 214
Charlemagne 173
Chateaubriand, R. de 216
Chennells, A. 130
Cherry, R. D. 9
Chew, P. G.-L. 130
Chiang Kai-Shek 133
China 129, 132–4, 150–4, 158–9, 231–2
  see also Hong Kong
Chinese 45, 129, 132–9, 144–7, 150–1, 158–9, 177–81, 184, 225, 231–2
Chinese identities 141–4, 177–9
  northern vs southern 152–4
Choi, P.-K. 158
Chomsky, N. 25–6, 32–3, 35, 56, 88–9, 184
Chow, L. 135
Christian identities 173–6, 194–200, 203–10, 213–23
Christianity 106, 109–10, 166–7, 172–9, 200–3, 217–23
  Catholic vs Protestant 109–10, 166, 174, 213, 220
  Middle Eastern 173, 200
  Orthodox 110, 173, 197–8
  see also Maronites
Cicero 21, 148
Cifuentes, B. 131
Cillia, R. dè 128
circumcision 173
city and country *see* rural vs urban
civilised and primitive 46
Clampitt-Dunlap, S. 131
Clark, W. J. 187–8

Clarke, D. C. 228
class x, 12, 36, 50–1, 59–64, 68–9, 79, 83, 90, 97, 119–23, 130, 138, 151, 162, 167, 170, 180–2, 229
  division, and nationalism 119–20, 138
  lower-middle, and linguistic nationalism 121, 138, 174
Clyne, M. 131
code-switching/mixing 134, 139, 166, 183
cognition 11
cognitive psychology 32, 56
Cold War 97, 119, 183
collocation 56–7
Colombia 169
communication (as function of language) 15–16, 20–5, 30, 36–9, 78, 96–8, 184–8, 191, 225–6
Communication Accommodation Theory 12, 38, 72–3
Communication Theory of Identity 80–3, 185
communities of practice 65, 167–8
competence and performance 31–3
computer programs 32
Condillac, E. Bonnot, abbot of 11, 44
Congo 130
consciousness of self 8, 11, 13, 80
construction of reality, child's 89
constructionism vs essentialism 42, 83–91, 106, 114, 119, 124–5
context of situation 17
Conversi, D. 127
Cook-Gumperz, J. 78
Cooper, T. 96
Cornish 126–7, 166
Corsican 127
Covino, S. 127
Cratylus (Plato) 15
Creole English 79, 130–1
Critical Applied Linguistics 58
Critical Discourse Analysis 57–8
Croatia 128
Crowley, Terry 131
Crowley, Tony 126, 214
Crystal, D. 183
Cuba 131
culture 23, 35–6, 73, 77, 105, 134, 167–71, 181, 214, 220
Cyprus 129

Dagher, J. 129
Danilevsky, N. 163
Dante Alighieri 98–102, 104
Darmesteter, Mme J. 216–18, 233
Darwin, C. 16, 26, 36, 63, 122
Dau, Rev. B. 199–200, 215, 219
Davies, A. 182
Delbridge, A. 131
Deng Xiaoping 151
Denmark 111
Der-Karabetian, A. 129
Descartes, R. 25, 44, 84
desire 5, 211, 215
Dessalles, J.-L. 28
Deutsch, K. W. 96–7
dialect 99–100, 104, 120, 133, 225
dialogism 50
Dickens, C. 21
discourse (as producer of self) 10
discourse analysis 62, 68
disposition 75–6
Dollerup, C. 128
Dominican Republic 131
Dravidian 129, 175
Druze 197–8, 204, 217
Du Bellay, J. 106–8
Dunbar, R. 27–8
Duranti, A. 131
Dutch 128, 183

Eckert, P. 65
education 12, 36, 68–9, 80, 108, 121, 133–4, 137–9, 147–8, 165–6, 184, 186, 192, 198, 206–7, 231
  as agent of 'linguistic genocide' 182
Edwards, J. R. 79–80, 229
ego and superego 38
Ehret, R. 130
elaborated and restricted code 69
Elizabeth, Queen (consort of George VI) 157–8
Elizabeth II, Queen 154–8
eloquence 102–7
Eminem 21

emotions 16–17, 19, 21–2, 39, 76, 118
empiricism vs rationalism 97
endangered languages *see under* language
England 93–4, 97, 106, 189, 213
English 45, 57, 70, 94, 126, 184, 186, 192, 197–8, 203–6, 212–14
  Caribbean Creole 79, 131
  Chinese Englishes 129
  'decline' in Hong Kong 134–9, 160: vs 'emergence' 147–50, 160
  as ex-colonial language 130–61
  Hong Kong English 139–51, 232
  International Corpus of (ICE) 149
  South Asian identity in 129
  spread of 23, 129–31, 181–92
  World Englishes 142, 149
Ennaji, M. 130
Epicurus 42–4, 110, 115, 168
Erfurt, J. 131
Errington, J. J. 129
Erse *see* Gaelic, Irish
Escalle, M.-C. K. 126
Esperanto 187
essentialism *see* constructionism vs essentialism
Estonia 128
Ethiopic 202
ethnographic research 71
ethnography of communication 77
ethno-symbolism 231
Etruscan 187
Europe, Central 97, 128
European Union 126, 165
evolution 16, 25–39, 63, 122–3
  'great divide' vs continuity 26, 32
  and racism 122–3
  social aspects of 27–8
exchange theory 70
exogamy 37, 169, 172
expression (as function of language) 16

face 59, 68
Fairclough, N. 9, 57–8
Faroe Islands 127
feudalism 106
Fichte, J. G. 98, 109–15, 122, 171
field, social 10, 74
Filipinos in Hong Kong 232
Firth, J. R. 19, 56–8, 229
Fish, S. 65, 118
Flanders 127
forgetting 114, 117–18, 210
Foucault, M. 9, 58, 73–4, 78, 211
Fowler, R. 57
Francard, M. 127
France 92–3, 96–7, 106–11, 120, 127, 148, 186, 194, 208, 212, 216–22
Franco, F. 127
François I, King 107
Franco-Prussian War 111–12
Frangoudaki, A. 128
Frantzen, A. J. 126
Frawley, W. 86
French 70, 74, 104–8, 148, 183, 186, 192, 195–8, 203–8
  as ex-colonial language 129–31, 149
French Revolution 96–7, 108
Freud, S. 2
Friedman, E. 152
Friedman, V. A. 128
Friggieri, O. 127
Friulan 127
Furfey, P. H. 61

Gaelic
  Irish 80, 166, 213–14
  as language of Adam 214–17
  Scottish 94, 166, 192, 212–16
Galician 127, 165–6, 214–15
Garde, P. 128
Gardt, A. 128
Garuba, H. 130
Gellner, E. 113–15, 119, 122, 231
generative grammar 31–3, 36
genetic conditioning 29, 37–8
genius
  of language 45–6
  national 44–6, 229
German 98, 128, 171, 183
Germany 97–9, 108–13, 128, 171, 173, 208, 214

gesture 72
Ghaleb, M. L. 129, 204–6
Gibbons, J. 134, 232
Giles, H. 71–2, 76
Gilman, A. C. 59
globalisation 182, 188–90, 220
Goffman, E. 9, 59, 67–8
Gordon, D. C. 129
Gorham, M. S. 128
Görlach, M. 126
gossip as grooming 27–8
Graddol, D. 182
grammar(s) 84, 99, 102–3, 131
Gramsci, A. 182
Granada 221
Grantham, Sir A. 154
Great Britain *see* UK
Greece 128
Greek 99–100, 103–4, 107–8, 173, 201–2
Greimas, A.-J. 222
Grossenbacher-Schmid, R. 128
Guenier, N. 198
Guimaraes, E. 131
Gumperz, J. J. 77–80
Guneratne, A. 129
Gutschmidt, K. 128
Guyana 131

Haalpulaar 130
Haarmann, H. 126
Haas, M. R. 61
Habermas, J. 58, 211, 229
habitus 74–5, 167–8
  shared 168
Halliday, M. A. K. 57–8, 69
Hamann, J.-G. 44
Hannan, K. 128
Hardie, K. 127
Harris, R. 148
Harris, R. G. 182, 190, 233
Hasan, R. 69
Havlíček Borovský, K. 163–4
Havránek, B. 52
Haynes, L. M. 131
Hebrew 129, 173–4, 201–3, 214
Hecht, M. L. 80–2
hegemony 58, 182, 186
Henley, N. 62
Herder, J.-G. 44, 112, 115, 121, 171, 215
heteroglossia 50, 123
Hindu identity 129, 175
history 49–50
Hitler, A. 98, 111
Hobsbawm, E. J. 119–25, 138, 174
Hodson, T. C. 228
Hoffman, C. 126
Holborow, M. 182, 229
Holman, E. 128
Holt, M. 233
Holy Roman Empire 173
Homans, G. 72
Homer 232
Hong Kong 129, 132–61, 184, 231–2
  universities 137–9, 149, 158
Hopf, C. 128
Hopi 55, 228
Huang, S. 129
Humboldt, W. von 45–6, 66, 115, 171
Huss, L. 127
Hutton, C. M. 171–2, 232–3
Hvitfeldt, C. 130
Hylland Erisken, T. 130
Hymes, D. 77, 86, 184, 228

Iban 130
Icelandic 127
identity
  age *see* generational
  analysed as: assertive claim 20, 118–19; distinctive function of language 20–5, 226; ethos, persona, self vs person 9; identifying, identification 10; linguistic phenomenon 11–14, 225; making sense of oneself 222; process vs product 84, 126; representation and as communication 16, 225–6; sameness or difference 37–8; signifier/signified *see* signifier; subject, subject position, positionings 9–10, 74
  colonial 154–8
  communal 81–2

Communication Theory of 80–3
conflict 179–80
construction of 6–11, 19, 30–1, 84
crossing 179–80
'deep' (as meaning of one's name) 2–3, 5, 172, 176
definitions of 1–2, 9–11, 37–8, 40, 76
educational 138
enacted 81–2
ethnic/racial 6, 8, 13, 20, 37, 44–8, 62–3, 79, 117, 120–3, 130, 159, 162–72, 181, 185, 190–1, 194–5, 199–200, 209–23: dangers of 46, 170, 222; defined 162–3
false 4
functions of 15–25
gender/sexual 7, 20, 36, 53, 61–3, 79, 83, 167, 198
generational 20, 36, 53, 139, 167
group (communal) 4–5, 46, 76
hybrid 156
individual: demands variation and prefers comprehension 191; and habitus 168; not possessed by 'primitive' peoples 46; not possessed by working class 69; vs social 76, 168
in-group/out-group 76–7, 106, 169, 174
interpretation of 2, 20–8, 81, 83, 118, 219, 225–6
layers/levels of 80–3, 185
local 117, 163
multiple 8, 73, 79
national 7, 12, 20, 46, 57, 62–3, 80, 83, 92–131, 134, 138–9, 147–68, 173, 185, 188–91, 195–7, 216, 221, 224–5: construction of 94; dangers of 46; fluidity of 93, 122; formed by language 94; and name 95; vs ethnic 163; vs religious 213
occupational 79
other people's 81, 83, 118, 221, 226
personal 81–2
'reading' and 'over-reading' of 20–8, 30–40, 83
regional 13, 36, 117, 163: as performative discourse 20
relational 81–2
religious/sectarian 117, 129, 166, 168, 172–6, 182, 185, 194–210, 213–23: linguistic performance of 174–5: non-traditional 176
repertoires of 9
self- 4, 20, 80, 83: sub-national 93; types of 3–4
ideology 50–1, 57, 65, 117–18, 121–2, 130, 135, 144, 167
see also language, ideologies of
Igbo 130
Iglesias Álvarez, A. 127
illiteracy 198
imagined community 65, 113–18, 123–5, 191–2, 211
imperial/colonial expansion 44, 103, 109–12, 128–9, 132–5
incomprehensibility (as a function of language) 192
India 129, 148, 160, 175, 208
Indo-European languages 45, 187, 195, 212, 215
Indonesia 129–30, 179–80
in-group and out-group *see under* identity
in-law relationship 38
innate ideas 44
institutions, national/governmental 80, 108, 138, 225
see also education
intercomprehension 186, 192
interlanguage 139, 145–7
Internet 177, 190
interpretation 30–40, 87, 190–1, 219, 225–6
interpre(ta)tive community 65, 118
interpreter, privileged 81–2
intersubjectivity 73
intonation 21, 31
Iraq 199, 223
Ireland 63, 80, 92, 126, 166, 176, 189, 213–14

Irish Gaelic *see under* Gaelic
Isabella, Queen 102–3
Islam 129, 167, 173–6, 183, 197, 200–3, 210, 216, 221, 233
Israel 129, 207, 210–11, 223
Istria 127
Italian 99–102, 104, 127, 183, 197
Italy 99, 107–9, 127, 164–5, 186–7, 208
Ivanič, R. 9–10

Jackson, M. 82
Jaffe, A. 127
Jahn, J.-E. 127–8
Jakobson, R. 19, 87
Japanese 129, 183
Jeffery, A. 201–3
Jenkins, R. 75
Jensen, J. B. 127
Jespersen, O. 51–2, 60, 228, 232
Jesus, etymology of name 203
Jewish identity 171–4
Johnstone, B. 86
Jones, M. C. 127
Jónsson, E. M. 127
Jordan 199
Joseph, J. E. x, 10, 15, 19, 42, 53, 56, 58, 65, 67, 89, 125, 127, 129, 134, 150–1, 187, 204–6, 208, 220, 226, 228–9, 232

Kachru, B. B. 129
Kamusella, T. D. I. 128
Kant, I. 113–14
Kasper, G. 58
Kayan 129
Kaye, J. 130
Keane, W. 129
Kedourie, E. 96–8, 109, 113–14, 119
Kerala 175
King, L. 131
kinship terms 175
Kirk, J. M. 126
Kloss, H. 144, 150, 165, 232–3
knowledge produced by power 73–4
Kohn, H. 97, 113, 163
Koller, W. 128
Koran 174, 194, 201–3, 208
  attempts to find Arabic origin for entire vocabulary 201–3
Kosovo 223
Kreindler, I. 128
Krio 130
Kristinsson, S. 127
Kroskrity, P. 65
Kuipers, J. C. 129
Kumari, T. C. 175
Kuter, L. 127
Kwok, H. 129

Labov, W. 60, 63–4, 72, 79
Laitin, D. D. 128
Lakoff, R. 61–2
Lambert, W. 70–1
Lammenais, F.-R. de 216
Lane, E. W. 218
language
  accommodation *see* Communication Accommodation Theory
  acquisition 26, 30–1, 35–6, 86–9
  analysed as: abstraction 211; culturally loaded or neutral 167; imagined community 124–5; institution 47; nation/republic 107–8
  attitudes research 12, 24–5, 70–1
  borrowing 104, 107–8, 173
  change 45, 48, 232
  child's construction of 86–9
  choice 166
  colonial and ex-colonial 128–61, 192
  concept of a 12, 34–6, 98–9, 176–7, 208, 211, 225
  conflict 79–80
  courtroom 61–2
  death 209
  egocentric vs communicative 86–7
  endangered 23, 56, 185–6
  heritage 80, 94
  ideologies of 53, 65, 120–2, 135, 144
  maintenance 80
  minority 80, 94, 126, 185

mixture 111
national 12–13, 98, 105, 117–21, 124, 126, 183–4, 208, 225
native *see* mother tongue
non-standard *see* vernacular
official 132–3
origin of 18, 43–4, 47, 114–15
policy 133, 165
political nature/function of 23, 28, 49–51, 56, 59, 62, 103–4, 107–8
powerful/powerless 61–2, 167
public and formal 69
purity of 104–5
'real' 33, 36, 52, 71
recognition of a 139–40, 144, 147–50, 165, 224
shift 79–80, 129, 181–92
standard x, 12, 52–3, 74–5, 99, 102, 120–5, 150, 225: and respectability 121
teaching 58, 84, 127, 161
and thought 47, 62; *see also* Sapir–Whorf Hypothesis
typology 45, 187
variation 144, 166
women's 61–3, 167
world 94, 183, 190–1
written, and nation 116–17
langue and *parole* 48–9, 51, 59
Lantolf, J. P. 86
Latin 99–108, 139, 148, 173, 186–7, 201
Lau, C. K. 160
Lear, E. 57
Lebanon 129, 193–200, 203–23
Lecercle, J.-J. 83
Lee, P. 228
Leo III the Isaurian, Emperor 173
Leo X, Pope 221
Le Page, R. B. 79–80, 131
Lestel, D. 26
Levinger, J. 128
Levinson, S. C. 59
Lévi-Strauss, C. 73
lexicography 131
Libya 223
Lin, A. M. Y. 134–5
Lindgren, A.-R. 127
linguistic diversity 104, 181–92
see also language, endangered
linguistic imperialism 186
linguistics 17, 36, 46, 48, 60, 62, 68, 78, 84, 135, 176, 224–7
applied 147, 182; *see also* Critical Applied Linguistics
critical 57–8
literary characters 1, 4
literary criticism 16
literature 130, 165–6
Lithuania 128
Llull, R. 165–6
Lo Bianco, J. 131
Locke, J. 44
Longmire, B. J. 129
Lord, C. 128
Lord, R. 138
Lotherington, H. 131
Lucretius 43
Luther, M. 98
Luxemburg 128

Maalouf, A. 220–3
McConnell-Ginet, S. 65
Macedonia 128
McGarty, C. 76
McLaughlin, F. 130
Malay 130
Malayalam 175
Malaysia 130, 149
Maley, W. 126
Mali 130
Malinowski, B. 17–19, 24, 55, 190
Malta 127
Manchus 152
Manx 166
Mao Zedong 133, 151–2, 158
marginality 215–16
Maron (or Maro), St 200, 213
Maronites 193, 196–200, 203–4, 215–19
Martha's Vineyard 60, 64
Marx, K. 96–7, 229
Marxism 49–51, 57–8, 62, 64, 73–4, 97, 119, 162, 167, 182, 211, 220, 229
Masuria 128
matched-guise testing 70–1

Mauritius 130
Mawkanuli, T. 129
meaning
  includes speaker 56–7
  textual 83
Médicis, J.-L. de *see* al-Wazzan, H.
Meinhof, U. H. 182
Melka, F. 126
membership 76, 174
memory 35, 208, 219
Menke, H. 128
Mennonites 174
Mexico 131, 169
Meyerhoff, M. 65
migration, early human 37
Millán-Varela, C. 127
Milroy, L. 63–4, 79
Minang 180
Minangkabau 180
Mitchell, J. C. 63
mixture of race/language 111
modernity 23, 151, 182, 231
Morocco 130
Morris, N. 131
mother tongue 98, 171–2, 183–5
Mozambique 130
Mufwene, S. S. 191
Muhammad 200–1
Mukařovský, J. 52
Müller, F. M. 46–7
Muslim identity 173–5, 179–80, 197–210, 215, 220–3, 233
Myanmar 129
mythology 47

Nahkla, R. 198
name 1, 4, 11–13, 172, 176–81
  deictic function of 4
  of language, identity value of 130, 209, 213
  and national identity 95
  as text of ethnic and religious identity 178–81
Napoleon Bonaparte 96, 109–12
Napoleon III 217
Nasser, G. A. 220
nation
  analysed as: based on forgetting 114, 117–18, 210, 218–19; based on sharing of common language 110, 114, 117, 120, 123–5, 224–5; community of social communications 97; daily plebiscite 114, 211; defined by language 110; grammatical being 96; historical product 97, 101–2, 113–14; interpretive community 118; memory plus will 112–13, 208, 210, 215, 218–19; soul, spiritual principle 112, 211, 218–19
  character of 105
  definitions of 92
  myth of as ancient/authentic 115–16, 119
  nation-state 92, 98, 165: myth of 98
  Romantic conception of 111
  symbols of 117–18
  without state 92, 165
  written language and 116–17
  see also identity, national
nationalism
  analysed as: act of consciousness 97; discursive vs real 123–5; doctrine 96–7, 113–14; tied to socio-economic factors 119, 123; voluntaristic vs organic 97
  banal 117–18, 121, 225
  Chinese 151
  and class division 119–20
  origins of 95–8, 109, 119–23
nationality *see* identity, national
natural 13, 34, 84, 96, 102, 105, 109, 113, 115, 118, 125
Nauerby, T. 127
Nazi-era ethnography and linguistics 171, 232–3
Neanderthals 37
Nebrija, A. de 102–3, 107
Nepal 129
Nerlich, B. 228
Newton, G. 128
New Zealand 131, 148, 189
Ngonyani, D. 130

Nigeria 130
Nihtinen, A. 128
Niles, J. D. 126
Nkweto Simmonds, F. 176
nominalism vs realism 84
Noreen, A. 51
norms 64–5, 74–5
Norton, B. 161
Norway 63, 127–8

Oakes, L. 127
Ó Baoill, D. 126
O'Barr, W. M. 61–2
occidentalism 219
Ogden, C. K. 17, 55
Omar, A. H. 130
Omoniyi, T. 130
onomastics 176
oratory 21
O'Reilly, C. 166
orientalism 194, 218–19
Orlandi, E. P. 131
Osama Bin Laden 93
Ostler, N. 185
Ottoman Empire 196–7, 203, 223
'over-reading' 38–9, 225
  see also identity, 'reading' *and* 'over-reading' of)

Paine, T. 120
Palestine 199, 223
Palestinians 210
Pan-Africanism 130
Pan-Arabism 129, 163, 233
Pandian, J. 129
Pan-Slavism 163–4
Paraguay 131
Parakrama, A. 149
Parry, M. M. 126
passions 16, 42
  see also emotions
Patten, C. 133
patriotism 151–2
Pavlov, I. 28–9, 36
Payton, P. 126
Pêcheur, J. 198
Pennycook, A. 58, 75, 182, 192
performative (as function of language) 19–20
Perta, C. 164–5
Peru 169
Petrarch (Petrarca, F.) 102
phatic communion (as function of language) 17–19, 24, 27, 190
Phillipson, R. 182, 186
Phoenicians 194, 199–200, 210–18
Piaget, J. 11, 32, 86–7, 184
Pictish 212, 216
Pinker, S. 26
Plato 15, 43
Platt, J. 149
Poedjosoedarmo, G. 130
Pol Pot 181
Polish 128
politeness 59
Portugal 165
Portuguese 104–5, 127, 166, 183, 208, 230
  as ex-colonial language 130–1, 149
post-structuralism 73, 114, 162, 229
power and power relations 58–9, 73–4, 78, 90, 186
pragmatics 19
Prague 128
Prague Linguistic Circle 52
prejudice 39, 46, 169
prescriptivism 135
Presley, E. 21–2
Press, J. I. 127
print-capitalism and nation 116–17
pronouns
  and politeness 59
  and religion 174
propaganda 17
propositional content 19, 21–2, 24–5, 190–1
Propp, V. 222
Proudian-Der-Karabetian, A. 129
Provençal 127, 165
Prussia 111
psychoanalysis 16
psychology 16
  see also cognitive, social psychology
Puerto Rico 131
purism 104–5, 174

Quakers 174
Quebec 70, 149
questione della lingua 208

race 83, 110, 163–4, 169, 214
  mixture 111, 169
  see also identity, ethnic/racial
racism
  and evolution 122–3
  motivated by cross-racial desire 169
  and Renan 219–20
  'scientific' 111, 122–3, 171–2
Ramaswamy, S. 129
Rampton, B. 171
Rastorfer, J.-M. 129
rationalism vs empiricism 97
reader response 83
'reading' *see under* identity
realism vs nominalism 84
Redouane, R. 130
reflection 115
regionalist discourse as performative 20
Reid, T. 228
religion 116, 220
  see also identity, religious/sectarian
Renan, E. 112–17, 194–5, 208–12, 215–20, 223, 231, 233–4
Renan, H. 217–19
renegades 210
representation (as function of language) 9, 13, 15–16, 20–5, 30, 36–40, 184–5, 191, 225–6
reproduction 75, 78, 117
resistance 160, 192
rhetoric 16, 21
Richards, I. A. 17, 55
Robins, R. H. 57
Rohfleisch, I. 128
Romance languages 99, 101, 139, 148, 165, 186–7
Romania 128, 139, 209
Rousseau, J.-J. 44
Rowley, G. G. 129
rural vs urban 52, 108
  rural to urban population shift 52, 185, 192, 231

Russia 128, 152, 164
Russian 183
Russian formalism 49

Sacks, H. 61
Sacy, S. de 218
Saddam Hussein 93
Safran, W. 127
Said, E. 118, 218–19
Samara, M. 128
Sanskrit 45, 129
Sapir, E. 53–6, 58, 85, 228–9
Sapir–Whorf Hypothesis 55–6, 62, 68, 228
Saussure, F. de 5, 47–9, 51, 78, 106, 228
Sawaie, M. 209
Sayer, D. 128
Scacchi, A. 131
Scandinavia 127, 208
Schama, S. 21
Schieffelin, B. B. 65
Sciriha, L. 129
Scotland 92–4, 106, 126–7, 166, 189, 212–16
Scots 94, 127–8, 166, 212–13
Scottish Common Sense philosophy 11, 228
Scottish Gaelic *see* Gaelic, Scottish
Second World War 97, 232
segregation 46
self 9
  as product of discourse 10
  structure of 67–8
Self-Categorisation Theory 76–7
self-concept 76, 82
self-hood, possibilities for 10
semiotic receptivity 28, 30, 32, 35–6
Semitic identities 194, 210, 215, 218–20
Semitic languages 195, 212, 215
Senegal 130, 164
Serbia 128
Sercombe, P. G. 130
Sériot, P. 128
Seton-Watson, H. 116
Shafer, B. C. 96
Shakespeare, W. 96
Shaw, W. 214

Shepard, C. A. 72
Shetland Islands 67
Siebenmann, G. 127
Sierra Leone 130
sign, relationship to reality 49–51
signifier and signified 5, 12, 37, 48, 106
signs, natural 11, 228
Silesia 128
Silverstein, M. 123–5
Singapore 129, 143, 148, 160–1, 176–9
Siu, H. F. 152
Skinner, B. F. 36, 88
Skutnabb-Kangas, T. 182, 186
Smith, A. D. 231
Smuts, J. C. 7–8, 10–11, 80, 84
So, D. W. C. 136
social
  anthropology 78
  as binding vs divisive 48–9, 51, 54, 59
  bonding 27–8
  class *see* class
  constraint 9–10, 74–5
  distance 59
  field *see* field
  myths/ideologies 76
  network 63–5
  psychology 12, 61, 72, 76, 79–83
  reproduction *see* reproduction
Social Identity Theory 76–7, 106
social science methodology 71, 77, 81–2
society 84
sociolinguistics 24, 30–1, 33–8, 60, 68, 71–4, 78, 83
  evolutionary 33
sociology 67–72, 118
Socrates 15
Solé, Y. R. 131
South Africa 130, 189
South America 131, 169
Spain 127, 165–6, 186, 208, 214–15
Spanish 102–5, 127, 165–6, 173, 183, 230
  as ex-colonial language 130–1, 149
Spanish Empire 103
speech accommodation *see* Communication Accommodation Theory
Spender, D. 62
Spenser, E. 126
Speroni, S. 107
Spires, S. 128
Spivak, G. C. 222
Springsteen, B. 21–2
Srage, M. N. 198
Sri Lanka 149
state without nation 165
status 53, 64, 72
Stefanink, B. 128
Steinke, K. 128
Stephens, T. M. 169
stereotypes 72, 76, 169
Stevenson, P. 128
Strassoldo, R. 127
Street, B. 9
Strietska-Ilina 128
Stroud, C. 130
structuralism 10, 26, 48, 56–9, 73–5, 228–9
Stubkjaer, F. T. 128
style 58, 72
subjectivity 10, 17, 76–7
Suleiman, Y. 129
Sumba 130
Swahili 130
Sweden 127
Switzerland 128, 231
symbol, national 117–18
symbolic representation 18
Syria 199, 207–9
Syriac 173, 194, 197, 202, 216, 233
systemic-functional grammar 57

Tabouret-Keller, A. 79, 126, 131
tabula rasa 44
Taiwan 129
Tajfel, H. 76–7, 106, 117–18
Tamil 129
Tannen, D. 62, 77
Tanzania 130
Taylor, T. J. 26, 65, 228
teaching 34
  see also education
telephone, cellular/mobile 190

television 189–90
Thailand 129
Thakerer, J. 72
Tharu 129
Thompson, J. B. 74
Thorne, B. 62
thought and language *see under* language
thought transmission 18–19, 22
Todorov, T. 49
Toribio, A. J. 131
Tory, G. 107
toscano *see* Italian
translation 108, 190, 233
Tristram, H. L. C. 126
truth value 24–5, 39, 191
Tse, J. K-P. 129
Tsou, B. K. 232
Tu, W.-M. 151
Turkey 129, 208, 214
Turkish 197
Turkish–Mongolian language family 45
Turner, G. W. 131
Turner, J. C. 76
Turville-Petre, T. 126
Tuva 129

UK 25, 92–4, 126, 152–8, 166, 176, 208, 211–16, 232
unconscious 19, 29, 60, 84
universal grammar 32–3, 36, 88
urban vs rural *see under* rural
USA 93, 106, 108, 120, 131, 148, 159, 164, 170, 176, 189, 223
  11 Sept. 2001, significance of 93
USSR 93, 126, 128
Uzbekistan 128

Valdés, J. de 103–5, 230
Valencian 104–5, 127, 165–6
Vallancey, C. 214
Van Bijlert, V. A. 129
Van den Bersselaar, D. 130
Vanuatu 131
Venezuela 149, 169
vernacular 64, 99–100, 104–5
  maintenance of 64
Verschueren, J. 65
violence, symbolic 75
Virgil 149
'voice' 21, 168, 226
volgare illustre 99–100, 104
Voloshinov, V. N. 49–51, 59, 72, 78, 167
Vygotsky, L. S. 86–7, 184

Wagner, R. 172
Wah, S. 141
Wales 92–4, 126, 159, 166, 189, 212
Wallonia 127
Wang Gungwu 151
Warsaw Pact 126, 128
Weber, H. 149
Wenger, E. 65
Western Samoa 131
Whitney, W. D. 46–8
Whorf, B. L. 55–6, 123, 185, 228–9
  see also Sapir–Whorf Hypothesis
Wiesinger, P. 128
will 19, 28, 40, 47, 75, 81, 84, 109, 112–13, 177, 181, 210–11
Williams, C. H. 126
Winichakul, T. 129
Wittgenstein, L. 15
Wodak, R. 65, 128
Wolof 163–4
Woods, D. R. 130
World Bank 189
Wright, R. 148
Wright, S. 126
writing 35
  and nation 116–17

Yau, S. C. 116–17
Yiddish 98, 171
Young, R. J. C. 169
Yugoslavia 128

Zimbabwe 130
Zoubir, A. 130